VALUING ANCIENT THINGS

Archaeology and Law

John Carman

Leicester University Press
A Cassell Imprint
London and New York

LEICESTER UNIVERSITY PRESS
A Cassell Imprint
Wellington House, 125 Strand, London WC2R 0BB
215 Park Avenue South, New York, NY 10003

First published 1996

British Library Cataloguing-in-Publication Data
A catalogue record for this book is available from the British Library.

ISBN 0-7185-0012-1

Library of Congress Cataloging-in-Publication Data
Carman, John, 1952–
    Valuing ancient things : archaeology and law / John Carman.
      p.   cm.
    Includes bibliographical references and index.
    ISBN 0-7185-0012-1
    1. Archaeology – Law and legislation – Great Britain. I. Title.
KD3740.C37   1996
344.42'094 – dc20
[344.20494]   95-24873
                                                                              CIP

Typeset by Mayhew Typesetting, Rhayader, Powys
Printed and bound in Great Britain by Biddles Limited, Guildford and King's Lynn

Contents

List of tables and figures

Abbreviations

Legislation and law

AMAA79	Ancient Monuments and Archaeological Areas Act 1979
AMCCO81	Ancient Monuments (Class Consents) Order 1981
AMCCO84	Ancient Monuments (Class Consents) Order 1984
CA88	Coroners Act 1988
EGCO87	The Export of Goods (Control) Order 1987
HBAM53	Historic Buildings and Ancient Monuments Act 1953
ICM55	Inspection of Churches Measure 1955
IECP39	Import, Export and Customs Powers (Defence) Act 1939
MS94	Merchant Shipping Act 1894 (part IX)
NH80	National Heritage Act 1980
NH83	National Heritage Act 1983
Overton80	Attorney-General of the Duchy of Lancaster *v*. G. E. Overton (Farms) Limited 1980
Overton82	Attorney-General of the Duchy of Lancaster *v*. G. E. Overton (Farms) Limited 1982
PLBC90	Planning (Listed Buildings and Conservation Areas) Act 1990
PM68	Pastoral Measure 1968
PMR86	Protection of Military Remains Act 1986
PW73	Protection of Wrecks Act 1973
RC69	Redundant Churches and Other Religious Buildings Act 1969

Others

AAI	Area of Archaeological Importance
AHM	Archaeological heritage management
ARM	Archaeological resource management
CRM	Cultural resource management
HBMCE	Historic Monuments and Buildings Commission for England (English Heritage)
NHMF	National Heritage Memorial Fund
RCHME	Royal Commission on Historic Monuments for England

Preface

WHAT THIS BOOK IS
This is a book about archaeology. In particular, it concerns the management and preservation of what is known variously as the archaeological heritage, the archaeological resource base, the cultural resource base, or the archaeological record. As such, it is a contribution to a growing body of literature in the field variously called archaeological heritage management (AHM), archaeological resource management, cultural resource management (CRM) or, more simply and directly, the management of archaeology. Archaeology, however, does not stand alone in its concern with the management and preservation of its object, and so this book also forms part of the wider literature concerned with the environment generally, with environmental studies into policy-making in particular, and especially in respect of the historic environment. It also has things to say about the so-called natural environment. In this way, the book additionally constitutes a contribution to the developing but rather ill-defined field of 'heritage studies'.

The book is about archaeology in two senses of the term. In one sense it concerns the very stuff of archaeology – the archaeological heritage, archaeological resource base or archaeological record itself. In this sense, it seeks to provide an understanding of what these terms mean, what types of materials they consist of, and what happens to those materials in the processes of management and preservation.

In the second sense of the term archaeology, it concerns the field of practice that is archaeology, the field of study or the discipline that is archaeology. In this sense, it seeks to identify how archaeologists came to preserve the material that is the object of archaeology, how archaeologists think about it, why archaeologists seek to preserve it, and – most importantly – how archaeologists give it value.

The subject matter of the book is English law as it relates to archaeological material. This consists not only of ancient monuments law (first dating from 1882, and in its current form from 1910), but also: the law of treasure trove, covering the discovery of valuable movable objects (from time immemorial); planning law, which regulates building development (from 1947); environmental protection legislation and countryside management (from 1949); export controls on antiquities, antiques and art-works (from 1939); national heritage funding and administration (from 1980); donations of antiquities, antiques and artworks to the state in place of tax-payment (from 1910); preservation of ancient wrecks (from 1973); and the preservation of military remains (from 1986). All of these very different branches of law affect archaeology, and despite their differences apply very similar principles to their treatment of ancient material. In part, this is due to the manner in which such laws came into being and the underlying idea of how to treat ancient material that they represent.

The book examines this collection of laws from two complementary perspectives. From the perspective of history, it seeks to understand how laws to preserve ancient things came into being in the first place, why we have them, how the idea of preservation was first established, and what the original promoters of such laws sought to achieve. In so doing, it contributes not only to the history of environmental preservation, but also to the history of archaeological theory. From a contemporary analytical perspective, the book seeks to identify how these laws affect archaeology – both the stuff of archaeological concern, and also the practice of archaeology. In particular, it seeks to identify how laws to preserve archaeological remains affect the ways in which archaeologists consider, understand and treat their material. The book proceeds from the recognition that the effect of laws on archaeology is less at the level of day-to-day practice than at the level of understanding and feeling. In this sense, laws constitute something that changes the way archaeologists think and feel about their object – in the language of this book, laws are a 'vector of moral change' of archaeological remains. In so doing, the book contributes to an understanding of the contemporary relevance and meaning of archaeological material and archaeology as a discipline.

In the phrase 'a vector of moral change', the word 'vector' carries the same meaning as in the expression 'a vector of disease' – that is, as a means of transmission, a mode of moving something from one place to another, a cause of change. Here, then, laws change the ways archaeologists perceive their object. The word 'moral' here carries a similar sense to that in which Napoleon Bonaparte is purported to have used it when he supposedly said of war that 'the moral is to the physical as three is to one'. In 'moral', here, are contained all those things which relate to thinking and feeling: attitudes, expectations, beliefs and understandings, the cognitive and conceptual. In 'physical' are contained the practical and logistical aspects: available resources and their disposition. Here, then, the change wrought in archaeological material by laws is in the way it is thought about, the attitude taken towards it, the expectations made of it, and particularly the value it is considered to have.

Questions of value loom large in this book, because it is primarily as a means of giving value to ancient things that the law is considered. In considering value, a specific theoretic model – that of Rubbish Theory – is outlined which, when considered in the light of English law as it applies to archaeological material, provides an understanding of how and why components of the historic environment are considered important and thereby constitute components of 'the heritage'. In so doing, this book is an attempt to contribute to current debates in archaeological theory by considering the contemporary relevance of archaeology and archaeological material.

WHAT THIS BOOK IS NOT

This, then, is a book about archaeology, specifically concerned with the law in England as it relates to archaeological material. It is a contribution to the literature of heritage management and archaeology generally.

This book is not a manual of archaeological heritage management practice. It does not, nor does it seek to, provide guidance on how to go about preserving or managing archaeological remains – whether individual objects, archaeological sites, ancient monuments or ancient landscapes. It is not, therefore, a contribution to the literature of archaeological conservation except at the level of theory. It does not tell you how to preserve things, but if that is what you are interested in, it may tell you why you are interested. Still less is the book a manual on the organization of archaeology. It is not concerned with what ought to be done, but why certain things are done, how they come to be done a certain way, and why those ways are considered proper.

The book is also not a guide to English law as it affects archaeology. It is in no way a legal text, since the approach is substantially different from that which any lawyer would consider taking. If legal advice is what you seek, then refer to the legislation itself, an appropriate legal text book, or – better still – consult a qualified lawyer. What the book does do is to take the law in England apart and put it back together again in a way that reveals the manner in which it acts as a vector of moral change on archaeological and other ancient material.

. The book limits itself to a consideration of English law alone. It does not address the very similar laws in place in other parts of the UK – in Wales, Scotland, or Northern Ireland, where very different laws apply. Nor does it seek to compare English law with the laws of other countries. Instead, the book carries out the first detailed contextual study anywhere of the rise of archaeological preservation legislation, the ideology represented by that legislation, and the manner in which that legislation affects archaeology. In so doing, the book lays the first firm foundation for a truly comparative study of such laws internationally. It also provides the first effective counterblast to those critics of archaeological heritage management who seek to dismiss it as trivial or dysfunctional.

HOW THIS BOOK IS ORGANIZED: THE HOUSE THAT JACK BUILT

The familiar form Jack is short for John or, via the French Jacques, James. The body of archaeological preservation legislation in England can be considered the bequest of one of two individuals from the nineteenth century: James Talbot, Baron de Malahide, promoter of the first legislation to appropriate Treasure Trove law for archaeology; or John Lubbock, promoter of the first Ancient Monuments Bill. Their efforts culminated in the laws we have in place today. As such, the laws in force in England today constitute the 'house' either (or both) of them built.

The metaphor of house-building, from choice of location through vertical structure to interior design and sale, can be carried forward into the chapters of this book. Chapter 1 outlines the current state of the field of AHM and the locus of this contribution, constituting the location or setting for the property. Chapter 2 provides the information necessary on which to proceed and the materials required – the blueprint for the construction. Chapter 3 discusses Treasure Trove, the first law to be used for the purpose of archaeology and the underlying model of all such law – the foundation. Chapter 4 describes the processes by which the first law specifically designed to protect archaeological material came into existence – the ground floor. Chapter 5 outlines the subsequent processes by which such law reached its current state – the superstructure. Chapters 6, 7 and 8 analyse the paths of archaeological material through the structure so built – entrances, rooms and exits. Chapter 9 outlines the application of this work, its implications for archaeology in general and archaeological heritage management in particular, and the future lines of enquiry it opens up – the property development as a whole.

Structurally, the work is divided into five parts: four parts constituting the main text, and the fifth the three Appendices. Part One – consisting of Chapters 1 and 2 – is introductory and outlines the context, purpose and approach of the work. Part Two – consisting of Chapters 3, 4 and 5 – is very largely historical (but not entirely so) and reviews the relationship between archaeology as a discipline and laws governing the protection and ownership of archaeological material over time. Part Three – Chapters 6, 7 and 8 – is analytical and concerns the effect of current law in England on ancient material and what this means for archaeology. Part Four – Chapter 9 – presents a summary and some conclusions as well as outlining future lines of research revealed in the course of this work. Part Five – the three Appendices – constitutes the basic building materials out of which the work as a whole is constructed.

Together, they represent everything the laws studied have to say about the heritage in England.

The book as a whole is intended as a contribution to understanding the place of archaeology in the contemporary world and to providing a basis on which to build the specialism of archaeological heritage management into a field of research rather than mere practice.

ACKNOWLEDGEMENTS

No work such as this is ever really the product of a single individual. Throughout, the contributions of others are evident. In particular, the advice and assistance of Professors Colin Renfrew, Martin Jones and Tim Darvill, together with those of Dr Marie-Louise Stig Sørensen, have been invaluable.

I am deeply indebted to Dr Nathan Schlanger for pointing me in the direction of Rubbish Theory and to its author Dr Michael Thompson for his enthusiastic reception of the use to which I put his ideas and for directing me towards Cultural Theory. Dr Matthew Edgeworth generously confirmed that I had not misused his own work and also made very helpful and incisive comments, as did Dr Mark Edmonds and Mr Peter Gathercole. Discussions with Mim Bower, Dee De Roche, Antony Firth, Dr J. D. Hill, Dr Alinah Kelo Segobye and Dr Anthony Sinclair were always useful and frequently challenging: I am also deeply grateful to them all for their continuing friendship.

I need also to thank Professor Susan Pearce and Dr Jane Grenville for allowing me to try out some of the ideas contained here on their students, and to several years of postgraduate students at the Universities of Cambridge, Leicester and York for keeping me on the straight and narrow path by sceptical and incisive questioning. The members of Darwin and Clare Hall Colleges, Cambridge, provided stimulating and friendly environments for the production of this work. In addition, I am grateful to Vanessa Harwood and Janet Joyce of Leicester University Press for their untiring assistance to an inexperienced author and to Professor Norman Palmer for his generous comments on an early draft. I must once again thank Professor Susan Pearce for all her support in helping to get this work into print.

Last, but by no means least, I must thank my wife Patricia, who has lived with this book as long as its author. I am sure she will be delighted to see it on shelves and out of her hair. Her untiring support and enthusiasm for my work, and this book in particular, put its author to shame.

John Carman
Clare Hall, Cambridge, UK
June 1995

Part One
Law and the archaeological heritage: key issues

1
Archaeological heritage management and law

The field variously designated archaeological heritage management (AHM; Cleere 1989a), archaeological resource management (ARM; Darvill 1987) and cultural resource management (CRM; McGimsey and Davis 1977) has spawned a large and growing literature since the 1970s. A conservative count of the content of six prominent academic journals available in the Haddon Library in Cambridge (Table 1.1) revealed a total of no less than 113 papers of relevance to AHM published in the years 1974 to 1989 – an average of over 7.5 per year, more than 1.25 per year per publication; of the three journals publishing most in this field, the average is over 5.5 per year, more than 1.8 per year per publication; these figures emphasize the wide interest in aspects of the AHM field. In addition to these, *British Archaeological News* and *Rescue News*, the newspapers of the Council for British Archaeology and Rescue: the Trust for British Archaeology respectively, are largely devoted to such concerns, as are regular publications of English Heritage and two recently founded journals: *The International Journal of Cultural Property* and *The International Journal of Heritage Studies*. Also conferences, conference sessions and training courses in aspects of management now abound in archaeology. On top of all these are the many books covering aspects of AHM currently in print. The subject matter of this literature and discussion is largely limited to technical matters or the reiteration – via descriptive case studies – of core principles.[1]

The principles of AHM reflected in this material are very few and derive from a limited number of key works of the 1970s and 1980s. According to these basic principles, the archaeological heritage is:

1. 'a finite and non-renewable resource' (Darvill 1987, 1); 'archaeological sites are one of a state's non-renewable resources' (McGimsey 1972, 24); 'the non-renewable stock of cultural resources' (Cleere 1984c, 127).
2. a matter of public concern: 'There is no such thing as "private

Table 1.1   PUBLICATIONS CONCERNING ISSUES IN AHM 1974–89

Issues addressed	CA	JFA	AJA	AA	ANT	ADV
Conservation/preservation	4	12	–	9	3	1
Archaeology and law	–	3	–	1	–	–
Public image	9	10	1	9	4	1
Professional ethics	–	9	–	2	–	–
Contract/rescue versus research	1	–	–	–	–	1
Inventory/sampling/salvage/rescue	–	2	–	2	–	5
Organization of archaeology	–	–	1	–	–	–
Introduction of management techniques	–	1	–	–	–	–
International comparisons	2	7	–	–	4	–
'Significance'	–	–	–	5	–	2

Notes:
CA = *Current Anthropology*
JFA = *Journal of Field Archaeology*
AJA = *American Journal of Archaeology*
AA = *American Antiquity*
ANT = *Antiquity*
ADV = *Advances in Archaeological Method and Theory*

archaeology". . . . It follows that *no individual may act in a manner such that the public right to knowledge of the past is unduly endangered or destroyed*' (McGimsey 1972, 5; emphasis in original).
3. 'governed by legislation' (Cleere 1989b, 10); 'depends for its very survival upon close interaction with the realm of law' (McGimsey and Davis 1977, 9); exists in a 'legal context' (Fowler 1982, 4); or a 'legislative context' (Schiffer and Gumerman 1977, 3–9); or against a 'legislative background' (Darvill 1987, 32); and relies upon 'legal mandates [for its] intelligent management' (Adovaiso and Carlisle 1988, 74).
4. subject to assessment for its archaeological 'significance' (Cleere 1984c, 127; Dunnell 1984; Schaafsma 1989).

The logic of these plausible but untested assertions leads to the managerial imperative to preserve a representative collection of archaeological material in the face of commercial pressures for the exploitation of the landscape – hence the appearance of the word 'management' in the various versions of the name of the field of AHM. As well as the word, a ragbag of associations comes with it. As argued by Darvill for monuments in the English countryside (1987), the application of specific tools is required in the conduct of archaeology – especially the tools of methods of identification and measures of significance (cf. Cleere 1984c,

127). The results of this process then allow choices to be made as to the most appropriate type of management treatment for individual sites: curatorial management, exploitative management or (as a last resort) rescue excavation (Darvill 1987, 25–31).

This kind of treatment of the archaeological heritage encourages calls for the increased professionalization of the discipline (Green 1984; Kristiansen 1989, 28) and specific training for archaeologists in the techniques and approaches of archaeological management (Alexander 1989; Davis 1989a). Professional associations of archaeologists are formed (the American Society of Professional Archaeologists in 1976; the British Institute of Field Archaeologists in 1982), which then propagate codes of professional practice and codes of ethics (Green 1984, 22–35; IFA n.d.). In turn, the discipline absorbs approaches from industrial and commercial management, leading to the introduction of guidance documents for archaeological projects and discussions of project planning and management (English Heritage 1991a, 1991b; IFA/English Heritage 1993; Cooper 1992). The net result is that AHM is perceived to be something distinct from academic archaeology and – particularly damaging – a realm of mere practice (Carman 1991).

This relegation of the field of AHM to mere practice is reflected more generally in the literature of archaeology. There is no reference to AHM in significant recent texts concerning the theory of archaeology (Hodder 1986; Lamberg-Karlovsky 1989; Trigger 1989). Similarly, Lewis Binford tends to ignore AHM unless treating it scathingly: he associates it with what he calls 'Yuppie' archaeologists – those who build their reputations by a reliance on unintelligible acronyms for complex pieces of technology (Binford 1989) ; and the only reference to AHM in his work is in a footnote to a discussion of Schiffer's work on site formation processes:

> [the] popularity of Schiffer's position with [AHM] archaeologists arises from its use as a basis for writing off most of the archaeo-logical record as 'insignificant' since it does not approach the idea of little prepackaged Pompeiis. (Binford 1983, 241)

In the light of this, it is interesting that Schiffer's own book on *Formation Processes of the Archaeological Record* (1987) also contains no specific reference to AHM.

AHM is served little better in undergraduate textbooks, where it is either completely ignored or relegated to a separate chapter where its scope is limited to relations with a phenomenon called 'the public' (Rahtz 1991; Renfrew and Bahn 1991). On the other hand, and perhaps surprisingly, the more 'radical' wing of archaeological theorists consider AHM (especially in its guise of rescue archaeology) at some length. Shanks and Tilley (1987a, 24–5, 93–4) devote some four pages to the subject. They are not, however, sympathetic to the field:

> central to the management of the past is the assessment of individual items . . . [and] this is seen as a problem of significance. . . . In effect this is a pricing of the past turned into a commodity. (Shanks and Tilley 1987a, 24)

Others criticize AHM for encouraging the growth of bureaucracy in archaeology (John Barrett, pers. comm.) or as a form of neo-colonialism (Byrne 1991).

Such comments, however, do not constitute an effective critique of AHM since they entirely fail to discuss, engage with, understand or challenge the four basic principles of the field. The appropriate response to Shanks and Tilley, Barrett and Byrne from AHM archaeologists is not: 'Yes, we are wrong; we shall stop what we are doing'; but 'Yes, we know; but (given the basic principles from which we start) what else can we do?' – and none of these critics provides any answer.

What all these failures to critique AHM amount to is the view that AHM has little or nothing to contribute to archaeology as an academic discipline: it is simply 'applied archaeology' (Embree 1990, 31); it takes the fruits of research and useful techniques from 'real' archaeology and applies them in practice; but, having thus borrowed, it puts nothing back. Despite the fact that worldwide the survey and rescue field is the one employing most archaeologists, this is the area which is seen as impacting the least on the discipline as a whole in academic terms.

The problem here – as all archaeologists will recognize – is that the archaeological heritage is being destroyed at an alarming rate. This being so, what is currently capable of being preserved for the future will constitute the entire archaeological record for the future (Lipe 1984, 3). This surely places AHM in an important position in the discipline, which requires it to be treated seriously. Such treatment can only begin with an effective – but not scathingly destructive – critique which aims to build a useful body of theory for AHM.

TOWARDS AN EFFECTIVE CRITIQUE OF AHM

As mentioned above, the principles of AHM have never been subject to any form of critique. Rather, they have been accepted at face value as statements of unassailable truth. As such they are open to criticism (in the popular usage of the term) – *pace* Shanks and Tilley (1987a, 24), Barrett and Byrne – but not analytical critique. This section attempts a beginning to the process of such critique with the aim of opening up the entire field of AHM to the possibilities of research rather than rhetoric.

Finite and non-renewable?

AHM has as its concern all 'the material *things* produced by past human activity' (Lipe 1984, 1; emphasis in original). For Lewis Binford, what archaeologists study is 'simply artefacts' (Binford 1989, 3), and for David Clarke 'the archaeologist's facts are artefacts and the information observed about their contextual and specific attributes' (Clarke 1978, 13). All of these ideas about the subject matter of archaeology are very similar, and raise the question as to whether there is any distinction to be made between the 'archaeological heritage' (Cleere 1984a, 1989a) or the 'cultural resource base' (Lipe 1984, 3) which is the focus of AHM, and the 'archaeological record' with which archaeology the discipline is concerned (Patrik 1985). Treating all three as synonymous is the more effective course since any barrier between AHM and conventional (or 'real') archaeology is thus breached, and the focus turns towards the object of archaeology as a conceptual unity rather than dividing it up into spurious discrete realms.

On the face of things, the assertion that the archaeological heritage (and therefore the archaeological record) is finite and non-renewable appears to be true. Every site, artefact, monument or trace is unique in itself and – once destroyed – is lost for ever. 'Unlike natural flora and fauna, the archaeological resource is non-renewable because it cannot reproduce itself, recolonize decimated areas, or be transplanted' (Darvill 1987, 4).

There are, however, three ways in which the archaeological record (as a category of material) can be considered in some way 'renewable':

1. by the deposition of new 'rubbish' material to become the archaeology of the future (Schiffer 1972, 1987; Rathje 1981);
2. by the discovery of new archaeological sites;
3. by the discovery, recognition or identification of entirely new classes of archaeological remains.

The first and second in this list are obvious to all archaeologists, and the third only slightly less so, but unlike numbers one and two it is very little regarded in AHM. It is arguably the most significant way in which the archaeological record can increase in extent. Nevertheless, studies of the process by which material already classed as 'archaeological' comes to the attention of archaeologists are very new (Edgeworth 1990); this issue will be further addressed in Chapter 6.

The possibility for research such questions open up is to enquire how certain types of things come to be considered specifically 'archaeological' and the attendant processes of identification and recognition. It will be shown below how this fits into a research programme in AHM, and will be the focus of detailed consideration in Chapters 4 and 5.

Public concern?

McGimsey's (1972) book *Public Archaeology* argued the case for legislation to protect archaeological material on the basis that such material was a matter of public concern. This principle is the position from which AHM practitioners proceed: they act as the guardians of items representing a 'public good' (Fowler 1984, 110), and of items preserved 'in the public interest' (Cleere 1989b, 10). What is not clear is from where this 'public interest' derives and why it is given such emphasis in AHM.

The conventional argument that 'the past belongs to all' (Merriman 1991, 1) does not lead logically to the conclusion that all humans have an interest in the preservation of archaeological remains. Merriman's survey of public attitudes to the past in Britain established one connection between the kind of knowledge of the past generated by archaeology and certain groups of people; and a separate connection between a very different – much more personal, family-oriented – past and other groups of people. These findings suggest that a general public concern with archaeology does not exist. Accordingly, there is the perceived need to create such an interest by various means, and this is recognized by writers in the AHM field: both McGimsey (1972) and Cleere (1984b, 61–2; 1984c, 128) press the case for programmes of public education, and McGimsey (1984) offers advice as to how to 'sell' archaeology to non-archaeologists.

Such thinking opens up the possibility of inquiring where the 'public' interest in preserving archaeological material derives from and resides. It will be shown below how this fits into a research programme in AHM, and will be the focus of detailed consideration in Chapters 4 and 5.

Governed by legislation?

This question relates closely to the previous one, since both Cleere (1989b, 10) and McGimsey (1972) justify legislative action on the grounds of 'public interest'. In particular, Cleere (1989b, 10) uses the term to explain and justify the management of the archaeological heritage 'in the public interest'. His historical introduction to the theme of AHM (Cleere 1989b, 1–5) emphasizes the importance of law:

> Archaeological heritage management may be deemed to have begun with the Swedish Royal Proclamation of 1666, declaring all objects from antiquity to be the property of the Crown. (Cleere 1989b, 1)

The theme of legislation also plays a large part in comparative studies in AHM (Cleere 1984a).

Law, then, is an important factor within the field of AHM; but to what extent is the heritage reliant upon legislation? In this context, what does the term 'governed' (as used by Cleere 1989b, 10) mean? His use of the term – and the overall reliance placed upon law by others – could be taken to imply some priority of law over other elements of AHM. If this is the case, then AHM is not archaeology at all but an arm of bureaucratic administration – and the critics cited above would be correct. At the very least, it would be correct for writers on 'real' archaeology to treat the field with a certain disdain as outside their legitimate area of interest. However, as noted above, AHM has very real consequences for very real archaeological material and it must be in the interest of all archaeologists to maintain control over developments. 'Governance', then, cannot mean the subvention of AHM within the field of law. Accordingly, the close relationship between archaeology and law within AHM must mean that law is a tool of AHM which in turn raises the question, 'what does law do for archaeology?'

It is clear from McGimsey and Cleere that the law in AHM is related to the notion of 'public interest' in archaeological material and its preservation. What is by no means clear is whether that public interest depends upon the law for its existence, or whether the law exists because of some pre-existing public concern. If the latter is the case, then presumably there would be no need for programmes of public education specifically to advocate the importance of archaeology (see above). If the former, then the question arises where the initial impetus to legislate came from.

The question of 'governance' thus raises the issue of the natures of the current and historical relationships between the fields of law and archaeology. It will be shown below how this fits into a research programme in AHM, and is the focus of detailed consideration throughout this work.

Measures of significance?

It is argued that the archaeological heritage cannot be preserved in its entirety:

> If . . . we were to declare that all cultural materials more than two years old were to be preserved, our societies would undoubtedly come rapidly to a halt, and we would soon stifle in our own refuse. (Lipe 1984, 1)

> It would be utopian to consider that all cultural resources must be preserved in perpetuity – nor, indeed, would it be in the interests of contemporary and future societies. (Cleere 1984c, 127)

Accordingly, the heritage is subject to a process of selection based upon 'identification and recording of that heritage' (Cleere 1989b, 11):

> Selection of the best and the representative is imperative, but this can be brought about only by adequate survey and inventoriz-ation. (Cleere 1984c, 127)

After such survey and inventory comes the process of judging each item's archaeological 'significance'. The term 'significance' is borrowed from the United States literature, where it has a very precise and strict legal meaning which makes it dangerous to use in any other context (King *et al.* 1977, 95–104; McGimsey and Davis 1977, 31; Schiffer and Gumerman 1977, 245–6). What is legally 'significant' in the USA may not also be in the UK – although this fact does not prevent attempts to export the concept to other non-US jurisdictions (e.g. Africa, Wester 1990; and Australia, Smith in press). In addition, to a large extent what is to be considered 'archaeologically significant' (in a strict legal sense or otherwise) will vary depending on context and the use to which it is to be put: a flint scatter in a ploughed field may be of limited significance in an area well known for prehistoric occupation but may be of great significance in indicating such occupation in a region previously thought to be sterile; similarly, what data any such flint scatter will reveal to the prehistorian will depend on a number of factors, including simply its accessibility to that prehistorian. Accordingly, 'significance' is not a simple concept to be applied easily despite its growing appeal to realms outside of mainstream archaeology (e.g. in museums, Young 1994).

The concept of significance has been subject to some strong criticism in archaeology, especially in the United States and Australia where it is applied most widely. In general, such criticism takes the form of chal-lenging the usefulness or applicability of the concept for measuring the value of archaeological sites. One problem identified in particular is that its application requires, in effect, the designation of certain sites as being insignificant. To overcome this, Schaafsma (1989) urges archaeologists to consider all sites 'significant until proven otherwise'. In considering the epistemological status of significance, Tainter and Lucas (1983) point out that 'significance' is not 'an essential attribute of a cultural property, [and thus] observable and recordable' (ibid., 711) but is rather a quality ascribed to that material by archaeologists. They nevertheless emphasize its importance by way of enshrinement in law (ibid., 707–9) and trace its power as a concept from its ultimate derivation from the Western philosophical tradition of empiricist science (ibid., 711). Leone and Potter (1992) follow this line in recognizing that significance is not a quality inherent in archaeological material. Instead, they argue, we are forced to 'understand significance as growing out of the needs of contemporary societies rather than as existing independently, within the relics of past cultures' (Leone and Potter 1992, 143). This, they say, requires us to engage in a dialogue about significance criteria 'with [those] whom they effect' [*sic*] (Leone and Potter 1992, 141). Similarly, in respect of significance as applied in Australia, Smith calls for archaeologists to be 'explicit about the political agendas we may wish to pursue; and for these agendas to be successfully implemented we need to critically understand the hegemonic structures which both provide authority for, and marginalize, archaeological concerns' (Smith in press). In thus criticizing the application of the significance concept, what none of these commentators does is to enquire into what precisely it is that site assessment or evaluation actually does in respect of the material that is its object. To achieve this means examining the concept of value underpinning the entire process, and accordingly an understanding of value will emerge as one of the main themes of this book.

An English example of testing for significance
Under a combination of law and archaeological practice, various classes of monument (a legally defined concept in Britain: Ancient Monuments and Archaeological Areas Act 1979, s. 61) are recorded and a set of decision criteria are then applied for the purposes of assessing them for their 'national importance' (the value ascribed by law to a scheduled monument which is then subject to restrictions on its use: Ancient Monuments and Archaeological Areas Act 1979, s. 1). In order to facilitate and standardize this procedure, the Secretary of State published in 1983 a set of eight non-statutory criteria for deciding 'national importance' (Darvill *et al.* 1987, 395; Department of the Environment 1990, Annex 4; English Heritage 1991a, 54; Startin 1992) (listed below). Subsequently, in an effort to increase the numbers of field monuments given legal protection in England, the Monuments Protection Programme (MPP; originally the 'scheduling enhancement programme') was initiated by English Heritage (Darvill *et al.* 1987; Startin 1992, 1993, 1995) and, for the purposes of the MPP, the eight non-statutory criteria were expanded and increased in number (Darvill *et al.* 1987, 396). The expanded MPP criteria are divided between three distinct stages of evaluation, designated as: characterization (concerned with ensuring that monuments scheduled are a representative sample of all eligible classes of monuments) (Darvill *et al.* 1987, 396); discrimination (concerned with identifying monuments of 'national importance' from those in the same class not worthy of such importance) (Darvill *et al.* 1987, 397); and assessment (concerned with identifying the management needs of individual monuments) (Darvill *et al.* 1987, 398). Similar sets of criteria

are currently in the course of production to cover urban archaeology (Darvill, pers. comm. 1992) and relict landscapes (Startin 1992, 203; Darvill *et al.* 1993).

Secretary of State's evaluation criteria

Period
Rarity
Documentation
Group value
Survival/condition
Fragility/vulnerability
Diversity
Potential

By contrast with the more sophisticated MPP criteria, the Secretary of State's few criteria are now used for three different purposes: for classifying monuments as of 'national importance' for scheduling (and hence protection) under UK national law; for deciding grant aid to rescue archaeology projects; and as guidance to local authorities for urban and rural planning purposes (Department of the Environment 1990, Annex 4; English Heritage 1991a, 54).

The use of such criteria in these different ways reflects many of the weaknesses of AHM as currently understood and practised. First, if 'national importance' is not a simple concept, a list of only eight criteria is unlikely to reflect the complexity of the decisions to be taken (this being one of the reasons behind the establishment of the MPP). Second, application of these identical sets of criteria for three different purposes – two of which lie outside the original intention of the criteria (Darvill *et al.* 1987, 394) – will inevitably result in gaps in coverage. Even assuming the adequacy of the criteria for assessing the significance of monuments for national legislation, the same monuments will also be assessed as significant for local authority planning and rescue archaeology purposes. Accordingly, anything lying outside these few criteria will be equally ineligible for either curatorial management, exploitative management or rescue excavation at the national, regional and local levels (Darvill 1987, 25–31). The net result will be the loss of archaeological material rather than its protection, together with distracting arguments among archaeologists and others as to the appropriate level of treatment.

In addition, the object of this process – the components of the archaeological record/resource/heritage – is necessarily treated as a wholly known body of material rather than one which is renewable by the deposition of new material and the identification of totally new classes of material. The result is a static evaluation process which cannot cope easily with changes in archaeological understanding. Moreover, it may serve to limit the capacity for such change by enshrining a limited version of current understanding in a procedure that needs to be fairly rigid in order to ensure the application of common principles over the (long) life of the evaluation project – that is, perpetuity. This applies also in the case of 'new' projects that derive directly out of the scheduling process. One such is the Monuments At Risk Survey (MARS; MARS News Release 1994) which aims to construct a model of the natural and cultural forces at work which damage and ultimately destroy components of the archaeological resource. In doing so, however, and like the MPP, the project considers only known material – monuments legally defined and previously recorded – and is concerned not to develop new evaluation criteria (as the MPP might) but to more closely define those already being applied.

The function of the Secretary of State's eight evaluation criteria are to allow 'points' to be awarded to any monument for its characteristics but examination of the criteria themselves reveals that they contain certain potential contradictions which cannot easily be resolved.

Secretary of State's evaluation criteria – potential contradictions

Survival/condition	Fragility/vulnerability
Documentation	Rarity
Group value	Low diversity
High diversity	

The categories 'survival/condition' and 'fragility/vulnerability', for example, may be exclusive. If the likelihood of survival in good condition is high (thus gaining points) then the monument may not be particularly fragile or vulnerable (for which it would also be awarded points). Other criteria are equally potentially contradictory. A monument acquires points for having documentation concerning it, for being part of a group, for having a number of attributes. But it can also gain points for being rare and for only having one special attribute. For example, a rare monument about which little is known is not likely to be considered in the same light as one on which a great deal of information is available.

The result of the application of these criteria will accordingly be an inability to compare meaningfully the significance scores of different monuments: a monument scoring high on the criteria shown on the right-hand side of the above list will be a very different one from a monument scoring high on the left-hand side criteria; any choice to be made between them will have to be based on criteria other than those included in the scheme, rendering the scoring procedure redundant.

In practice, overcoming these potential contradictions simply requires the ranking of the criteria so that one factor is given more importance than another. This is despite the fact that the criteria themselves are not officially listed in any order of ranking (Department of the Environment 1990, Annex 4). But the weighting will need to be different for every monument or type of monument encountered. To do otherwise would guarantee the exclusion from coverage of monuments in particular sets of circumstances. This throws the burden once more on the subjective assessment of the individual inspector. In fact, the judgements of evaluators prior to the introduction to the MPP have in general been upheld (Startin, pers. comm. 1994). In reviewing potential contradictions among the criteria, it becomes possible to suggest that these criteria are not a set of decision criteria so much as a means to justify decisions already made on other − possibly quite different − grounds.

In contrast with the potential for contradiction among them, it is evident simply from looking at the criteria that certain of them are similar in kind and so can be conveniently grouped together. Seen from this perspective, 'survival/condition' and 'fragility/vulnerability' relate to the physical condition of a monument. By contrast, the 'period' criterion covers questions of the representativeness of a site type and the degree to which it characterizes (or stands for) a particular historical period. The question of 'rarity' value is deeply implicated here: a single unique monument can characterize a period (e.g. Stonehenge for the later Neolithic and early Bronze Age) but so can a common and widespread type (e.g. the round barrow for the Bronze Age, the hill-fort for the Iron Age, the castle for the Middle Ages). This relates quite closely to the 'group value' criterion which connects the monument to associated features of the same period or other periods, and thus to the 'documentation' criterion which concerns the existence of contemporary written records. In turn, this suggests the idea of the criterion of 'diversity', which distinguishes a single attribute from grouped ones. Collectively these criteria − period, rarity, group value, documentation and diversity − concern questions of meaning and interpretation rather than mere physical existence.

Secretary of State's evaluation criteria −
models of the archaeological record represented

'Physical' model	*'Textual'* model
Survival/condition	Period
Fragility/vulnerability	Rarity
	Group value
	Documentation
	Diversity

Determining criterion
Potential

Two sets of evaluation criteria from the same assessment scheme thus appear to relate to both of Patrik's (1985) incompatible textual and physical models of the archaeological record while leaving no room for the alternative 'field of discourse' model (Barrett 1987). There is, however, a way out of this impasse by way of the final evaluation criterion – one not allocated to either model. This is the criterion of 'potential', described as the 'nature of the evidence' a site can be expected to produce (English Heritage 1991a, 54). This 'evidence' is not merely things or remains because the idea of evidence contains the notion that it shall be evidence of or for something (Barrett 1987) – in other words, that the evidence represented by or contained within the site or monument shall be used for some purpose. This purpose will vary depending on the model – physical, textual, or 'field of discourse' – of the object of archaeological enquiry being brought to bear by the individual assessor. In this way, the final criterion of 'potential' 'acts back' on the other criteria to determine the manner in which they are understood and applied and the degree of weighting to be attached to each. Once again, therefore, the subjective and personal vision of the individual archaeologist is brought to the fore in the application of the evaluation criteria to sites.

This brief consideration of the measurement of archaeological 'significance' thus reveals some of the complexities of linking the concept of the archaeological resource with that of the archaeological record. In terms of research it opens up questions concerning the values we place on archaeological material – and how we place those values. It will be shown below how this fits into a research programme in AHM, and will be the focus of detailed consideration in Chapters 2 and 8.

Summary
The field of AHM is separated from academic archaeology to the detriment of both, since, while academic archaeology depends on an effective AHM for its future – by the preservation of its study material – AHM remains ineffective without critique. The four basic principles of AHM – that the archaeological resource is finite and non-renewable, is a matter of public concern, is governed by legislation, and is to be assessed for its significance – have been accepted as truths without question. This has caused AHM to become increasingly detached from mainstream archaeology. A critique of these four principles reveals their shortcomings, but it also opens up wide-ranging questions which can be made the subject of research. These four areas of potential research – into how material comes to be considered 'archaeological', into the nature and origin of the 'public interest' in archaeology, into the nature of the relationship between archaeology and preservation legislation, and

into the valuation of archaeological remains – are necessarily related since they each derive from the principles of AHM, which follow each other in logical progression.

TOWARDS A RESEARCH PROGRAMME IN AHM
Since the four large research areas opened up by a critique of the basic principles of AHM are related, to start on any one inevitably leads to the others. This interlocking set of problems can be envisaged as an 'archaeological rhizome' (cf. Shanks 1992, 47) in which the choice of entry point may be arbitrary but the track of which necessarily involves engagement with other research questions. In the case of the study that is the subject of this work the route so traced was as follows:

the nature of the relationship law ↔ archaeology → history of that relationship → history of the development of archaeology → how certain materials became the subject of archaeological enquiry → how those materials became considered to be valuable → the role of law in that process → the function of law in archaeology → how the law works on archaeological material → the values ascribed by law to archaeological material

Such a route thus addresses the issues not only of the function of law in AHM, but also of the definition and identification of archaeological material, of 'public interest' in that material and finally of the valuations placed on that material. All of these will be addressed in the chapters that follow, with the intention of opening up yet further routes of enquiry.

The study of law in AHM
The initial decision to research the relationship between law and archaeology was made on a number of grounds. First, the very centrality of law in the field of AHM makes it a priority for examination. If the 'governance' of law in this field means the domination of archaeological concerns by legal ones, then no change can be wrought in the understanding of AHM without a close review of that relationship. Second, the lack of previous enquiries into aspects of AHM from a critical perspective have resulted in the failure to build a useful data set for such purposes. Not only this, but the methodology of constructing such a data set is also lacking. The law as written – being already extant and available – provides a ready-made source of data which can be constructed and used for the purpose of research into AHM. Third, the existing literature of AHM provides much coverage of aspects of the law

relevant to the preservation of archaeological remains. This provided a convenient starting point for research.

A comparative approach was eschewed from the outset. Comparative studies (cf. Cleere 1984a; Czaplicki 1989) tend to be merely descriptive in content as a result of the problems inherent in such an approach. First, fundamental differences between legal systems must be taken into account and neutralized. For example, whereas US federal legislation requires to be read in the light of its preamble (which sets out the intention of the legislators), English law must not be so read. Similarly, the fundamental differences between a system of common law (applicable in England) and of Roman law (applicable on much of the European continent) – which rely on very different underlying assumptions for their application and interpretation – must be catered for. Second, any differences in the nature of the archaeological record covered by the legislation must be carefully considered since this will affect its interpretation and treatment. For instance, prehistoric remains in England can largely be considered the remains of the ancient (but no longer extant) predecessors of those currently inhabiting that country; the same cannot be said for the United States, Canada or Australia where the prehistoric archaeology is that of an extant but different culture who may lay claim to it (cf. Layton 1989a, 1989b). At the same time, laws covering upstanding field monuments may not also apply to standing buildings, buried sites or movable objects, and any assumption of such coverage will be inappropriate. Third, the historical development of archaeology in a territory will affect the nature, range and style of the relevant laws. Accordingly, it will be necessary also to take this into account in researching such law in comparative perspective.

The cumulative result of such problems is that it will take a detailed knowledge of the history and nature of archaeology and of the legal system in at least two separate countries to compare their archaeological legislation meaningfully. To fail to undertake this massive amount of work will mean that there is no certainty that like is not being compared with something totally unlike. Accordingly, jurisdictions will need to be dealt with separately. However, this does not mean that no comparative study can ever be undertaken or have relevance. Rather, the task is one of seeking to understand the law as applied in AHM in one country in order that the understanding so gained can be compared with the understanding of another country's laws acquired by a similar means. Only by sets of detailed individual contextual studies – such as this work intends to provide for England – can we be certain that a subsequent comparative approach is genuinely comparing like with like. Such detailed contextual studies of archaeological law will require much work since this cannot be done simply from a review of the current literature concerning AHM.

Current approaches to law in AHM

Much of the relevant coverage of law is contained in the general body of AHM material where the place of law in AHM is unquestioned (Cleere 1984a, 1989a; McGimsey 1972; McGimsey and Davis 1977), but more specific works reflect the general attitude toward legal regulation taken in the field. Historical studies of the development of law start from the premise that such law is necessary and inevitable and the only surprise is that it takes a long time to come into being (Boulting 1976; Chippindale 1983a; Kennet 1972; Saunders 1983). The rare challenges to such a view come from two sources: those adopting an oppositional stance to the current regime, who charge those promoting legal developments with narrow political interests (Wright 1985); and institutions responsible for the implementation of legislation who, when under threat, emphasize the long struggle involved in gaining this legislation (Countryside Commission 1989) – although such an argument serves to confirm the necessity of such legislation rather than challenging it.

General reviews of relevant branches of law abound. The laws relating to museum collections internationally are particularly well covered (Malaro 1985; Williams 1978) although more general coverage of all cultural property is also available (Burnham 1974; O'Keefe and Prott 1984). Other reviews concern themselves with specific jurisdictions (US Dept. of the Interior 1989–90) or with specific classes of material perhaps also limited by jurisdiction (e.g. for the laws relating to human remains in the US, Price 1990). This type of work is invariably descriptive rather than analytical but has its use in advertising the existence of the laws cited. The overriding problem from the point of view of this rather limited use function is that this literature tends to go out of date very quickly as laws change. Like so much of this material, exemplified in England by the literature on Treasure Trove as it applies to ancient remains (Hammond 1982, Palmer 1981, Sparrow 1982), the bulk of it is written by lawyers with a side interest in archaeology rather than archaeologists with an interest in the application of law to their field; the only exception to this rule is Hill (1936), who used it to justify the transfer of the administration of Treasure Trove to the British Museum, of which he was then Director.

Equally descriptive are shorter papers which briefly outline the current situation with regard to law in relation to specific bodies of material (e.g. Chippindale and Gibbins 1990; Priddy 1991) or institutions charged with conservation duties (National Rivers Authority 1991; Somerset County and District Councils 1989). Longer such pieces can also be used to justify the status quo (Torres de Arauz 1987). A more critical stance to such an approach is sometimes taken, either to point out failures of the system and recommend remedies (Ziedler 1982) or to encourage wider compliance (Price 1984). Like the wider reviews available, such material is useful in indicating the presence of laws, but neither challenges its *raison d'être*, nor analyses its mode of operation.

Summary
The current literature relating to law in AHM – while helpful in indicating laws of relevance to archaeology – does not provide a useful framework for its analysis and critique. This analysis and critique is nevertheless required because of the centrality of law in AHM, and because law provides the source of the data lacking for an approach to the other research questions identified in the field. A comparative study of law is currently inappropriate because of the inherent problems of such an approach, requiring not only a detailed knowledge of the legal system but also of the history and nature of the archaeology in at least two different territories. Accordingly, research limited to a single jurisdiction is called for. Such research will nevertheless involve a consideration of the three other research questions identified, and therein lies at least part of its value.

THE WAY FORWARD
The problem of opening up research directions in AHM can in part be addressed by a study of English law as it relates to archaeology, both in the sense of archaeology the academic discipline and archaeology as archaeological material. The relationship between archaeology and law is examined from two perspectives in this book. From the historical perspective, the very close relationship between the historical development of the discipline of archaeology and the appropriation or creation of bodies of law which allow archaeologists to gain control over their material is demonstrated. From an analytical perspective, the underlying principles on which such current law is based and the effects of its implementation on archaeological material itself are revealed.

As outlined above, the route of the research process through the field of AHM encounters the concept of value at a number of points. In what follows, it will be argued that the primary role of law in relation to archaeology is to ascribe a modern social value to archaeological material and thus vicariously to archaeology the discipline and archaeologists themselves. To begin, then, it is necessary to acquire some insight to the social processes by which things gain and lose value – and this is the subject of the first part of the next chapter.

NOTE
1. See: Adovaiso and Carlisle 1988; Andah 1990; Ashley-Smith n.d.; Ashworth and

Tunbridge 1990; Chippindale and Gibbins 1990; Cleere 1984a, 1989; Cracknell and Corbishley 1986; Creamer 1990; Cunningham 1979; Darvill 1987; Darvill *et al.* 1978; Fawcett 1976; Fowler, D. D. 1982, 1986; Fowler, P. J. 1992; Gale 1990; Green 1984; Greeves 1989; Hughes and Rowley 1986; Kennet 1972; King *et al.* 1977; Knudson 1986; Lipe 1974, 1977; McGimsey 1972; McGimsey and Davis 1977; Marsden 1972; Messenger 1989; Mills n.d.; National Trust for Historic Preservation 1980; Newcomb 1979; Priddy 1991; Raab 1984; Rahtz 1976; Rowley and Breakell 1977 [2 vols]; Schiffer and Gumerman 1977; Silverman and Parezo 1992; Uzzell 1989 [2 vols]; Wildesen 1980; Wilson 1987; Wilson and Loyola 1982.

2
Value and law

Questions concerning the value of archaeological remains are central to AHM but have received scant attention other than in terms of assessing 'significance' (Chapter 1). In order to develop, AHM requires to consider valuation as an essentially dynamic social process.

To understand this social dynamic requires, among other things, a study of the historical trajectory of the valuation of archaeological material. Accordingly, as outlined in the Preface, it is appropriate to divide the major portion of this work into separate 'historical' and 'analytical' segments. The apparently clear division between past and present reflected in this organization, however, is merely a literary convenience. The concepts that inform the approach to the work are common to both the historical and analytic sections. Accordingly, as well as describing the methodology of the research, this chapter will introduce the important concepts which inform it throughout – both in terms of the valuation process (an issue which recurs throughout the thesis) and of law (the starting-point for enquiry and the source of data).

VALUING ARCHAEOLOGICAL MATERIAL
From the point of view of AHM, archaeological remains – although able to inform us about the past – are a body of contemporary material. Accordingly, the processes which result in the ascription of particular kinds of value to archaeological remains are the same as those which ascribe value to other classes of material. To understand one, then, is to understand the other. In this section, examples will be chosen from both archaeological material and other categories of object – whichever is most appropriate – to illustrate the process of valuation at work in our society. The whole question of the valuation process requires a close involvement with the concerns of a number of other social sciences.

The public domain: public people are to private people as 'heritage' is to family history
The archaeological heritage consists of things and, from an economic point of view, things are goods. Unfortunately, economic theory does

not have much to say about how people become attracted to one kind of thing as opposed to another. Economists have very powerful tools for analysing choices between similar things (one car and another car, for example) but when it comes to the choice between a car and a holiday they rely on others. It was this disability that led Mary Douglas and Baron Isherwood to try and construct an 'anthropology of consumption' in *The World of Goods* (1979).

After outlining the strengths and weaknesses of economics in the understanding of saving and consumption, Douglas and Isherwood move to a more explicitly anthropological approach. They start by classifying goods – that is, things – as 'an information system' which say things about the people who choose them. They also point out that 'needs' are socially determined and relate to one's social position rather than being constant across social boundaries (1979, 95). In an interesting example, they quote the take-up of telephones as opposed to television sets in the United Kingdom:

> In 1948 the percentage of households owning television sets was 0.3 percent. By 1958 it was 52 percent while the telephone, introduced in 1877, by the same date was installed in only 16.5 percent of households. . . . Two years later [1960] the proportion of all households owning television sets had gone up to 65 percent. By contrast, telephone penetration had actually reached no further than 21.4 percent by 1965. (Douglas and Isherwood 1979, 99–101)

This pattern of take-up results in a very steep curve for televisions and a much shallower one for telephones which, although spread over a much longer time, does not reach such a high level. The distribution of these items across social groups is a related factor. While the television has a fairly even distribution across social groups, the telephone is clustered in the top social group. This is explained in terms of the need to create and maintain social linkages (Douglas and Isherwood 1979, 185–94). Those at the top end of the social scale are in control of the resources which maintain their position, but to keep their position they also need to retain control of those resources. Accordingly, Douglas and Isherwood refer to them as 'social controllers'. To keep control they need to have a widespread network of contacts – professional, political and social – with whom they are regularly in touch. Communication is therefore a key requirement and any means to facilitate this will be accorded a high value. When the telephone was invented and taken up by one member of such a social network, all the other members did so in order not to be excluded. Those who were already excluded from the network had no need for such a device and were much slower to take it up. By contrast, the television was fairly rapidly taken up by all social groups more or less equally.

The point of this difference in take-up is that the television is a form of home-based entertainment while the telephone relates to communication outside the home. An emphasis on the importance to social controllers of contacts outside the residential base is given valuable support by the fact that as social class goes down, more time is spent watching television; while as social class goes up, membership of clubs, contact with friends and even hours worked go up (Douglas and Isherwood 1979, 91). The upshot is an emphasis among the 'upper set' – the better off, the better educated, and so on – on activities outside the home. By contrast, those further down the social ladder show a tendency to concentrate their activities around the hearth.

This pattern of external orientation versus internal orientation is similar to that identified by Merriman (1991) in his survey of public attitudes to the past. What his work revealed was that the higher a person's place in society, the more likely they were to visit museums and various kinds of 'heritage' display and to value 'history' in the sense of world-shaking events, battles, monarchs and the like. Those lower down the scale placed a higher value on local concerns, and especially on family history rather than national history.

Analysis reveals, then, two sorts of people. On the one hand there are those with a wide network of social contacts – well off, well educated, with much 'cultural capital' (Bourdieu 1984), who show an interest in national heritage (Merriman 1991) – and whose activities concentrate outside the home. On the other are those whose world concentrates on the home – the television set, family history, and a much narrower range of social contacts. The former are the politicians, the business people, the academics, the 'social controllers'. The latter are not. These two sets can be characterized as 'public people' and 'private people'.

The core of my argument is that the public domain is fundamentally a different phenomenon from the private domain. In dividing people into those who are public and those who are private, I am suggesting that these realms are to some extent inhabited by different kinds of people. Public people are Douglas and Isherwood's 'social controllers' and private people their 'socially controlled'. Social controllers tend to enjoy 'cultural capital' as well as 'economic capital' – that is, social know-how and the money to exploit it (Bourdieu 1984). This means that they can move fairly easily between social worlds as they choose – including the public and private domains.

The division between public people and private people reflects a conceptual distinction between the public and private domains of life. I will argue in Chapter 4 that the public domain was expanded at the expense of the private in the nineteenth century as part of a wider project related to the creation of a new, more broadly based political unity within the British state. It was as part of this process that the archaeological heritage first acquired legal protection and that by doing so it was 'lifted' into the public domain.

The distinction between the private domain of economic activity and the activities of the State has been recognized by Giddens, who says:

> [A] 'private' sphere of 'civil society' is created by, but is separate from and in tension with, the 'public' sphere of the state. . . . Civil society is the sector within which capital accumulation occurs, fuelled by the mechanisms of price, profit and investment in labour and commodity markets. (Giddens 1984, 197)

Peter Berger (1973, 104) says that 'the cleavage between private and public spheres is a basic principle of modernity' – in other words, it is a defining characteristic of the world as we have created it. Accordingly, as one analysis puts it, the distinction 'between publicness and privateness is a practical one, part of a conceptual framework that organises action in a social environment' (Benn and Gaus 1983b, 5). The two spheres are also normative categories, applied in relation to social context (ibid., 11), and so there is a problem of assessing the degree of continuity between them – 'more' public versus 'more' private (ibid., 13–18). There are three dimensions along which such measurements can be made – interest, agency, and access.

Interest is measured in terms of public interest – the degree to which the entire community is concerned with something. There is a large element of circularity of argument in this – things that are in the public domain are deemed to be matters of public interest; and the reason they are in the public domain is because they are a matter of public concern. The public interest itself is 'a diverse cluster of rights of ownership and control' mediated by agency (Benn and Gaus 1983b, 9–10).

Agency relates to the powers of action in relation to the matter that is of public interest. In many cases, the power of a public official may exceed that of the private individual citizen, but the actions of the official are constrained by the law which gives the official the authority to act. The element of limited competence on the part of the official (Berger 1973, 46) results in referral of specific problems elsewhere for coverage by the appropriate agency. There is a strong emphasis on proper procedure, individual anonymity, orderliness, organizability, predictability and the non-separability of means and ends (ibid., 47–8, 50–5).

Access in this context is not just physical access – to a site or monument, but also to knowledge and a general awareness of its presence. This relates to public interest in the sense that anything in the public domain is felt to 'belong' to one – or that one belongs to it (cf. Christopher Chippindale on Stonehenge, pers. comm.) – but not exclusively. This is the quality exhibited by all public goods as recognized by economists – that of externality, defined as the effect of an action by one individual person on another (Ordeshook 1986, 211). Public goods are capable of consumption freely or at no marginal cost; in other words, they are non-excludable in the sense that access cannot be denied except with difficulty (ibid., 212).

Benn and Gaus (1983a, 39) consider the important institutions of the two domains. In the private sphere we are essentially concerned with the individual. In the public sphere, it is the group which is the important thing, and especially the state which stands for the entire society. Thus, in the public sphere the group acts as a single body, and in the case of the state it acts for everyone. This brings us back to Douglas and Isherwood who consider the differences between individual and corporate savings. Of the strong corporate group, they say:

> Because its legal existence is eternal, it can make its demands in the name of unborn generations. . . . No individual acting on his or her own behalf can entertain dreams of such a long-term future. Only the group can develop a full-fledged otherworldly morality, for the group outlives its members. (Douglas and Isherwood 1979, 37)

This is the way to view the archaeological heritage – as a form of corporate saving. The heritage can be seen to exist in the public domain, the realm of the group rather than the individual, endowed with an 'otherworldly morality'. The idea of the 'otherworldly' expresses the aura of the public domain quite nicely. It is not of the everyday in which things are used up, discarded, bought or sold, or just ignored. The public domain is a special place – above and beyond the reach of the individual and yet something in which the individual has a legitimate interest and rights. This raises issues concerning the importance we ascribe to the heritage and how we should apply to the archaeological heritage ideas about the 'social life of things' (Appadurai 1986b) and how things gain and lose value (Carman 1990a).

The 'social life' of things
The notion that objects have social 'life histories' in the same way as people is an idea that has emerged from, among other areas, work in

economic anthropology. This insight has been applied in particular to the commodity, that is, an item 'with use value which also has exchange value' but which is not merely a thing (a material object) but 'also culturally marked as being a *certain kind of thing*' (Kopytoff 1986, 64; emphasis added).

Appadurai (1986a, 13) thus distinguishes 'commodities' from other objects and seeks to identify the 'commodity situation' of the object by reference to the 'commodity phase' of its life cycle, the 'commodity candidacy' of the object, and its 'commodity context'. The 'commodity situation' of an object is defined as 'the situation in which its exchange-ability (past, present or future) for some other thing is its socially relevant feature' (ibid., 13). The economic value of the commodity is seen to result from its exchange between persons (rather than being immanent in the object itself) and 'the link between exchange and value is *politics*, construed broadly' (ibid., 3; original emphasis). In other words, the distinguishing feature of a commodity is its exchangeability for other commodities (including money), and the economic value of a com-modity is related to the social world in which it circulates. Accordingly, its economic value will vary depending on the social context in which it circulates.

In this scheme, the 'commodity phase' of the object's life cycle is to be distinguished from other such phases: the production phase in which the object comes into being, and the consumption phase in which it ceases to exist. The possibility remains, of course, of other non-commodity phases in which the object has no exchange value, is not exchanged between persons and yet remains extant. Thus, a truly priceless artwork (which can be considered as too valuable to exchange with any other item) or worthless waste, although extant, are neither of them com-modities in this sense. Nevertheless, they are objects and the 'priceless' and 'waste' phases of their life cycle may be only one of several.

In the case of certain objects one such phase may perhaps be called the 'archaeology phase'. Michael Schiffer (1972) distinguishes between the 'systemic context' of an object and its 'archaeological context'. For him, archaeological deposits 'are no longer part of an ongoing society' (Schiffer 1987, 3). The systemic context corresponds to an object's place in an ongoing society while the archaeological context corresponds to the phase after this – after the object has ceased to be part of an ongoing social situation. He traces (1972) the life cycle of objects through phases of procurement, manufacture, use and maintenance, recycling and discard (all stages in the systemic context) to the final position of the object as refuse (in the archaeological context).

Schiffer does not, however, make explicit the point that, once dis-covered in the archaeological record, an object again becomes part of an ongoing society. This is not the society in the past – the society in which it was made and originally used – but our modern society. Accordingly, the life cycle of such an object does not end with discard and refuse, but continues through discovery and archaeological study, museum display or whatever subsequently happens to it.

Archaeological objects are held to be items of value. They are the source of an archaeologist's knowledge and understanding of the past. For certain very large expanses of time, they are our only source of knowledge concerning the human past. The value that is thus ascribed is not solely derived from the physical events in the life of the object – Schiffer's various stages from procurement to discard – but from the new social context in which it finds itself. In other words, as with a commodity, the value of an object is not immanent in the object itself but is the result of its place in a human, social context. Nevertheless, the new value ascribed to the object by the archaeologist is different from that ascribed to the object in its previous systemic context. Since the value of the object is not immanent in the object itself, then to understand this process of changing valuation, some other scheme must be found that will explain it.

Michael Thompson's (1979) book *Rubbish Theory* aims to explain how objects, as well as ideas, gain and lose value. It culminates in the use of a model derived from Catastrophe Theory to explain sudden jumps between styles of educational curricula. Thompson considers the transfer of various types of object from a period of use and declining value to one of preservation and increasing value. Such objects include 'Stevengraphs' (Victorian mass-reproduced pictures), an old car, inner city housing, the ruinous country house at Grange Park, Hampshire, and artworks.

The scheme posits three possible kinds of value which can be ascribed to objects (Thompson 1979, 8). Transience (in which value is declining) and durability (in which value is increasing) are both regions of fixed assumptions in which a person's categorization of the object determines the action they take towards it (thus, an antique cabinet will be treated differently from a secondhand chest-of-drawers, although physically these may be identical). The category of rubbish (in which the item has nil value) is a region of flexibility in which action towards the object determines the view of it that is taken. In this scheme, the terms 'durable', 'transient' and 'rubbish' do not refer to the physical life expectancy of an object: something which is transient for Thompson may be as physically robust (or more so) than something durable. The terms refer instead to the values placed on objects. Something for use only today is transient, however robustly it may be made; something to be kept – however fragile – is durable. Thus, a washing machine (a

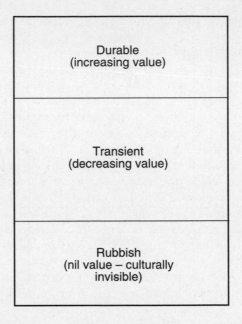

Figure 2.1   Rubbish Theory (after Thompson 1979)

consumer durable in the jargon of trade) is merely transient; but a Zuni war god, while rotting in the earth, is durable.

Rubbish, as defined by Thompson, is deemed by cultural convention to be invisible and therefore non–existent. However, rubbish (whether outdated fads in popular decoration, decrepit motor vehicles, or slum housing) does occupy space in the real world and can be used by people in the same way as any other item. Its very invisibility renders it an ideal tool for manipulation to restructure expectations of and ideas about the world. Accordingly, a slum occupied by a 'knocker-through' will become a period townhouse. Similarly, an old banger when carefully restored becomes a vintage car.

The bottom part of Figure 2.1 – the rubbish box – is where items of no value reside. As rubbish they are valueless and deemed to be invisible. This means that they are held by common agreement not to exist – like the person defecating in an Indian city street, or the dust on the top of a door which we all ignore, or the stained paper that did not get flushed away in a toilet bowl. All these things have a physical existence, but we choose (unless we are being perverse) not to see them. Not seen, not discussed. Rubbish exists in a realm below that of discourse. This is very useful, because Thompson's model is a dynamic one that attempts to explain how things shift from one value category to another. The rubbish

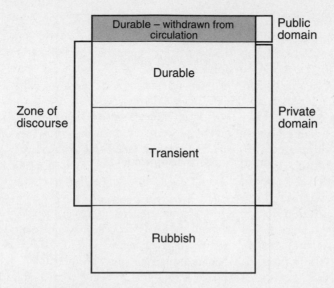

Figure 2.2   The public domain in Rubbish Theory

category is particularly important in this, since it is by being reduced to rubbish – culturally invisible, not considered or discussed – that items can be manipulated so as to re-emerge with a new value placed upon them. Thompson provides numerous examples of this process.

Many (if not most) archaeologists will be conversant with the idea that any form of material culture can operate in the social environment at a level below that of discourse (cf. Hodder 1982). However, the archaeological heritage can be said to reside in the durable box. Durable items are deemed to have a permanent existence and constantly increasing value. What happens when they reach a level of value that can no longer be measured is that they are withdrawn from circulation. This is not rubbish – they are not culturally invisible. Instead, they become hyper-visible, highly prominent in the cultural landscape. This lifts such items out of the zone of normal, everyday discourse and into another, higher realm – that of the public domain.

The distinguishing characteristic of material in the durable category is that, over time, its value is rising. Things that become so valuable that they are literally priceless – beyond price – are removed from circulation. To extend Thompson's diagram, they are lifted into a special part of the durable box beyond that of items in circulation (Figure 2.2). They are lifted out of circulation, out of the everyday world and into a special realm where conventional language breaks down. Unlike rubbish, however, they are not placed below discourse but above it.

The origin of value

The question remains, however, how things are given value – the processes involved. The need is for a device that can show how people operate in the social environment.

The principle of the Grid/Group diagram devised by Mary Douglas (1982) is that you can locate people in any society along two dimensions: in terms of how prescribed their field of action is – the 'Grid' dimension; and how involved they are in relations with others – the 'Group' dimension. Michael Thompson and his collaborators (Schwarz and Thompson 1990; Thompson 1990; Thompson *et al.* 1990) go one stage further and define five positions in the Grid/Group matrix. This they call Cultural Theory.

Each position in the Grid/Group matrix (Schwarz and Thompson 1990, 9) constitutes a separate rationality comprising related sets of behaviours and beliefs, in which each mode of thought or action supports the others in that rationality. This contextually dependent rationality is the filter through which we respond to the world. Thus, when any question arises, we look at it through this particular filter and we try to match the problem to our current understanding of how the world works, which in turn depends on our current social context.

Thompson and his collaborators have applied this approach to understanding disputes about technological issues – especially energy policy disputes (Schwarz and Thompson 1990) – and in particular why estimates of expected benefits or harm can be so widely divergent between one expert and another. They have this to say:

> the clue to why some people give credence to one perception and other people to other perceptions [is that] if resource estimates are clumped in order to provide justifications for energy policies then energy policies are best understood as arguments for ways of life, as rationalizations for different kinds of desired social arrangements. If this is the case, then the conventional sequence will have to be reversed. (Schwarz and Thompson 1990, 91)

The conventionally accepted sequence is this:

facts $\longrightarrow$ policy formulation $\longrightarrow$ selection of best policy

> Instead, you start with a socially induced predilection that leads you to favour the sort of social arrangements promised by one policy. . . . Having chosen [the policy] you then look around for justifications for it. (Schwarz and Thompson 1990, 91–2)

In terms of managing the archaeological heritage, the usual assumption is that archaeological material is valued and as a result is given protection. If, however, there is a parallel here with Cultural Theory then the sequence needs to be reversed. The conventional sequence is:

valued material $\longrightarrow$ methods of protection $\longrightarrow$ selection of

appropriate protection

To reword Thompson:

> Instead, you start with a socially induced predilection that leads you to favour the sort of social arrangements promised by protecting a particular class of material. . . . Having chosen you then look around for ways to value that class of material over others.

What this means for our purposes, then, is that the legal value which is given to archaeological remains comes at the end of the process of protecting them. First they are chosen for legal protection, then they are valued – not the other way around.

The spaces in the Grid/Group matrix are each occupied by people holding very different views of the world. What follows from this is that the people in each will see the same material object in a different way. It will mean different things to each of them, it will be valued differently. Not only will one ascribe something a high value, another a low value, a third no value at all, but the kinds of value ascribed to the object will also be very different. On the principle that 'birds of a feather flock together' the same will apply to institutions, which are made up of largely like-minded individuals organized along their preferred lines.

This potential for differential valuation introduces the useful concept of value gradient – or rather gradients – since there will be a different one for each kind of value. In introducing this idea, Michael Thompson considers the old Gracie Fields song 'I'm a lonely little petunia in an onion patch' (Thompson 1990, 125). Onions are an important agricultural food crop with much economic value; petunias are not. The poignancy of the song lies in placing the aesthetic but not very commercial petunia among all these powerful rivals for attention. He points out that the force of the idea would have been lost if the protagonists had been reversed: would 'I'm a lonely little onion in a petunia patch' be remembered? He suggests not: onions are far more powerful than petunias and as he points out

> songs about power, as a rule, are very tedious. . . . [I]t is displacement down an aesthetic (and an almost exclusively anti-

> economic and anti-power) gradient that [Gracie Fields] was
> singing about so memorably. (Thompson 1990, 125)

In a similar way Louisa Buck and Philip Dodd have examined how the
category 'art' receives a different valuation – and indeed a different
identity – depending on its context (Buck and Dodd 1991). Thus, they
point to the changing perception of what it is to be an 'artist' over time
and space, what art means to the commercial art market, to collectors
individual and corporate, to the state, and to art museums. What
emerges is that the single category 'art' does not have a single meaning,
nor a single kind of value, but a different one in each context, and even
different ones to different people in the same context.

The same applies to archaeological material. A polished Neolithic axe
which provides much valuable data to a researcher is desirable to a
museum because of its aesthetic quality while the man who runs the
coin shop in Bridge Street, Cambridge, may want it because he can sell
it. There are three quite different views of the axe here and for each
person it sits on a very different value gradient. The same axe from a
different (unprovenanced) context would be worth less to a researcher,
but would be equally valued by the museum officer responsible for
displays and by the man in the coin shop. If broken, the axe might be
worth the same to a researcher but less to the museum and maybe
nothing to the man in the coin shop. The value given to the axe
depends not on the axe itself but on the filter of attitudes and
behaviour patterns through which it is seen. This filter is in place before
the axe is encountered. So the axe is given value at the end of a
process, not at its beginning. That value depends not on any attribute
of the axe itself but on your expectations of the world and the place of
the axe in that world: as data source, as display object, or as saleable
commodity.

This raises the question of how we know what value gradient to place
things on. How do we know when something belongs or has been lost
to archaeology? One reason we are able to know is because we have set
up a system of procedures which allows us to identify when a decision
has been made, and – by taking part in that process – we bind ourselves
to accept its judgement. As Charles Smith has recently written about
auctions:

> Objects are reborn in auctions. They acquire new values, new
> owners, and often new definitions. . . . For these new identities
> to be accepted as legitimate, they must be seen as having a
> communal sanction. It is this search for legitimacy that underlies
> the communal character of auctions. (Smith 1989, 79)

The same words can be used about all decision-making processes that concern objects. All such procedures establish, first, the relevant value gradient for the object, and then its place on that gradient (that is, both the type and quantity of value). In this connection, the key functions of an auction have been listed as follows:

> They resolve ambiguities and uncertainties; they establish value, identity and ownership of items; they entertain; they shape social relationships; and they reallocate vast amounts of money. They also tell us a great deal about economic and social relationships. (Smith 1989, 162)

The most important of these functions are perhaps those of: resolving ambiguities and uncertainties; and the establishment of value, identity and ownership. Smith (1989, 33) points out that in the case of the auction the type of uncertainty to be resolved is that of price, and this in turn depends on the category of the object (as art, as a collectible or as a commodity). But the categorization of the object itself depends on how it is viewed. So even before entering the realm of uncertainty (the auction), some kind of decision about the object has already been made.

This suggests that in any decision process there are at least three phases. First, objects are chosen for a particular form of treatment. Second, they are categorized. Only at the end of this process are they given value. This is the same process as follows from the logic of the Cultural Theory scheme. This is also the process that is in operation when the law is applied to archaeological material and will be examined and discussed in the chapters that follow.

LEGAL PROCESS AND ARCHAEOLOGICAL MATERIAL

Before tackling the issue of how to approach the law, it may be appropriate to consider briefly what the phenomenon of law is. Following Newan (1983) after Durkheim, one can see the law as a set of social norms backed by coercive force. As one legal commentator has put it

> law is fundamentally an instrument, a tool for the achievement of social purposes. The purposes are not those of the law as such, but of people who make and enforce the law. . . . [Accordingly] law is an instrument of policy . . . but . . . there are many circumstances in which the precise nature of these goals or values is not a matter of great importance . . . to the law and lawyers. (Atiyah 1983, 74–80)

It follows from this that the law in any field is not the sole preserve of legal study. In particular, the study of law from an anthropological perspective has a long history and, specifically, anthropologists approach the law as a process (Moore 1978; Snyder 1989). Simon Roberts provides a useful summary of English legal theory from an anthropological perspective:

> Legal rules . . . have the dual purpose of prescribing approved avenues of conduct for people to follow and of providing criteria whereby disputes can be settled where these arise. (Roberts 1979, 19)

The operation of the law is such that fixed rules determine the outcome of disputes, but crucially these outcomes do not provide for compromise so that always 'one party wins and the other loses' (Roberts 1979, 20). The form and course of the dispute are beyond the control of the disputants, and the 'precise issue in dispute is separated from any larger complex of relations between the two disputants and dealt with in isolation from other aspects of their relationship' (ibid., 21). For Roberts, the institution of 'the law' operates as a discrete sub-system, cut off from the rest of society but the 'pre-eminent authority of "the law" in its assigned area of operation' means that 'all other normative systems give way to legal rules' (ibid., 22). As Aubert points out, however, in his study of Norwegian law:

> Law has manifold functions in a modern society. . . . The growth of legislation . . . suggests that law is used as an instrument to further many interests other than peace-keeping and conflict resolution. (Aubert 1969, 282)

In summary, law is primarily a set of rules which are to do with the resolution of conflicts within a society in accordance with certain norms. However, as well as being set by norms, one of the functions of the law is to set those social norms and to give them coercive force. As a setter of social norms the law requires people to behave in certain ways – that is, to do certain things. The law acts, then, as a programme for action.

Michael Thompson injuncts us to 'look for the institution' in studying social process (Thompson 1990, 116). In terms of Cultural Theory, the institution that prefers to work through sets of structured rules – in turn backed by coercive force – is the high Grid/high Group hierarchy (Schwarz and Thompson 1990, 9), and in its most sophisticated form the bureaucracy. Peter Berger reminds us that bureaucracy is 'the imposition of rational controls over the material universe, over social relations, and finally over the self' (Berger 1973, 202). In the case of laws to protect archaeological material, then, the issue is one of control. Accordingly, it will be argued in Chapters 3, 4 and 5 that the development of systems of such law in England go hand in hand with the development of the discipline of archaeology and provide support for the frameworks in which archaeologists learnt to order and control their material. The application of current law (Chapters 6, 7 and 8) serves to reaffirm this system of order and control.

Archaeological law in England

This study is limited to the law in England and this needs to be distinguished from UK law. The United Kingdom of England and Wales, Scotland and Northern Ireland comprises three separate jurisdictions with independent bodies of law: England and Wales; Scotland; and Northern Ireland. The rules governing archaeological material are quite different in each of these jurisdictions and are not easily comparable. For instance, while English law (which also covers Wales) is a system of common law, Scottish law is heavily influenced by the Roman law of the European continent. There are as a result significant differences between them, such as the rules relating to the ownership of land and (of particular relevance to this study) Treasure Trove. The law in Northern Ireland is also constructed on a common law base, but specific requirements reflect the peculiar circumstances of that province and its closeness to the Irish Republic. The same rules, then, do not apply in these three territories. To confuse matters further, even when the same legal regulations apply (as they do in England and Wales), the responsibility for putting them into effect rests with different agencies – for example, English Heritage and Cadw.

This study is concerned specifically with English law, which is directly concerned with archaeological material in England. The currently applicable law in England comprises a number of branches of law, both case law and Parliamentary legislation, which are listed below. The division of the various components of the law in this field (individual Acts of Parliament and court cases) into their separate branches is arbitrary but conventional. Where individual laws do not readily fit any category, they are placed in the one into which they most conveniently fit (for example, the Protection of Military Remains Act 1986 would conventionally be classified under 'military law', a category otherwise irrelevant here; accordingly, it is more convenient to list it under 'ancient monuments' with which it has some affinity).

This enormous corpus of legislation and case law is overwhelmingly large. In order to complete the research project in a reasonable time, some selectivity was inevitable. Accordingly, while the historical part of the work charts the development of all relevant branches of law, the analytical part concentrates on the items shown below in **bold** type; opposite each is shown the abbreviation by which it will be referenced in the Appendices and Chapters 6, 7 and 8. Nevertheless, enough is covered in the analysis to reveal the manner in which all such laws work, and to demonstrate that they all work the same way.

ANCIENT MONUMENTS
**Historic Buildings and Ancient Monuments Act
1953**   **HBAM53**

**Ancient Monuments and Archaeological Areas Act
1979**   **AMAA79**

National Heritage Act 1980   **NH80**

Ancient Monuments (Class Consents) Order 1981   AMCCO81

National Heritage Act 1983   **NH83**

Ancient Monuments (Class Consents) Order 1984   AMCCO84

Protection of Military Remains Act 1986   **PMR86**

ECCLESIASTICAL LAW
Inspection of Churches Measure 1955   **ICM55**

Pastoral Measure 1968   **PM68**

**Redundant Churches and Other Religious
Buildings Act 1969**   **RC69**

Cathedrals Measure 1990

ENVIRONMENTAL PROTECTION AND COUNTRYSIDE MANAGEMENT
Commons Act 1876 (section 7)

Coast Protection Act 1949 (section 47)

National Parks and Access to the Countryside Act 1949

Coal Mining (Subsidence) Act 1957 (section 9)

Land Powers (Defence) Act 1958 (section 6)

Mines (Working Facilities and Support) Act 1966 (section 7)

Forestry Act 1967 (section 40)

Countryside Act 1968

Wildlife and Countryside Act 1981

Agriculture Act 1986 (sections 17 to 21)

Electricity Act 1989 (schedule 9)

Water Act 1989 (sections 7 to 10)
and Code of Practice on Conservation, Access and Recreation

Environmental Protection Act 1990

EXPORT CONTROLS
Import, Export and Customs Powers (Defence)
Act 1939   **IECP39**

The Export of Goods (Control) Order 1987   **EGCO87**

FINANCE AND TAXATION
Inheritance Tax Act 1984 (sections 25 to 28 and schedules 3 and 4)

PLANNING
Town and Country Planning Act 1990
Planning (Listed Buildings and Conservation
Areas) Act 1990   **PLBC90**

SALVAGE AND WRECK
Merchant Shipping Act 1894 (part IX)   **MS94**

Protection of Wrecks Act 1973   **PW73**

TREASURE TROVE
Coroners Act 1988   **CA88**

Attorney-General of the Duchy of Lancaster *v.*
G. E. Overton (Farms) Limited 1980   **Overton80**

Attorney-General of the Duchy of Lancaster *v.*
G. E. Overton (Farms) Limited 1982   **Overton82**

Legal approaches to these laws tend to treat these different branches as discrete entities within the conventional scheme and to focus on individual legal provisions. *Halsbury's Statutes*, for example, is a tool designed specifically for use by qualified lawyers. These volumes, divided by branch of law, consist of annotated copies of current legislation. The annotations serve to show amendments to Acts made after passage (the official versions provided by HMSO do not include amendments), refer to other relevant legislation and terminological definitions, and guide users towards relevant cases in the field. The focus is on specific provisions which although annotated in this way remain to be fully interpreted by their professional users.

A similar approach is taken by other professional writers in the field, such as Suddards (1988). The focus here is on that specific body of town and country planning legislation which affects historic buildings. Although opening and closing chapters take an 'overall' view, there is very little attempt to relate separate bodies of legislation. Thus, for instance, there is a chapter on ancient monuments and another on conservation areas, but neither of these relates the legal constructs to one another nor to listed buildings. Suddards seeks out the key terms and provisions and interprets them but – like *Halsbury's Statutes* – only for the professional legal community.

Parnell (1987) aims to interpret the legislation for a non-legal profession – architects and builders. Built around practical case studies which can be taken to represent examples of best practice and success in meeting the requirements of conversion for current use and legal protection, Parnell seeks to describe the law in terms that are meaningful to his readers. This is an exercise in interpretation but it is limited only to laws as they affect historic buildings (so no ancient monuments law or environmental protection legislation) and is couched in language which can be turned into action by its readers.

Greenfield's (1989) approach to the issue of the return of cultural property is also interpretive, but in a different way. Hers is a comparative approach across international boundaries. She seeks to isolate the key issues in the field and then the key legal provisions that will answer the case. She then interprets the relevant provisions and provides a solution to the issue based upon that interpretation.

O'Keefe and Prott (1984) also take an international comparative approach. Drawing on the legislation relating to archaeology in all the countries of the globe and international law they address the question of how specific questions or problems are answered in different places. Like Greenfield, they isolate the key provisions from each body of law and compare them with one another. Both Greenfield and O'Keefe and Prott seek to isolate the key elements in the law that will answer specific questions or provide a result in specific cases.

The purpose of this study contrasts with the legal approaches of *Halsbury*, Suddards, Parnell, Greenfield and O'Keefe and Prott. Whereas these writers seek to identify and interpret individual legal provisions – whether for professional intra-territorial use (*Halsbury*, Suddards, Parnell) or in a comparative study across jurisdictional boundaries (Greenfield, O'Keefe and Prott) – my purpose is to identify the approach that the entire corpus of English law takes to archaeology. Whereas Greenfield and O'Keefe and Prott compare individual provisions across international borders, this study is comparative across branches of law within a single jurisdiction. Accordingly, separate branches of English law (for example, ancient monuments legislation versus Treasure Trove) will not be distinguished except in terms of their historical development (Chapters 3, 4 and 5) or where the approach to archaeological material can be demonstrated by analysis to be different.

Historically, the study concerns the relationship between the development of the legal regulation of the treatment of archaeological material in England and the development of the discipline of archaeology. The study will approach the questions of how such law came into being, the disciplinary and political context in which it came into being, how the disciplinary and political context affects the change and development of key concepts over time, and the extension of legal coverage to different components of the archaeological heritage.

Analytically, the study will seek to identify the key terms and phrases contained in the law which operate in relation to archaeological material. These terms will be examined by reference to their context in specific branches of law and by their relation to other terms and phrases in that branch and others. The focus will be on their effect on components of the archaeological heritage as follows:

- as terms which define components of the material to be affected by law
- as terms which may result in a physical change to that material (a physical change either to the material itself or to its environment)
- as terms which may result in a moral change in that material (in the way it is valued, perceived, or understood).

The key terms identified in the analysis will be related to the relevant phase of the tripartite sequence derived from Cultural Theory in which they have effect and their consequences for subsequent phases described. The end result will be a scheme which analyses the 'path' of components of the archaeological heritage through the legal process.

The law as 'gatekeeper'

A useful analogy for the law as it operates in relation to archaeological material can perhaps be drawn from the sociological concept of the 'gatekeeper'. Derived in part from the work of Erving Goffman (1961, 1969), the concept has been most often applied in relation to so-called 'gatekeeper interviews' which take place at times in the life of individuals when career path decisions need to be made (Erickson 1976; Erickson and Schulte 1982). Each possibility has certain consequences for immediate action which have the effect of closing other options which are otherwise open. Since the counsellor is also in a position of authority, failure to take the counsellor's advice as to an appropriate course of action has consequences for future success. In other words, gatekeeper encounters result in real effects in the real world.

The concept has also been applied in a looser sense in relation to aspects of material culture. Leah Greenfeld's (1989) study of the art market in Israel applies the term 'gatekeeper' to those who control access to the category 'art' – dealers, critics and gallery curators. The task of these gatekeepers is to keep 'bad' art out of the places where it could be encountered (galleries) and to promote 'good' art, the selection process being based on criteria of current stylistic fashion.

This gatekeeping function is a similar one to that of the law in relation to archaeological material. The processes of selection, categorization and valuation serve to guide components of the archaeological heritage towards appropriate treatments. The processes of selection and subsequent recategorization each serve to close certain options for the treatment of that material. Similarly, failure to meet a criterion for inclusion within any category has the effect of casting that particular component out of the legal process altogether. The legal process, then, has real effects in the real world on real archaeological material.

The idea that selecting, categorizing and valuing things from the past has the effect of changing them is not new. As David Lowenthal has argued, the identification of material as old 'locates the antiquity on our mental map . . . [and] distinguishes it from present-day surroundings' (Lowenthal 1985, 265). Similarly, display, protection, reconstitution, removal and adaptation all serve to change objects of antiquity (ibid., 265–88). Overriding mere physical transformations in importance are perceptual ones. As Mary Douglas puts it:

> Anything whatsoever that is perceived at all must pass by perceptual controls. In the sifting process, something is admitted, something rejected and something supplemented to make the event cognisable. The process is largely cultural. A cultural bias puts moral problems under a particular light. Once shaped, the individual choices come catalogued according to the structuring of consciousness, which is far from being a private affair. (Douglas 1982, 1)

We have returned once more to the field of the public domain and the Grid/Group diagram as the tool of Cultural Theory. Law is a means for the perception of archaeological material. It is a tool for the application of standards but also the device by which they are set. As a gatekeeper the application of law has real consequences for real material. The delineament of these consequences is the ultimate purpose of this work.

SUMMARY
This chapter has outlined the concepts involved in Cultural Theory and Rubbish Theory which provide a framework for understanding the process of the valuation of archaeological material, which is a concern of some importance in the field of archaeological heritage management. The tripartite sequence of selection, recategorization and valuation derived from this framework can be applied to the study of English law as it affects archaeological material. This study is undertaken from both a historical and an analytical standpoint, the former seeking to place the development of such law in the context of the development of the discipline of archaeology as a whole and the latter seeking to identify the underlying principles of such law by a detailed intra-jurisdictional comparison of key terms across branches of law. The idea of the law as 'gatekeeper' opens the possibility of examining the pathways by which archaeological material passes through the legal process.

Part Two
The idea of preservation by law

3
Treasure Trove

Treasure Trove is the first law to have been appropriated by archaeologists in the attempt to build national collections of antiquities. This
opened the way for the further development of legal measures as a tool
by which archaeologists could gain control of their material. As a
consequence, the structure of Treasure Trove is reflected in all the
branches of law to have been devised or appropriated for application to
archaeological material. The doctrine works in three ways: it first selects
a body of material to which it can be applied, excluding other bodies of
material; second, it recategorizes this body of material, transforming it
from a class of material to a legal category; third, by this process of
recategorization, it adds value to the material, specifically as Treasure. It
will be argued in the following chapters that all the laws applied to
archaeological material in England similarly select, recategorize and add
value to that material.

The underlying principles of Treasure Trove will reappear in Part
Three of this book, to be related to their counterparts in other branches
of law as part of the general analysis of the law as it stands today. For the
purposes of this chapter, however, Treasure Trove will stand alone as
the epitome of 'heritage law'.

THE DEVELOPMENT OF THE DOCTRINE
Treasure Trove is perhaps the most ancient law applied to the archaeological heritage. As Henry Cleere has pointed out, it was a 'widespread
medieval fiscal prerogative' (at least in Europe), extended in Sweden by
the Royal Proclamation of 1666 which declared all objects from
antiquity to be the property of the Crown (Cleere 1989b, 1). This may
be the first deliberate application of law to recognize the value of such
items as objects from the past rather than merely as sources of revenue.

In the only full-scale study of the doctrine, Sir George Hill identifies
three 'periods' of Treasure Trove, each based on a different diagnostic
operating principle (Hill 1936, vi–vii). The first (and most ancient) is the
'period of regality'; the second is the Roman period; and the third is the

'modern' period, dating in Britain roughly from the end of the Middle Ages. These are not solely chronological periods but also represent attitudes and approaches towards the doctrine and systems of thought under which it was applied. Accordingly, under the regality system the sovereign automatically owns all treasure even before discovery. By contrast, modern understanding allows the state (as successor to the person of the sovereign) to acquire treasure only after discovery. Under medieval continental law Treasure Trove was one of the rights attaching to the person of the ruler: in modern times this right is 'enjoyed by the State but exercised for the common weal' (Hill 1936, vii). Roman law sought to limit the exercise of royal rights and accordingly declared that treasure should go either to the finder or to the owner of the land on which it was found in accordance with equitable principles; this view ceased to apply in Britain after the departure of the legions (Hill 1936, 1–47).

The medieval period

Nevertheless, as Hill makes clear at the opening of his book, Roman influence is not entirely lost. The word treasure derives from the Latin *thesaurus* which very specifically is used in Roman jurisprudence to mean masterless wealth (that is, items of value of which the ownership is undetermined) (Hill 1936, v). This is the sense in which it was understood throughout the medieval period in England. 'Trove', derived from Old French *trover*, means simply found or discovered. Thus, Treasure Trove means literally 'masterless wealth which has been found (by someone)'.

The importance of the ownership of treasure in the medieval period cannot be underestimated. Treasure was a measure of wealth which consisted of precious items. Precious metals, in particular, were physically durable, divisible into smaller lots without loss of value, and portable. Individual treasures were artefacts made out of precious materials that, in case of need, could be broken up, melted down and sold. As such, treasures were sought and kept by powerful individuals and by institutions such as the Church. Thus, the ownership of treasures indicated wealth, and treasures were the containers of wealth (Hooper-Greenhill 1992, 48). In accordance with late medieval patterns of thought,

> the signs that indicated wealth and measured it were bound to carry the real mark in themselves. In order to represent prices, they themselves had to be precious. They had to be rare, colourful, desirable. (Foucault 1970, 169)

Treasures were literally fabulous. Those that came 'unbidden' from the ground would be doubly so – gifts from unknown benefactors. Thus treasures were not only material objects, but also the legends accruing to them. They were, as Hooper-Greenhill (1992, 48) points out, a technology for the maintenance of power relations. As monarch, one had the right to claim treasures from the earth as one's own; and laying successful claim to such treasures served to confirm one's royal authority. This is why Treasure Trove was sought by the monarch – as treasure it represented wealth; as treasure trove it was tinged with an air of mystery; by laying claim to it one confirmed one's own position. It was thus triply valuable as a sign of royal mystique.

The first written statement of Treasure Trove in England is found in the *Leges Henrici* (the Laws of Henry I) set down between 1114 and 1118, under which all treasure belonged automatically to the monarch. However, the *Leges Edwardii Confessoris*, another section of the same document (purporting to deal with the laws of the Saxon King Edward the Confessor), provides that this general doctrine will be modified if the find is made in a church or church cemetery so that while all gold goes to the King, silver is apportioned equally to Church and King. The *Retractatus* (yet a third portion of this same document) specifies that the doctrine applies only to treasure specifically hidden in the earth rather than merely lost or abandoned. It seems that these laws were set down in writing precisely at this time (that is, the twelfth century) because of the discovery on the European continent of documents containing Roman laws which directly contradicted the right of the sovereign to claim treasure (Hill 1936, 189).

In reaction to this discovery of Roman law, later twelfth-century documents – the *Dialogue of the Exchequer* of 1179 and the *Tractatus de Legibus et Consuetudinibus Regni Angliae* of 1187 to 1189 – sought to expand the doctrine in favour of the King's treasury. By the mid-thirteenth century, in the works of Henry de Bracton called *De Legibus et Consuetudinibus Angliae* of 1250 to 1258, the principle was well established that finds of treasure were reportable and subject to a Coroner's inquest to decide whether they were indeed Treasure Trove (Hill 1936, 193); this principle was restated as recently as 1988 in the Coroners Act of that year. Indeed, it was not until the passage of the Theft Act of 1968 that 'concealment of Treasure Trove' ceased to be a criminal offence (Sparrow 1982).

The modern position
The medieval documents cited above – although probably keenly consulted in their own day – are no longer regarded as 'very reliable or of high authority' (Dillon, J. in *Attorney-General of the Duchy of Lancaster*

v. G. E. Overton (Farms) Limited, Weekly Law Reports 1980, 872). Much greater reliance is placed upon more recent legal works, which in turn rely on the great jurist of the Jacobean period, Sir Edward Coke.

Coke was Chief Justice of the King's Bench until his dismissal by King James I in 1616. He was a founding member, along with William Camden and others, many of whom were lawyers, of the (first) Society of Antiquaries in London in the late sixteenth century (Piggott 1989, 14; Trigger 1989, 47). The Society was suppressed by King James I in the early seventeenth century (Piggott 1989, 1; Trigger 1989, 47). It is clear that this suppression was because the King was displeased with its activities, in particular its involvement in the political debates of the time – especially those over the relative rights and duties of monarch and subject, Crown and Parliament, Church and state (Trigger 1989, 47). Coke himself, as a student and compiler of English Common Law and concerned with questions of political rights and duties, was involved in all these debates and his work played a large part in providing the philosophical justification for Parliament's rebellion against the misuses of royal prerogatives in the 1630s which led to the English Civil War. His statement on Treasure Trove provides the foundation for the modern understanding of the doctrine. He relied heavily on Bracton's *De Legibus et Consuetudinibus Angliae* for his authority. Coke's understanding of the doctrine is set out in his *Institutes*, written after his dismissal from office:

> TREASURE TROVE is when any gold or silver, in coin, plate, or bullyon hath been of ancient time hidden, wheresoever it be found, whereof no person can prove any property, it doth belong to the king, or to some lord or other by the kings grant or prescription. . . . Gold or silver.] For if it be any other metal, it is no treasure; and if it be no treasure, it belongs not to the king, for it must be treasure trove. (Quoted by Lord Denning, Master of the Rolls in *Attorney-General of the Duchy of Lancaster v. G. E. Overton (Farms) Limited, All England Law Reports* 1982, 527)

Subsequent authorities have followed Coke. In 1762 John Comyn, Chief Baron of the Exchequer and 'the greatest lawyer of his time' (Lord Denning, Master of the Rolls in *Attorney-General of the Duchy of Lancaster v. G. E. Overton (Farms) Limited, All England Law Reports* 1982, 527), published his *Digest*. He wrote that:

> *Treasure-trove* is when a Man finds Coin or Plate, of Gold or Silver, the Owner of which is not known, then it belongs to the King. . . . But, it is not said to be *Treasure-trove*, if it be other than gold or silver. (Quoted by Lord Denning, Master of the Rolls in

Attorney-General of the Duchy of Lancaster v. G. E. Overton (Farms) Limited, All England Law Reports 1982, 527)

Similarly, with some additions which have not been accepted subsequently, Sir William Blackstone wrote in his *Commentaries* in 1768 that:

> treasure-trove, (derived from the French word, *trover*, to find,) called in Latin *thesaurus inventus*, which is where any money or coin, gold, silver, plate, or bullion, is found hidden in the earth, or other private place, the owner thereof being unknown; in which case the treasure belongs to the king. (Quoted by Lord Denning, Master of the Rolls in *Attorney-General of the Duchy of Lancaster v. G. E. Overton (Farms) Limited, All England Law Reports* 1982, 527)

In 1820, Joseph Chitty removed Blackstone's additions – those concerning (any) money or coin – and reverted in his *Prerogatives of the Crown* to Coke:

> Treasure trove, is where any gold or silver in coin, plate or bullion is found concealed in a house, or in the earth, or other private place, the owner thereof being unknown, in which case the treasure belongs to the king. (Quoted by Lord Denning, Master of the Rolls in *Attorney-General of the Duchy of Lancaster v. G. E. Overton (Farms) Limited, All England Law Reports* 1982, 527)

Whereas in the medieval period, 'treasure' referred to all items of value of which the ownership could not be established, since Coke it has become limited to items only of gold and silver. Throughout most of its history, the doctrine of Treasure Trove was never designed to play a part in the protection or management of the archaeological heritage. It was a device whereby the monarch could obtain financial benefit and bolster his position from items of value which were discovered within the borders of his territory: a form of taxation of secret wealth long after the death of the taxee. It was not until the mid-nineteenth century that this law began to be used in Britain for the purpose of state acquisition of antiquities.

Appropriation for archaeology

As Hill tells the story, the nineteenth century was a period of progress in which it gradually dawned on the minds of state authorities that treasures had uses other than to be melted down as bullion. As the pecuniary value of items became of less interest to the state and the costs of inquiries rose, the Treasury ceased to recover such items for the Exchequer unless they were of exceptional value or doubts existed as to the legal ownership. A system of rewards was instituted to encourage the reporting of finds, and the assumption gradually took hold that finders would only deliver their finds if they could expect remuneration (Hill 1936, 239). The reality may have been a little more complicated than that.

In 1858 James Talbot, first Baron de Malahide, proposed a Parliamentary Bill to give to the finder the full antiquarian value of honestly reported finds of Treasure Trove items. The Bill also provided for police powers of seizure and search in cases of failure to report, and for the lord of the manor to take possession of the find if he could prove ownership and paid the full antiquarian value to the finder (Hill 1936, 239). The effects of the Bill if passed would have been fourfold: first, to remove Treasure Trove from the realm of royal prerogative into that of Statute law, thus making it subject to Parliamentary authority; second, to shift the emphasis in Treasure Trove away from the acquisition of wealth to the acquisition of ancient objects by the spending of wealth; third, to have increased the power of the state authorities (particularly the police) to seek out such objects; and fourth, where the ownership of the object by the state could not definitively be established, to provide a means whereby such objects could be concentrated in the hands of those most likely to allow their study.

According to Hill, the Bill failed for 'technical reasons'. In fact it received its first reading in the House of Lords on 5 July 1858, never reached its second reading, and accordingly was never debated, since Parliament was dissolved for a General Election on 23 April 1859 (Hill 1936, 239; *Hansard (JHL)* 151, 910).

The promoter of the Bill, Lord Talbot (1805–83), was the son of the third Irish Baron Talbot de Malahide. He was educated at Trinity College, Cambridge, gaining his BA in 1827 and his MA in 1830. In 1832 he stood and was elected as the Member of Parliament for Athlone. As a keen and loyal supporter of Palmerston's Tory government he was advanced to a United Kingdom peerage on 19 November 1856. His House of Lords career was marked in particular by social reform measures, such as the Acts to prevent the adulteration of food (1855–60). He was appointed Lord-in-Waiting to the royal household from 1863 to 1866 (*Dictionary of National Biography* XIX, 318).

As well as his political career, Talbot was an active student of the material past. From 1845 he was a member of the Archaeological Institute (subsequently, and still, the Royal Archaeological Institute) of which he became short-term President in 1851 (because of the death of the previous incumbent, the Marquis of Northampton) and again in 1863 until his death. He acted as Chair of meetings of its Section of

Antiquities (the section concerned with the study of ancient objects) on numerous occasions (*The Archaeological Journal*, passim). He was elected a Fellow of the Royal Society in 1858 and was also a Fellow of the Society of Antiquaries as well as, at one time, President of the Anthropological Society. His particular interests lay in the field of Roman and Irish antiquities.

A study of the contents of the Archaeological Institute's annual publication, *The Archaeological Journal*, for the 1850s is instructive. In 1851, Charles Newton argues in its pages that the subject matter of archaeology is threefold: 'Oral, Written, and Monumental' (Newton 1851, 2). The bulk of the paper is taken up with the discussion of the merits of written and inscribed material followed by a detailed study of the merits of what today would be called an 'art-historical' approach to architecture, burial monuments, stelae and the like. Only on the penultimate page are the 'remaining material products' (Newton 1851, 25) covered. The point of the paper, however, seems to be not to dismiss this apparently residual category – which would contain all the materials studied by modern archaeologists – but to elevate its study to the level of the other material listed. As he puts it:

> To collect the implements, weapons, pottery, costume, and furniture of races is to contribute materials not only to the history of mining, metallurgy, spinning, weaving, dyeing, carpentry, and the like acts, which minister to civilisation, but also to illustrate the physical history of the countries where these arts were practised. . . . A museum of Antiquities is to the Archaeologist what a botanical garden is to the Botanist. . . . A society [such as the Archaeological Institute] which would truly administer the ample province of British Archaeology should be at once the Historian of national art and manners, the keeper of national record and antiquities, the Aedile of national monuments. (Newton 1851, 25–6)

If antiquarianism is defined in Piggott's (1989, 21) terms as 'historians, using exclusively documentary sources for a study of the medieval and later past' and for whom objects merely illustrated this written documentation, then Newton's paper contains many antiquarian overtones. But the importance placed upon national collections of objects and the possibility of studying them in their own right opens up the possibility that here we have one of the first statements in England of something we can recognize as a distinctive discipline of archaeology.

The trend towards placing an increasing importance on the object as the focus of study continues through the decade. Also in 1851, a Mr Yates proposes to the Institute's Section of Antiquities a resolution 'for the public collection of casts from antique statues, and *other objects of value to those engaged in archaeological enquiries* [emphasis added]. . . . Lord Talbot de Malahide submitted to the meeting the proposed resolution' which was passed and agreed should go to the Council of the Institute (*The Archaeological Journal* 8, 334–5). In 1852, the Opening Address by Edmund Oldfield commends the collection of British antiquities (*The Archaeological Journal* 8, 1–6). In the same year and the two subsequent years A. W. Franks, already emphasizing the need for a Department of British and Medieval Antiquities at the British Museum, reports on the growing number of British antiquities being collected by the Museum (Franks 1852, 1853, 1854). In 1853 he writes:

> I think we may congratulate ourselves on the promising com-
> mencement of the British collection. . . . The law of treasure
> trove, as it exists in this country, has no doubt caused the
> destruction of many interesting relics, and led to the concealment
> of many more. (Franks 1853, 13)

In 1859 Talbot observed to the Institute that it 'had been earnestly desirous to impress on every locality. . . the importance of developing local institutions, and had even sought to stimulate an interest in the preservation of national monuments' (*The Archaeological Journal* 16, 370). In 1861 he felt able to announce something of a victory to the Institute when one of its supporters, the Duke of Northumberland, was appointed a Trustee of the British Museum: prior to this 'the working archaeologists of this country . . . had, on many occasions, felt aggrieved by the neglect of National Antiquities . . . whilst those of other races and foreign lands were diligently sought after' (*The Archaeological Journal* 18, 268).

Treasure Trove was at this time a mechanism whereby money in the form of rewards was exchanged for items of gold and silver of which the ownership was unknown and which would pass to the Treasury. The rewards made were consistently less than the value of the finds, hence the unwillingness of finders to declare them. Talbot's 1858 Bill can be seen as an abortive attempt to provide a tool to be used for the collection of ancient objects to fill a national collection. As Chapman sums up the situation by 1871:

> within a ten year period . . . archaeology had progressed from an
> essentially dilettantist avocation to an organised discipline, and
> ethnology had resuscitated altogether as a new field, with a
> decidedly archaeological orientation. . . . The British Museum
> collections were larger and more popularly supported than
> before, and 'prehistory' had found a place within a new and
> relatively popular anthropology. (Chapman 1989, 34)

Talbot's abortive attempt to transform Treasure Trove may have played a larger part in this than is immediately apparent. In 1858, after the failure of the Bill to reach its second reading, Talbot reported to the Institute as follows:

> I have felt for a number of years a deep interest in the matter [of Treasure Trove]. All archaeologists deplored the present state of the law, but knew not what to do in the emergency. My first impression was to move that a committee be appointed to examine witnesses and make inquiries upon the subject; but on further consideration there appeared to be great difficulty under the existing law of obtaining information from those who had given any attention to the subject. At the same time there would have been great impediments in collecting accurate evidence. Many would object to come forward, and others might be afraid that their property would be endangered for giving information. Then, on the other hand, it was evident, in order to have evidence of any value, we should not confine ourselves to vague generalities. Under these circumstances it struck me that the best plan would be to have a bill drafted and laid upon the table of the house [of Lords], which accordingly I have done. I think that the bill may meet the chief requirement of the case, although, certain amendments may doubtless appear requisite. My object was not to carry it into law in the present session. That would have been hopeless. I had caused the bill to be drawn without consulting Her Majesty's government. It was most essential however to obtain the concurrence of the government in any further proceedings. The bill would have very considerably modified rights and prerogatives, which, of course, could not be considered at length without the permission of the Crown. The bill has been presented on the table of the House of Lords, and has been read a first time and printed. I consider that, in doing so, for the present my object was gained, and I have no intention of pressing forward in the present year, but next session I hope to take it another step in advance. I trust it may be found highly beneficial to archaeology. (*The Archaeological Journal* 15, 367–8)

In fact, the Bill, despite Talbot's apparent intent, was never revived. Instead, an initiative by the Society of Antiquaries of Scotland resulted in finders in Scotland becoming eligible to receive the full value of finds handed in as the result of the issue of a formal notice of advice by the Treasury to the relevant authorities (*The Archaeological Journal* 16, 196–7). On 3 February 1860, Talbot was able to report to the Institute that a similar initiative on his part in Ireland had also met with a favourable response, and he 'entertained the hope that a speedy adjustment of the question [of the giving of full value to finders] might now be hopefully anticipated, by the extension of favourable concessions on the part of the Crown to the whole of the United Kingdom [that is, England and Wales]' (*The Archaeological Journal* 17, 69–70). This was not long in coming, but the circular formally announcing the concession, although drafted and first issued to the Chief Constable of Hampshire in 1860, was withdrawn and was not finally made public until 1871 (Hill 1936, 240).

It is not immediately clear quite why the Treasury suddenly became so amenable: Hill's explanation (1936, 240), simply the exchange of correspondence and Talbot's urging, is unconvincing. It is clear from Talbot's own words quoted above that the Bill was not an immediate attempt to bring about a substantive change in the law so much as a means to put the Treasure Trove issue on the political agenda; perhaps it was more than that – a form of political bluff to force a change of attitude at the Treasury. Certainly, as Hill notes (1936, 240–1), the Treasury concession made little financial difference to the state. In addition, it must be questioned whether the Bill as drafted would have passed through Parliament: a professional police force had been established less than thirty years, was unpopular and still widely considered as no more than a state spy organization; it is not likely that the granting of massive powers for the purposes of retrieving items that many would consider their private property would have been greeted with enthusiasm.

A Treasury Minute of 1886, issued to the police, established a revised procedure which directly benefited the British Museum and reflects in many ways the terms of Talbot's Bill:

- objects would be forwarded to the British Museum for valuation
- objects desirable for the national collection would be retained by the Museum, who would pay to the Treasury the market value
- the Royal Mint, local museums, and the owner of the land on which the find was made would be allowed to acquire such objects at the British Museum value
- the finder (if honestly reporting the find) would receive back all items not so desired or the antiquarian value of those retained by others. (Hill 1936, 240–1)

The role of Treasure Trove as a method of taxation of the wealthy dead was now transformed. By involving the British Museum as valuer and first claimant of any finds of gold or silver items, such items were no longer to be used to increase the wealth of Crown or state. Indeed, since the British Museum is largely supported by public funds, the effect of this transformation is to provide state finance for the acquisition of items for the Museum: while the account between the Museum and the Treasury remains in balance for this purpose, the net effect is to take money from Treasury funds. Accordingly, state funds were henceforth to be used to enrich, first, museums and, secondarily, where not wanted by a museum, private collections of ancient material. It was not until 1931 that the whole administration of Treasure Trove was placed in the hands of the British Museum (Hill 1936, 242), finally breaking the last (and by now fragile) link between Treasure Trove and the increase of state revenue.

Summary

Treasure Trove, an ancient legal doctrine, has undergone a series of transformations. Originally it was a device to increase the wealth of the monarch from stray finds of precious items of which the ownership was unknown. In the early seventeenth century, the scope of this royal prerogative was limited to items of gold and silver which had been specifically hidden rather than lost. In the nineteenth century, it was transformed from a means of increasing the wealth of the state to a device whereby items of archaeological interest could be acquired by museums and, where unwanted by museums, by private collectors who could demonstrate an interest.

The development in the 1850s of an approach to the study of the past through the study of objects, particularly by the members of bodies such as the Archaeological Institute, led to the creation of a discipline recognizably close to modern archaeology. The interest of such figures as James Talbot, Baron de Malahide and A. W. Franks, among others, in the building of national collections of ancient objects led in turn to efforts to transform the doctrine of Treasure Trove into a device for the benefit of the nascent discipline. From a means whereby the monarch, and then the state, could acquire wealth in the form of treasure, Treasure Trove has become a device whereby state treasure is expended to acquire items of gold and silver which have value to collections of national antiquities.

THE DOCTRINE IN OPERATION

Treasure

The current state of the law relating to Treasure Trove was conveniently restated in the case of *Attorney-General of the Duchy of Lancaster v. G. E. Overton (Farms) Limited* ('the Overton case') first heard in the Chancery Division in 1980 and subsequently on Appeal in 1982 (*Weekly Law Reports* 3, 1980, 869–75; *All England Law Reports* 1, 1982, 524–31). The Appeal Court held as follows:

> The Crown's right to Treasure Trove was limited to objects of gold and silver, and for an article to be so described it had to

contain a substantial amount of precious metal. Whether in fact an object contained a substantial amount was for the Coroner's jury in each case, but in the case of coinage the deliberate inclusion of precious metal at the time of minting did not affect the question the jury had to decide. (*All England Law Reports* 1, 1982, 524)

The case had concerned the find of a hoard of 7811 third-century antoniniani in a field at Coleby, Lincolnshire, owned by G. E. Overton (Farms) Limited. The field lay within the 'liberties' of the Duchy of Lancaster (that is, the Duchy – rather than the Crown itself – had the rights to Treasure Trove in that area). A sample of 923 of the coins had been examined at the British Museum where it was found that the silver content of the coins ranged between 18 per cent and 0.2 per cent. A Coroner's jury found that the coins were Treasure Trove and would therefore belong to the Duchy of Lancaster who would pass them on to the British Museum. The landowners contested this and appealed against the Coroner's verdict on the grounds that the coins were not Treasure Trove and therefore belonged to them as owners of the field in accordance with Common Law (*Weekly Law Reports* 3, 1980, 869).

The judgement hung on the issues of whether:

- the deliberate insertion of however small an amount of silver into the coins made them silver for the purposes of Treasure Trove, and
- the actual quantity of silver in a 'silver' coin made any difference.

The judgement settled these issues against the intention of the issuer of coins and in favour of a consideration of the actual amount of precious metal in the coins as found. In so doing, the Appeal Court redefined Coke's understanding of the doctrine to meet the needs of an age when coins are not all made of pure silver or gold (*All England Law Reports* 1, 1982, 527). The standard is high: in the judgement of Lord Denning, Master of the Rolls, 'an object should have a gold or silver content *of 50% or more* before it can be described as a gold or silver object' (*All England Law Reports* 1, 1982, 524; emphasis added).

The responsibility of Coroners' inquests for declarations of Treasure Trove was restated more recently in Section 30 of the Coroners Act 1988. This provides that a Coroner 'shall *continue* to have jurisdiction (a) to inquire into any *treasure* that is found in his district; and (b) to inquire who were, or are suspected of being, the finders' (emphasis added). The word 'continue' serves to emphasize that the doctrine is not, so far as the law is concerned, ever deemed to have altered in any way. The section does, however, limit the jurisdiction of the Coroner to finds – not of *possible* or *suspected* treasure – but to *actual* treasure. In other words, the fact of the item constituting treasure for legal purposes is established (or deemed to be so) prior to the Coroner's inquest. In practice, this leaves the way open for cases such as the Overton case to be referred to the higher courts, which are not bound by the findings of Coroners' inquests, and where the issue will turn on whether the items in fact constitute treasure or not.

Separation from the criminal law

Treasure Trove continues to be an issue seriously treated by the archaeological community. In 1987 the finder of the Donhead St Mary hoard in Wiltshire was prosecuted for the illegal use of a metal detector on a protected place and fined. Despite his criminality, the finder was given a reward for making the find, although not the full market value of the hoard (*British Archaeological News* 1.9, 73; 2.1, 10; 2.2, 17).

This example and that of the Overton case serve to emphasize the separation of Treasure Trove from the criminal law. In the Overton case, the finder of the coins was successfully prosecuted for theft since, although having permission to investigate the field where the finds were made, he did not report his find to the owners of the field and instead tried to deal in the coins. This had nothing to do with the judgements on first hearing nor on appeal and was included in Lord Denning's Appeal judgement as a colourful part of the story and explanation of how the find came to the attention of the authorities (*All England Law Reports* 1, 1982, 525).

Since Treasure Trove items belong specifically to the Crown – rather than to the state – 'concealment of Treasure Trove' was for a long period a different offence from mere theft. In 1968 – as part of an effort to tidy up and simplify the law in relation to the unlawful taking and holding of property – the offence was done away with in the Theft Act of 1968 (Sparrow 1982). The finder in the Overton case was thus prosecuted for the simple theft of items that, as a result of the Coroner's inquest, were deemed to be the property of the Duchy of Lancaster; the subsequent ruling that they were in fact not Treasure Trove and thus belonged to the landowner did not change this; the fact remained that at no time were the coins the legal property of the finder.

The separation of Treasure Trove procedures from the criminal law can, however, have unfortunate consequences. In the case of *R v. Hancock* (*All England Law Reports* 3, 1990, 183–90) a conviction for theft of Treasure Trove was overturned on appeal because the trial judge had incorrectly directed the jury that all they needed to decide was whether the objects in question could have been found to be Treasure Trove rather than whether they actually were Treasure Trove beyond a reasonable doubt, the normal standard in criminal cases. Since the case was brought on the basis that the defendant had stolen items that were Treasure Trove – rather than taking items that either were Treasure Trove or belonged to the landowner, but in any case were not the defendant's – such a decision on the part of the jury was necessary in order to determine if a theft had, in fact, taken place (*All England Law Reports Annual Review 1990*, 77). The jury acted on the judge's ruling rather than making a firm decision, and accordingly the conviction could not stand (*All England Law Reports* 3, 1990, 189). This ruling has consequences beyond the individual case, however, because in confirming and extending the principle enshrined in the Overton case that Coroner's inquests cannot bind a higher court, it establishes that (at least in cases of theft) there is no proprietary right of ownership by the Crown simply by virtue of a Coroner's inquest finding (*All England Law Reports Annual Review 1990*, 129).

An adversarial approach

In Britain, the criminal justice system is an adversarial one. This means that the criminal courts are not concerned to find the truth of an event, but merely to decide the guilt or innocence of a named person for a particular offence committed on a single day at a specific time. Accordingly, criminal trials take the form of verbal combats between different versions of an event. Although Treasure Trove is not directly related to criminal justice, this adversarial approach is contained within the operation of Treasure Trove law.

The purpose of a Coroner's inquest, and of any dispute which is then taken to the higher courts as in the Overton case, is simply to decide the ownership of items brought before the inquest. The ownership decision is an absolute one in the sense that once ownership is decided the other possible owner retains no rights over the object. Thus, if the item is held to be Treasure Trove it belongs – and has done since discovery – to the Crown. Neither the finder, nor the owner of the land on which the find was made, has any rights in the object. If it is not Treasure Trove the landowner owns the object and has done so since discovery. Neither the Crown nor any museum can claim any legal rights over the object or its destiny.

The ownership of the object is to be distinguished from any reward paid to the finder. Lord Denning outlined the procedure as follows in the Overton case:

> This is the modern practice of the Crown. If an object is Treasure Trove it is offered to the British Museum, or some other museum. If they decide to keep it the finder is paid its full market value

> forthwith. If they do not want to keep it, the object is returned . . .
> to do what he likes with it. (*All England Law Reports* 1, 1982, 529)

The use of the word 'practice' is significant. The Crown is not purchasing the item from the finder, but merely rewarding the finder for
reporting it. In the case of Treasure Trove, the Crown has always
owned the item in question.

Accordingly, the process of Treasure Trove sets up an opposition of
interest between the finder or landowner and the Crown. One or other
of these will receive ownership of the object, but there is no provision
for the maintenance of mutual rights in it. Ownership is absolute and
therefore open to dispute. It is this adversarial structure that opens the
way for such disputes to be presented in a higher court for resolution, as
in the Overton case.

Objects without contexts

Having confirmed that Treasure Trove relates only to finds of gold and
silver, a distinguished legal counsel has pointed out that the Overton
case was applied as if each individual item should be considered separately (Sparrow 1982). The potential archaeological value of the Overton
hoard was that it provided an accurate measure of the gradual debase-
ment of third-century coinage which could be applied for dating
purposes. By treating each coin as an individual item, the collection as a
whole would be split. A similar problem occurred in relation to a
twelfth-century hoard found near Colchester as discussed by Palmer
(1981, 181): the coins were declared Treasure Trove and went to the
Crown, while their lead container went to the landowner. Such finds
are thus effectively decontextualized.

The problem of divorcing objects from their context is exacerbated
by the rule that, to constitute Treasure Trove, such items need to have
been deliberately hidden with the intention of subsequent recovery.
This was not an issue in the Overton case, but assumed by all parties. As
Lord Denning put it in telling the story of the discovery:

> No doubt [the coins] had been brought over to England by some
> of the Roman legionaries or civilians and used as currency here.
> One of the Romans must have saved them up. . . . He put [them]
> into a 'safe place', as we always do, hoping to come back some
> time and get them. The Romans went. He went. He never came
> back. They remained there . . . hidden for 1600 years. (*All
> England Law Reports* 1, 1982, 525–6)

In *R v. Hancock* the likelihood that the objects in question were votive
deposits (and thus not intended to be retrieved) was taken as a basis for

assuming them not to be Treasure Trove (*All England Law Reports* 3, 1990, 186), and this issue arose again more recently in the case of the Snettisham hoards of Iron Age gold torcs (Stead 1991). This did not go beyond a Coroner's inquest, and all concerned seem happy at the verdict. Arguments concerned the lack of a clear votive context for the deposits since neither human remains nor a recognizable 'temple' site were found (Stead 1991, 458–9). The absence of evidence for Iron Age occupation was similarly adduced in support of deliberate deposition, since coin hoards 'were often buried in remote places' (ibid., 463). The conclusion is that the finds represent a single treasury, broken down into smaller lots and in some cases disguised by less valuable 'decoy' hoards buried above them for greater security (ibid., 463). This, at least, is the interpretation accepted by the Coroner's inquest. Nevertheless, it leaves the hoards themselves as individual finds, divorces them from other Iron Age finds at the same locations and in identical contexts, such as traces of wood and pottery (ibid., 450), and begs the question of why they were buried at all (except for some vague notion of 'safety'), and specifically why at that particular location. Other features in the field where they were found – such as Neolithic pits – are similarly relegated to the status of residual items; a more extensive excavation 'might have uncovered the bottoms of more Neolithic pits, but this was not the object of the exercise' (ibid., 450). In other words, the investigation of the field on Ken Hill, Snettisham was for the purpose of locating impressive Iron Age torcs of gold and nothing further.

A law for museums
We have seen that one of the aims of those who sought in the nineteenth century to appropriate Treasure Trove for archaeology was to use it to help build collections of national antiquities – especially a national collection in the British Museum. The British Museum was responsible for excavating five of the nine hoards at Snettisham (Stead 1991, 450–1) and for investigating the Overton hoard. Salisbury Museum was involved in the Donhead St Mary case, although unable to benefit from the declaration of the find as Treasure Trove because of compliance with a Museums Association Code of Practice covering the acquisition of illegally retrieved material; accordingly, the British Museum stepped in to take the items in question (*British Archaeological News* 2.1, 3).

The main drive of the doctrine is thus to acquire objects for museums. This relates closely to, and in a sense justifies, the decontextualization of Treasure Trove items discussed above. It is also in part a product of the history of the shift in purpose of Treasure Trove from a device financially to enrich the Crown to a means of acquiring ancient objects. The appropriation of the doctrine on behalf of the nascent discipline of archaeology took place at the time when 'classical' antiquarianism was being replaced by a more recognizably modern form of archaeology. Treasure Trove thus looked forward to the new discipline while retaining many elements of the old, especially a focus on the object alone, divorced from context, and serving to illustrate history rather than being studied in its own right as a source of new information about the past. The effect of the law in decontextualizing the object serves to focus attention on the object alone and to allow its transfer into a new context: that of the museum case. The law is also limited to items of silver and gold; such objects are ripe for display in the museum, less as items of specifically historic import than as valuable artworks.

SUMMARY
Treasure Trove remains an issue of concern to the archaeological community. It operates in some cases to reward the finders of objects obtained by criminal means; but this is irrelevant to the operation of the doctrine in terms of acquiring objects for museums. However, the adversarial approach adopted in the criminal justice system is present in the Treasure Trove procedure in that it sets up an opposition of interest between rival claimants. In its operations the doctrine serves to decontextualize objects, both in the process of treating separately each single object which together constitute the find; and by concentrating on the object alone, divorced from related objects and features. This decontextualization is in part the result of the historical circumstances of its adoption by the nascent discipline of archaeology. Nevertheless, decontextualization serves to ease the transfer of the object into its new realm, that of the museum.

Theoretical Interlude
Transformations: from archaeological object to museum treasure

The three processes of transformation from found object to Treasure Trove take place almost simultaneously during the Coroner's inquest. The first two processes – selection and recategorization – are phases of progressive decontextualization, and the third – adding value – a phase of recontextualization.

SELECTION

Section 30 of the Coroners Act 1988, as noted above, suggests that an item needs to be deemed to be treasure prior to consideration by a Coroner's inquest. As held in the Overton case, however, it is for the Coroner's jury to decide whether the quantity of precious metal present in the object is sufficient to make it treasure (*All England Law Reports* 1, 1982, 524). In practice, therefore, this is the first question the Coroner's jury will need to consider. This will be entirely a matter of fact: if Lord Denning's opinion in the Overton case is followed, nothing of less than 50 per cent precious metal will ever be passed to a Coroner's jury for assessment. It is much more likely that the archaeological community – and museums in particular – will continue to attempt to define the quantity required to be present at a level below the 50 per cent mark. In so doing, they will be asking Coroner's juries to select individual items for treatment in accordance with the doctrine. This is the first phase of decontextualization – a focus on single objects.

RECATEGORIZATION

Once selected for treatment, the item becomes legally 'treasure'. This is the phase of consideration of the circumstances of discovery, including the process of initial deposition, as required under Section 30 of the Coroners Act 1988. The archaeological context is taken into account at this stage – the Neolithic pits but lack of evidence for Iron Age

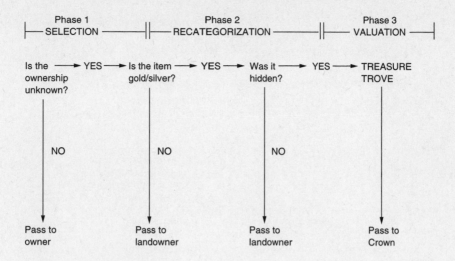

Figure 3.1   A Treasure Trove flow chart

settlement or ritual practice at Snettisham; the containers and dating at Donhead St Mary and Overton. Once considered to establish the intention of the depositor to retrieve the items in question, however, these contexts are put to one side. It is the single object that is important now, no longer the reason it was found, where it was, or how it came to be there. This is the second phase of decontextualization – the divorce from context.

ADDING VALUE

The object is now definitively classed as Treasure Trove. As in the medieval period, it is an object of wealth and (some) mystery. It will take its place in a museum as a valued relic of the ancient past. It has gained this new value by being isolated as a single object, removed from its former context, allowing recategorization, and being placed in a new one where it acquires new attributes and a new meaning. This is the phase of recontextualization – promotion to the status of museum object.

A Treasure Trove flow chart

The process of transition through these phases can be represented by a flow chart (Figure 3.1). This device serves to emphasize the manner in which each stage of the transformation process depends on the previous one, and accordingly the cumulative nature of this transition from initial selection, through categorization to final valuation.

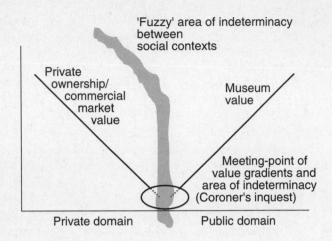

Figure 3.2   A Treasure Trove diagram

A Treasure Trove diagram

In terms of Rubbish Theory (Thompson 1979; and see Chapter 2), the phase of rubbish is the instant of time between complete decontextualization and recontextualization. As treasure, the item has one kind of value – a measurable commercial value in money terms. This value is removed during the process of transition to Treasure Trove and the declaration of the item as Treasure Trove causes it to shift to a new value gradient – that of the museum object. If the museum chooses not to take the item, it loses this museum value and regains its commercial one, or possibly a different one such as a 'personal prized possession'. Either way, the Coroner's inquest serves to transform the object from one status to another. If kept by the museum, it is raised into that higher realm of immeasurable value, not merely durable but existing in the upper part of the durable box – in the public domain.

This is the true meaning of the declaration of Treasure Trove. It serves to explain the great interest shown in such items by archaeologists, by the media and ultimately by the population at large. Treasure Trove items are still tinged with that air of magic and mystery which made them desired by medieval monarchs. But they no longer belong exclusively to the King: by placing them on museum shelves they become, in a sense, owned by us all.

This process of transformation can be represented graphically as in Figure 3.2. The vertical axis represents measures of value – however defined; they may be monetary, informational, aesthetic. The horizontal axis represents social contexts, in this case two only: the realm of private property (including the economic marketplace), and the realm of public property (including the museum). The divergent curves represent different value gradients along which the object may be located. The shaded area is the realm of uncertainty between social contexts and, in the case of Treasure Trove, is created by the Coroner's inquest in which the object is decontextualized. The place where the curves touch – within this area of uncertainty and emphasized by the ellipse around this junction – is the transfer point at which the object either is declared not to be Treasure Trove or is unwanted by a museum and so is returned to the private realm.

The value gradients diverge as a result of the adversarial approach contained within the Treasure Trove procedure. Ownership is absolute and cannot be shared. Accordingly, neither claimant can be expected to give the object away unless its value to that claimant is relatively low. As the object rises along the value gradient, the owner's resistance to parting with the object will increase. This will apply whether the owner is a private individual or a public museum. This is not to say that the measure of value for each is identical: the reason for two value gradients is that they measure different scales and types of value which are relevant to the social context in which they exist. The region between the two social contexts – the public and private realms – is a 'fuzzy' one and the two gradients do not meet neatly at a single point. Rather, it is an area of dispute and uncertainty – which is where the process of law comes into play.

SUMMARY AND CONCLUSIONS

Treasure Trove was deliberately adopted by the promoters of the nascent discipline of archaeology in the mid-nineteenth century as a device to collect objects specifically for museums. In doing this, it retains many attributes of antiquarianism. In particular it focuses on single objects which are removed from their context in the process of applying the doctrine to them. The processes of selection of items for treatment by the doctrine and recategorization in terms of the doctrine are phases of progressive decontextualization. The process of adding value is a phase of recontextualization in which the object is placed in a museum environment and thus raises it into the public domain.

The two chapters which complete this part of the book will examine the further development of bodies of law which apply to archaeological objects. Chapter 4 will focus on the efforts to provide legal protection for archaeological remains *in situ* and how this relates to the development of the discipline in late nineteenth-century Britain. It will close with the passage of the Ancient Monuments Protection Act of 1882.

Chapter 5 will bring the story up to date with the spread of legal coverage to other components of the archaeological heritage. In Part Three, Chapters 6, 7 and 8 will analyse the current body of law in terms of the three transformations noted above: selection; recategorization; and adding value.

4
A law for monuments

In 1858 James Talbot, Baron de Malahide addressed the Archaeological Institute at its meeting in Bath on the progress of his abortive Bill to amend the law of Treasure Trove (see Chapter 3). This Bill was concerned only with movable objects, but Talbot went on:

> I do not contend that [the Treasure Trove Bill] is the only thing wanted. No doubt greater attention to public monuments is absolutely required. One advantage of a society, such as the [Archaeological] Institute, is that it keeps watch on public authorities; and I must here admit that there are many corporations which do not take the same interest as the Corporation of Bath has shown in the preservation of its ancient monuments. Some of the worst acts of vandalism have been committed by such bodies. One of the great objects of such an association as ours is to maintain vigilant watch for such proceedings, and I have reason to think from my own experience, that when the evil apprehended is fairly stated, we seldom have difficulty in obtaining redress. It requires however great assiduity and promptitude in obtaining accurate and early information. It was, therefore, very desirable that we should have some public department to take an interest in the matter, and to be ready to interpose when any injury to National monuments is projected. It is very difficult, in this free country, to interfere with the rights of an individual, and compel him to do even that which everybody admits to be required; but I trust there will be well considered suggestions brought forward in regard to these questions, which may enable us to deal effectually with this important subject. (*The Archaeological Journal* 15, 368)

The term 'monument' had undergone a significant change of use since the *Archaeological Journal* paper of 1851 on the threefold subject matter (oral, written and monumental) of archaeology (Newton 1851; and see Chapter 3). For Newton, the term 'monument' covered anything that today we would call 'material culture' – all artefacts large and small. But in Bath in 1858, Talbot uses the term exclusively in the sense of large features, as is made clear by his reference to the monuments of Bath, and the two French examples which follow the passage quoted above, both of which concern ancient towers (*The Archaeological Journal* 15, 368–9). His call is thus for governmental responsibility for the preservation of large-scale landscape and townscape features. As in the case of Treasure Trove, the call is related to a concern specifically for 'National' monuments rather than those overseas (see Chapter 3).

In 1882 – nearly a quarter of a century later than Talbot's address and ten years after the first introduction of draft legislation to the House of Commons – the passage of the Ancient Monuments Protection Act marked the first successful piece of Parliamentary legislation in the field of conservation in England. It was exclusively concerned with large-scale landscape features and provided for a public official to be responsible for their preservation. Almost all histories of archaeology ignore the passage of this Act – despite its apparent importance to the archaeologists of the time, as reflected in the efforts to ensure its passage and Talbot's comments quoted above (see, for instance, Daniel 1978; Daniel and Renfrew 1988; Marsden 1984; Trigger 1989). Those works that do refer to it do so in passing, and the following are typical examples.

> Attempts to protect physical monuments ran aground on the same rock of the sanctity of private property as had the earlier Historical Manuscripts Commission. . . . Much modified proposals finally reached the statute book in 1882. (Levine 1986, 123)

> In Britain, the move towards the establishment of a governmental body responsible for the historic and archaeological environment was a gradual one. One of the main reasons for the [Act] to take so long to become law (ten years) was the fact that it was perceived by many Tories and Whig Liberals as an attack on the rights of private property. . . . [T]his group of right-wingers argued that such monuments were already well protected by landowners, and if a monument was not protected then such a monument was clearly not of great importance. . . . It should be realised that an issue which was contemporary with the Ancient Monuments Bill was Irish Home Rule; in the end Irish monuments were excluded from the Act. (Walsh 1992, 70–1)

Some recent work which examines the progress and effect of this statute has made the story rather better known in general and has concentrated on answering the question why it took so long for Parliamentary legislation on monuments to be forthcoming. As Saunders (1983, 11) puts it, 'it had been a long struggle against those who felt its objectives were an affront to the rights of private property'. Murray (1990, 55) concurs: 'it transpired that the Ancient Monuments Protection Bill was sorely to try [the promoter of the Bill, Sir John] Lubbock's patience and sap his optimism'. Similarly Chippindale (1983a, 11) comments that 'the Bill and its Schedules . . . was reintroduced . . . at every session until Lubbock lost his seat at the 1880 general election, to make eight attempts in all. By degrees it was "becoming itself an ancient monument".' And elsewhere Chippindale (1983b, 60) says 'Lubbock's Ancient Monuments Bill . . . never did become law. The landed interests in both the Commons and the Lords were too strong.'

The emphasis in these studies is on Lubbock's efforts to place legislation on the statute books and his struggle against opposition. The assumption in these works seems to be that it is naturally right that ancient monuments should be given legal protection and therefore the historical problem to be addressed is that of why it took so long to achieve. This question is addressed in detail by Saunders and Chippindale, and admirably so by Murray who relates it to the development of archaeological theory in the latter nineteenth century. In so doing all three – as well as Levine and Walsh quoted above – tell a story of the triumph of scientific progress over entrenched philistinism. However, they may be taking certain of the statements of those involved rather too much at face value. Talbot (*The Archaeological Journal*, 368) says there is 'no doubt' that attention to public monuments is required. Lubbock – in his address to the Royal Anthropological Institute in 1872 (quoted by Murray 1990, 55) – accepts that 'there seems to be a general wish throughout the country to take some adequate steps for the preservation of these ancient monuments'. And yet – as Saunders, Chippindale, Murray and the rest are at pains to point out – it took eight attempts and ten years for legislation to reach the stage of Royal Assent. At the same time, however, if legislation was so difficult to achieve, the question arises: how was Lubbock able to submit his Bill so many times and finally to force a vote requiring government legislation? From this point of view, the question becomes not why was legislation so long in coming, but how was legislation possible at all? It is the latter question that this chapter seeks to answer – and in so doing addresses those of the problems involved and the length of time it took.

A CONTEXTUAL HISTORY
I will draw here on the work of four writers in particular – Michel Foucault (1970; 1973; 1977); Philippa Levine (1986); Harold Perkin (1989); and Richard Shannon (1976) – to construct the framework of a contextual history in which to locate the efforts to bring legislation into being. In particular, this will relate to the political context of those efforts and the concerns of these four writers will be shown to be

reflected in the events which resulted in the Act of 1882. The term 'contextual history' is derived in part from the work of Tim Murray who conducts a useful critique of 'non-contextual histories of archaeology' (Murray 1990, 56–7).

The order of knowledge

This attempt at a contextual history – although influenced in large part by the work of Michel Foucault – is not a direct application of his interpretive scheme and so, while having some affinity with Eilean Hooper-Greenhill's recent volume considering the history of museums, it differs significantly from her approach (Hooper-Greenhill 1992).

Attempts at legislation in the archaeological field are limited to the latter part of the nineteenth century which locates them firmly in Foucault's Modern *épistème* (Foucault 1970), and a grasp of the relevant *épistème* is thus crucial to an understanding of the ideological and cognitive framework in which the passage of such legislation became possible. Foucault defines the *épistème* as 'the pure experience of order and its modes of being' (ibid., xxi). This 'order' is that of how things are organized in a system of thought. The *épistème* exists in a realm between the 'fundamental codes of a culture [which establish] the empirical orders with which [a man] will be dealing and within which he will be at home' and 'the scientific theories or the philosophical interpretations which explain why order exists in general, what universal law it obeys, what principle can account for it, and why this particular order has been established and not some other' (ibid., xx). Archaeology as a discipline is itself the product of this *épistème*, which is a dynamic one and in which previously broad areas of study break up into more specifically oriented ones. Archaeology – a human science along with Foucault's own list comprising psychology, sociology, studies of language and myth, psychoanalysis and ethnology – together with all the human sciences, can be located in the three-dimensional cognitive space which exists between biology (in which elements are ordered by function); economics (the field of competition and conflict for scarce resources, leading to the establishment of rules which control behaviour); and philology (the study of meaning which produces a system of signs).

This *épistème* also results in the phenomenon of professionalization. This process is particularly noted by Foucault in relation to the practice of medicine (Foucault 1973, 64–87). He describes how one effect of the French Revolutionary and Napoleonic Wars was the proliferation of quacks and inadequately trained medical personnel in the French countryside. This resulted in calls for new legislation to regulate medicine. Central schools of medicine were established: thus, theoretical knowledge and the practical experience of the hospital were for the first time combined in institutions open to medical students for training and to the public for the control of diseases. A failure to examine students in their knowledge led to the development of self-organized medical bodies for the control of medical practice. The end result was a division of the medical profession into officers of health who display practical knowledge, 'controlled empiricism' (ibid., 81) and doctors who emerge from the medical schools and reserve unto themselves the choice of entry of others to the professional training and expertise available in these clinics.

On a broader scale, the separating out of fields of study and the rise of the professional specialist was reflected in a new form of the exercise of power throughout society (Foucault 1977). In the switch from the Classical to the Modern *épistèmes*, there was a corresponding switch from the exercise of power by spectacle to the exercise of power by surveillance. In particular, the public torture and execution of criminals was replaced by the prison, where punishment takes place away from public view but within which the daily routine of the prisoner is closely watched. Originating in the techniques for disciplining members of the military, these techniques spread throughout society to become the new means by which power could be exercised. Operationally, spatial distribution is used to separate out individuals and groups of individuals from one another; there is control of activities over time, promoting efficiency of performance; judgement is normalized by the 'naturalization' of ranking systems, the institution of penalties for performance below some externally prescribed norm, and the grant of rewards for 'good' and 'proper' performance; and there is an emphasis on examination, especially a focus on the individual performance, and the progressive reduction of persons to 'cases' and 'functions'. All of this results in the uniformity in look and style of major social institutions – schools, hospitals, factories, prisons and military barracks. At the same time, 'the individual' as a category is created and maintained, and individuals thus created are subject to a discipline which not only prevents and limits 'bad' (unwanted) behaviour but which also actively promotes 'proper' (desired) behaviour. These mechanisms of discipline 'seep out' of institutions into society at large, creating the 'disciplinary society'. In economics, they promote efficiency; as law-like behavioural norms they control 'free' populations; as 'science' they allow the measurement of behaviour to promote the first two (Foucault 1977, 218–28).

What emerges from a consideration of Foucault's work is the realization that any academic discipline is at once constituted by but also allows and indeed promotes the Modern *épistème* and the broader disciplinary mechanism which operates across society at large. As 'science' the discipline performs the vital measuring role which is so important in the 'disciplinary society' and provides a point of entry for the rise of the professional specialism. An examination of Foucault's works opens up the search for possible similarities across disciplinary boundaries – the rise of professionalism, the application of legal controls and a first glimpse of how they became possible in the nineteenth century.

Professionalization

The rise of the salaried professional in the field of the study of the past has been examined in particular by Philippa Levine (1986). In her work she distinguishes between not only *The Amateur and the Professional* (the main title of her book) but also *Antiquarians, Historians and Archaeologists in Victorian England* (the sub-title). Her work concentrates

> first on an analysis of the social location of many historical prac-
> titioners . . . and second on the organizations and institutions in
> which they gathered. It was within this framework that the
> widening gap between amateur and professional . . . was realised.
> The emergence of new professions was a characteristic trend in
> nineteenth-century Western societies. . . . Attempts to limit entry
> . . . provided both a sense of community and of status for those
> within. (Levine 1986, 6)

Levine's analysis focuses on the factors which characterized those involved in the production of knowledge of the past in the period 1838 to 1886. In particular she is concerned with the social background of practitioners, the societies of which they were members, the precise definition of their specific disciplinary concerns, the role of government, and the role of the universities. 'The structural changes of intellectual institutions' she says 'are nevertheless only of interest . . . insofar as they throw light upon the status and state of knowledge in society. . . . The significance of these institutions leads inescapably back to . . . professionalisation' (Levine 1986, 6). She sees the rise of professionalism as 'an attack upon individual provincial cultures' (ibid., 174) with antiquarians increasingly marginalized by being 'rarely salaried to their historical interests and lacking access to the university community' which becomes of increasing importance (ibid., 173).

Her analysis results in a view of the relationship between anti-quarianism, history and archaeology somewhat at odds with the more traditional views of other historians of the discipline. The traditional view tends to regard antiquarianism as the more 'primitive' precursor of archaeology, which is replaced by archaeology during the nineteenth century, with history as a separate field of study altogether (cf. Stocking 1987, 71). Levine, on the other hand, treats them very much as related and parallel fields of study, with history and archaeology separating out from antiquarianism as the professional arms of the study of the past

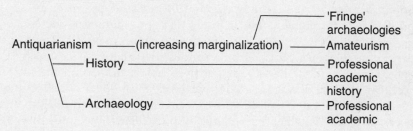

1. *The 'conventional' relationship*

Antiquarianism ——— (development and growth) ———Archaeology

History ————— (development and growth) ———History

2. *Levine's (1986) 'parallel' relationship*

Antiquarianism ———(increasing marginalization) ——— 'Fringe' archaeologies / Amateurism

History ——— Professional academic history

Archaeology ——— Professional academic

Figure 4.1   Possible relationships between antiquarianism and archaeology

while antiquarianism continues as an amateur pursuit. It is out of this remanent antiquarianism that ultimately grows so-called 'fringe' archaeology and modern 'treasure-hunting'. The differences between these two views are reflected in Figure 4.1.

Levine's approach can be criticized as being rather too rigid. She describes A. L. F. Pitt-Rivers, for instance, as an amateur (Levine 1986, 34) (which, like many in archaeology, he was to begin with) but without noting his entry to something like professional status as the first Inspector of Ancient Monuments under the 1882 Act (Chippindale 1983a, 1983b). Similarly, she dismisses Baron Talbot de Malahide as 'an antiquarian', ignoring his concern in the Archaeological Institute with archaeological remains, his efforts to appropriate Treasure Trove for archaeological and museum purposes and his quasi-professional status in 1882 as an inspector of manuscripts with the Historical Manuscripts Commission (Levine 1986, 121–3). Nevertheless, her approach success-fully highlights the significant changes taking place within disciplines concerned with the study of the past in this period – the rise of professionalism, the division of broad areas of study into more narrowly prescribed fields, and increasing restriction on entry to those fields.

The Rise of Professional Society: England since 1880 (Perkin 1989) charts these processes as they effect the entire country. Perkin notes through-out the earlier nineteenth century

> the continuing expansion of . . . 'the forgotten middle class', the non-capitalist or professional segment of the middle class. . . . They . . . mounted a critique of industrial society which began,

even at its height, to undermine the entrepreneurial hegemony
and reform its worst excesses, in the shape of factory legislation,
public health regulation, control of adulteration of food and drugs
and pollution of the environment, housing by-laws, state
educational provision and the like. (Perkin 1989, xii)

Perkin's argument is that from about 1850 onwards the capitalist society
dominated by class relations was gradually replaced by one centred on
professional hierarchies. He argues that pre-industrial society was
permeated by the aristocratic ideal based upon passive property and
patronage. This was replaced by an industrial society permeated by the
entrepreneurial ideal based upon active capital and competition. The
working-class ideal was the collective ideal of labour and cooperation.
Against these stood the professional ideal based on trained expertise and
selection by merit which emphasized human capital (but not simply the
labour theory of value) (Perkin 1989, 3–4).

The replacement of a class society by a new form does not represent
merely the old class society fitted out with a new ruling class. Instead,
'the matrix of the new society is the vertical career hierarchy rather than
the horizontal connection of class, and social conflict . . . takes the form
of a competition for resources between rival interest groups' (Perkin
1989, 9). The three classes of landowners, capitalists and workers were
identified and categorized by the new professional middle class who
were their 'theorists, apologists and propagandists. . . . Yet although they
"forgot themselves" as a class, nearly all of [the professional middle class]
. . . reserved a special place for their kind as the guides and mentors, the
Platonic guardians of society' (Perkin 1989, 118).

A professional society, says Perkin, is defined by a number of
characteristics. First, professional hierarchies reach 'well down the social
ladder' (Perkin 1989, 3) and are thus not just another ruling class. It is
permeated by a professional social ideal of how society should be
organized and a vision of the ideal citizen (ibid., 3–4). The transforming
device is always professional control of the market for a particular kind
of expertise (ibid., 7). The search is for status and power (ibid., 4) by the
techniques of persuasion and propaganda which make the service available a necessity (ibid., 6).

These characteristics can be conveniently mapped on to Foucault's
analysis of the 'disciplinary society' (Foucault 1977) and also on to
Cultural Theory (Schwarz and Thompson 1990; Thompson *et al.* 1990;
and see Chapter 2). The social ideals of organization and the ideal
citizen reflect the new techniques for the exercise of power – not
physical but by way of indirect control and surveillance. Similarly, the
chosen techniques of persuasion and propaganda serve to 'normalize'

hierarchical ranking and the provision of discrete types of expertise. As a domain of hierarchical structures which categorize others in the same terms, the professional society epitomizes the high Grid/high Group 'hierarchist' space in the Cultural Theory matrix. Perkin's analysis thus serves to link the underlying ordering of knowledge in the nineteenth century with the processes at work within the field of archaeology at the time legislation affecting archaeological material was first passed. As a model, however, it presents rather too strong a conspiratorial air – as if the process of professionalization was orchestrated in some deliberate fashion by a secret cabal of hierarchically oriented, middle-class social analysts. This is particularly so if it is placed alongside Levine's rather rigid approach. What is required is a less conspiratorial approach, one that injects a needed dose of contingency and the occasional unforeseen result. This can conveniently be found in the work of another historian of the later nineteenth century, Richard Shannon (1976).

Cultural politics

Shannon's view of the later nineteenth century as a period when attempts to maintain the status quo resulted in unforeseen, unintended but significant change is conveniently stated in the Introduction to his book *The Crisis of Imperialism 1865–1915* (Shannon 1976). Against a background of rising population, the spread of industrialization, the increasing concentration of population in industrial cities and the growth of trade, Shannon tells a story of nineteenth-century cultural politics.

> The developments of the . . . twentieth century have been essentially a working-out, a fulfilment of the themes which first began to assert themselves in the 1870s, 80s and 90s. . . . The problems of 'culture' and 'civilisation' assumed their place in the modern intellectual debate of the 1870s and 80s. . . . Contemporaries sensed the speed of the process. . . . By the beginning of the twentieth century the High Victorian synthesis of nature, art, society and culture had irretrievably broken down. . . . Very few people, if canvassed in 1865, would positively have chosen the end result in the early 1900s as the best of all possible worlds. . . . [Conscious political] aspects expressed themselves within . . . a domestic theme in which the central ambition was to adapt changing society to the imperatives of public policy but in which, in hard fact, the central necessity was to adapt public policy to the demands of a changing society, to cope with it by equipping it with institutions, services, structures of administration, necessary to enable it to function adequately as a society. And here 'adequately' meant a modest and negative achievement: avoiding such a breakdown or dislocation as

> would discredit the otherwise largely unchallenged ascendancy of the ruling class. (Shannon 1976, 12–16)

Two examples from the 1860s exemplify this process of status-quo maintenance which nevertheless resulted in massive unforeseen and unwanted change. In 1867, Prime Minister Gladstone presented a Franchise Bill in Parliament, the aim of which was to reduce the property qualification for the vote in Parliamentary elections. A reduction of £5 in this qualification added some 400,000 names to the electoral roll nationally, a significant increase. Shannon points out, however, that the spokesmen for the new working-class electors were merely:

> demanding entry to the club, not demanding that the club be demolished, or even that the rules be changed drastically. . . . The essence of the question of reform is thus to be seen in terms . . . of making the existing system of politics more comprehensive and not in terms of setting the existing system on a prescribed path towards twentieth-century democracy. (Shannon 1976, 60–2)

In 1870 Gladstone instituted the long-standing recommendations of a Commission that no person should enter the ranks of the Civil Service (other than the Foreign Office, which was excluded) without first passing a set of open competitive examinations. Rather than taking national administration out of the hands of the aristocracy, however, and placing it into the hands of a new meritocracy, Gladstone believed he was strengthening the ties between that administration and the current ruling class:

> for he had a 'strong impression' that 'the aristocracy of this country are even superior, in natural gifts, on the average, to the mass'; and that it was clear that with their 'acquired advantages, their insensible education, irrespective of book-learning, they have an immense superiority'. (Shannon 1976, 81–2)

The end result – as chronicled by Perkin (1989) – was increased professionalization and the take-over of the administration of the state by the educated middle class. One of the elements that made this take-over possible – despite the intentions and wishes of the actors involved – was the established credo of the actors themselves. Later nineteenth-century Liberalism was committed to the creation and maintenance of a 'legitimate' political regime and all Liberals agreed on the need for some measure of reform to ensure the maintenance of that legitimacy. Liberals were, however, divided over the issue of how far that reform should go, largely by arguments over the nature of 'legitimacy' itself. The more radical wing – exemplified by John Stuart Mill – were keen to 'establish a science of society that would provide guarantees of legitimacy for the new progressive politics of the future' (Shannon 1976, 32). Mill and his adherents believed in liberty – and especially in liberty of opinion, taking a line that good (correct) opinion would always drive out bad (incorrect) opinion. On the other hand, Matthew Arnold believed that 'tradition was the ruling social idea' and that the better approach was that of 'cultivating the nation by nationalising culture' (Shannon 1976, 33). This nationalization was to be achieved by the

> establishment of an intuited 'right reason', a kind of historically derived 'intelligence'. As Arnold defined culture as the best that has been known and said transmitted from the past and thus made available by tradition so 'right reason' was the historically conditioned intuition of society, [that is, of] the ruling class. . . . Arnold's *Culture and Anarchy* [of 1869] was the prime social text of the new English ruling class . . . for it provided . . . the intellectual basis on which aristocracy and bourgeoisie could adopt a common style. To this extent Arnold did in fact secure the nationalizing of culture. The authority of the one [the aristocracy] and the discipline of the other [the bourgeoisie] would be transmuted via a national culture into a very tough, resilient, self-confident and persistent new ruling class. (Shannon 1976, 33–4)

Practical efforts to nationalize culture can be seen in the extension at this time of the 'public' domain at the expense of the previously 'private'. This was one of the effects of the widening of the franchise in 1867 – the de facto dilution of aristocratic political control. It can also be seen in the professionalization of the Civil Service which began the process whereby control of the mechanisms of state was taken out of private aristocratic hands. This was further exacerbated somewhat later by the abolition of political appointments to the Civil Service altogether.

The origin of the split between the private and public domains has been traced back to the sixteenth century – the time of the first emergence of something recognizable as a modern nation state. This distinction was clearly recognized by the early nineteenth century. In 1832, Sir George Cornewall Lewis was describing the two areas thus: 'public, as opposed to private, is that which has no immediate relation to any specified person or persons, but may directly concern any member or members of the community, without distinction' (quoted in Benn and Gaus 1983a, 32). In the late nineteenth century there was a massive expansion of the public domain at the expense of the private. Many areas of life previously ignored by the state suddenly became areas of concern and there was legislation touching aspects of life previously left untouched.

The 1870s – the period with which this chapter is particularly concerned – was the period when the expansion of the public domain was most evident. It was in this decade, for example, that the monarchy started to develop its skills in ritual: as Cannadine (1983, 120) puts it 'there was a fundamental change in the public image of the British monarchy, as its ritual . . . became splendid, *public* and popular' (emphasis added). In 1872 the logic of a wider franchise required the introduction of the secret ballot (Shannon 1976, 62, 81), thus further lifting the business of government and politics out of private aristocratic hands. The effective creation in 1870 of a national education service by putting non-Church Board Schools 'on the rates' epitomized Arnold's 'nationalising' of culture. In 1880, elementary education became compulsory for all, and in 1881 fees for Board School education were abolished. This change was significant. As a number of recent historical works make clear, the whole notion of what it is to be 'English' was created in the forty or so years from about 1880 to around 1920 (Colls and Dodd 1986) and most 'ancient' British traditions date from no earlier than 1870 (Hobsbawm and Ranger 1986; Shannon 1976, 13).

Public health and cleanliness became an issue for legislation in 1875 with two Acts on Public Health and Artisans' Dwellings (Shannon 1976, 103). Licensing Bills were put up in 1871 and 1872 for reasons of public health (Shannon 1976, 93) and the 1870s saw a number of Parliamentary debates on the place of women in factories (Harrison and Mockett 1990, 142). They also marked an increased interest in regulating commercial and industrial life. Working hours were interfered with – the Bank Holiday was invented in 1871[1] and a Ten Hours Bill for female shopworkers was put forward in 1873. The exploitation of employees was addressed with the Employers And Workmen Act of 1875 (Shannon 1976, 105) and the Merchant Shipping Act of 1876 (Shannon 1976, 103). Previously private commercial documentation was to be given legal status and so enter the public domain with the Bankers Book Evidence Bill which was also presented during the 1870s (Mallet 1934). Commercial life was further regulated under the Employer's Liability Act of 1880 and the Corrupt and Illegal Practices Act of 1883 (Shannon 1976, 177, 180).

Whatever its ethical and ideological justifications, the purpose of this large-scale programme was ultimately to strengthen Britain against external threats. The programme as a whole is reflected in the reforms of the system of military recruitment following the defeats of the Austrian and French armies by Prussian forces in 1866 and 1870; the purchase of military commissions was also abolished (Shannon 1976, 83–5). In addition to this, 'there were plausible arguments . . . which stressed the correlation between success in education and success in war' (ibid., 86) and by giving more of the population a stake in the political system, the safer that system would be. All of this is tied up with programmes to create a positive sense of British national identity.

> Late Victorian Britain saw a sustained programme aimed at building cultural authority through projects creating and promoting a sense of national identity. . . . [The] politics of intellectual production . . . was to be exercised within a common public sphere of rational discourse; and it was an intellectual duty to initiate the uninitiated into its procedures. (Amigoni 1991, 146–7)

The aim of this cultural programme was to include as many people as possible within the cultural arena and to allow them to participate in its perceived benefits.

Summary: necessary conditions

This section has argued that the intense cultural and political activity in the latter part of the nineteenth century is all of a piece. Various aspects of life that were previously privately controlled – government offices, military promotion, commercial practices like the keeping of Bankers Books, labour contracts, working hours, building standards for homes – all became public concerns. At the same time there was a concerted effort on the cultural front – in particular the creation of a state education programme for all, and intense activity to give a public face to national institutions such as the monarchy – to engender a sense of national belonging among the entire population.

This process is closely linked to the rise of nationalism, but there is a very real sense in which nationalism is the effect rather than the cause. As Hobsbawm notes, there was something akin to English nationalism in existence as early as Shakespeare's time, whereas on the European continent nationalism does not appear as a significant political force until the French Revolution (Hobsbawm 1990, 75). The aim in the later nineteenth century in England – as made clear by Shannon – was to maintain the political status quo and political activity was directed to this end. The techniques employed derived from the Modern *épistème* and the disciplinary society as revealed by Foucault. The result was the rise of the professional in many and diverse fields of activity, including those relating to the study of the past as discussed by Levine, and ultimately of the professional society as described by Perkin. The massive expansion of the public domain at this time, in which professional expertise penetrates into all spheres of life, is both caused by and causes the proliferation of Parliamentary legislation.

Efforts to arrange legal protection for ancient monuments is a part of

this process and cannot be divorced from it if it is to be fully understood. As such, it forms part of and is directly related to other public
policy imperatives. This legislation would have three interconnected
effects. First, it would lift the object of that legislation into the public
domain. Second, by so doing, it would privilege that material and those
who are responsible for it over other material and persons. Third, it
would bring that material into the sphere of professional activity.

THE ART OF THE POSSIBLE

The previous section has been concerned to construct an image of the
wider socio-political background against which efforts to generate
legislation for the protection of ancient monuments can be set. By
drawing on the work of four writers it has been possible to construct a
context within which certain specific activities can be seen to be not
only possible, but also forming part of a range of similar activities at the
time – and even the necessary result of particular historical conditions.
Having established the existence of a socio-political context in which
legislation to protect ancient monuments is possible, we can turn to the
activities of a particular individual and his 'set' and demonstrate how
their efforts fit into this broader interpretive scheme.

Politics is – among other things – 'the art of the possible'. Attempts
at legislation are political activities. It is in political activity, therefore,
that the possible, the necessary and the achieved come together.

An archaeological politician

Sir John Lubbock – the father of the Ancient Monuments Protection
Bills – is in many ways a quintessentially public person. Although short
on formal education, he acquired much academic distinction and so is
regarded as one of the founders of modern archaeology and anthropology. He also had a long and distinguished political career which
culminated in his elevation to the peerage as Lord Avebury. Archaeologists, however, tend to forget that he was also distinguished in
commercial and professional banking life. Indeed, it was through
banking (the career of his father as well as himself) that Lubbock was
first able to enter the public domain with the creation of the first cheque
Clearing House in 1858 (Mallet 1934). What does seem to be clear, too,
is that his politics, his business and his academic activities all affected one
another and formed a consistent set of interests.

This is perhaps made nowhere clearer than in the final chapter of his
major – and most cited – work *Prehistoric Times*, first published in 1865
and subsequently re-issued six times (Lubbock 1900). In his 'Concluding
Remarks' to this book, Lubbock connects the technological development of a society directly to the mental condition of its members

(Lubbock 1900, 562). The simpler the available technology, the lower the moral state of the society. Drawing then on Darwinian evolution, he argues that the process of natural selection works to advance both physical and moral conditions over time (ibid., 567). Accordingly, technological advances lead directly to advances in learning, to greater understanding of nature and to increased happiness (ibid., 572). Reversing this process by a slick sleight of hand, he then suggests that scientific advances will necessarily lead to both physical and moral improvement among modern European populations (ibid., 573). Since 'science will also render man more virtuous' and there is no end to the improvement possible, then the poor and uneducated of the later nineteenth century were 'but on the threshold of civilisation' (ibid., 575). It follows from all this that 'Utopia [will] turn out . . . to be the necessary consequence of natural laws' (ibid., 577).

The concern to advance the welfare of his fellow human beings is also reflected in Lubbock's other works. In *The Use of Life* (Lubbock 1894) he seeks to provide an answer to 'the great question' – which is 'how to live' (ibid., 1). He provides detailed advice on many aspects of civilized existence – the importance of tact in dealings with others, on the benefits of thrift, on the importance and proper use of recreation, on the maintenance of good health. He follows this with four chapters on aspects of education – on the benefits of national education provision, on the value of self-education throughout all of life, on the great boon of the free lending library, and on the appropriate frame of mind in which to approach books and read them. This focus on education then leads into two chapters advising on what qualities and attributes constitute a proper patriotism and good citizenship. These various and acquired benefits of civilization are then related to appropriate sets of behaviour in social relations and at work. The moral high-point is reached in the final six chapters on 'Faith', 'Hope', 'Charity', 'Character', 'Peace and Happiness', and 'Religion'. All through, the benefits of Lubbock's own (largely self-acquired) education are apparent, in quotations from the classics. The overall programme presented in the book is entirely that of the later nineteenth-century Liberal, the ideas that underscored Gladstone's reformist politics in the 1860s, 1870s and 1880s.

On first entering Parliament in 1870, Lubbock's aims were threefold: to promote the study of science in primary and secondary schools; to quicken the repayment of the National Debt; and to secure some additional holidays and to shorten hours of labour in shops (Mallet 1934, 36). For a banker, the concern with the National Debt would be natural, and it relates to both the attitude towards thrift shown in *The Use of Life* (Lubbock 1894) and a concern for the improvement of the lot of others: the National Debt is a burden on all of society, including the poorest, and accordingly the value of thrift in personal life should be reflected in the conduct of national life. The other two aims similarly reflect a concern with the betterment of life for others and their moral and physical well being. If scientific advance and an understanding of nature lead to moral improvement, as argued in *Prehistoric Times* (Lubbock 1900, 573), then it follows that a scientific education should be made as widely available as possible. To be a good citizen requires one to be educated, argues Lubbock in *The Use of Life* (1894). Education, however, takes time to absorb and time must therefore be made available for it. In other words, people need more leisure time in order to gain the necessary scientific knowledge that will allow them to develop into good citizens. And it is this – the development of good citizens – with which Lubbock was concerned. In this he reflects the concerns of Matthew Arnold and Gladstone's administration, for throughout his thirty years in Parliament his efforts were 'highly favourable to the best elements in national life' (Mallet 1934, 37–8).

In concentrating on the Ancient Monuments Protection Act archaeologists tend to understate Lubbock's other legislative efforts. In fact, as a Parliamentarian, Lubbock was very busy. He was in full sympathy with the aims of the Liberal Party in the 1870s: Parliamentary reform, the extension of the franchise and later proportional representation (Mallet 1934, 55), Free Trade, and the provision of educational opportunity (ibid., 38). During the decade 1870 to 1880 no less than eleven pieces of legislation were guided by him through the House of Commons – not all successfully – and he was associated with at least one more (Mallet 1934). Of these eleven, nine are concerned with the regulation of professional, commercial or industrial life: the Apothecaries Acts Medical Act Amendment Bill; the Falsification of Accounts Bill; the Bankers Book Evidence Bill; the College of Surgeons Medical Act Amendment Bill; the University of London Medical Act Amendment Bill; the Factories Act Amendment Bill; the Bills of Exchange Bill; the Dental Practitioners Bill; and the Companies Act Amendment Bill. The Bank Holiday Bill and the Ten Hours Bill (concerned with shop working hours) reflect his concern to create additional leisure time but they would also have had an impact on commercial life: if the Bank of England were forced to cease business for a day, then all other banks would have to follow suit, making commercial activity virtually impossible; a limit on shop opening hours would provide shopworkers with increased leisure time but would also affect trade. This concern with working hours continued into the 1880s, with successful efforts to pass the Shop Hours Regulation Act in 1886 and his election as President of the Early Closing Association in 1892 (Mallet 1934).

Lubbock's wider political activities extended into his archaeological and anthropological concerns. In the 1860s he was closely linked with the younger intake at the Archaeological Institute who included John Evans and A. L. F. Pitt-Rivers, both of whom were also connected with A. W. Franks and accordingly Baron Talbot de Malahide. As William Chapman has recently outlined

> Pitt-Rivers, Evans, Lubbock and Franks worked closely with one another, supporting each other's candidacies for office within the Society of Antiquaries and the [Archaeological] Institute – all four eschewed the British Archaeological Association [from which the Institute had split in 1845 (Stocking 1987, 71)] – as well as pressing for more recognition of what we might consider the newer archaeological interests within the archaeological establishment. . . . All four pressed for reforms, encouraged a more active society role in protecting ancient sites and sought wider recognition of scientific topics. . . . It was partially through the pressure of this . . . group that British and Medieval Antiquities and Ethnography was recognised as a separate department under Franks at the British Museum in late 1866. (Chapman 1989, 27)

The hand of Talbot de Malahide can perhaps be detected in this programme – especially in the reorganization of the British Museum and the drive to protect sites, which followed from his efforts to appropriate Treasure Trove (see above and Chapter 3). The connection with Lubbock's political interest in scientific education is reflected in the group's aim of seeking the wider recognition of scientific topics.

Politics in the academic field also relates to a practical power politics, as suggested by Chapman's reference to mutual support in candidacy for office, and which extends also into the field of anthropology. Here, the Ethnological Society was at war with the Anthropological Association (Stocking 1987, 245–73), and the divisions were also internal to each of these bodies. On the one side stood the 'Ethnologicals' – comprising Lubbock, Pitt-Rivers and their cohorts, representing in general Nonconformist, middle-class backgrounds and a Liberal, 'humanitarian' approach – who would form the 'emerging intellectual aristocracy'. On the other stood the 'Anthropologicals', who occupied marginal positions within London high society and who were closely associated with colonial policy (Stocking 1987, 251–3). In party political terms, the Ethnologicals were dominated by Liberals, whereas the Anthropologicals were predominately Tory (ibid., 251). Battles were hard fought, with the Anthropologicals more regular attenders at meetings than Ethnologicals, although Lubbock was elected President of the Ethnological Society in 1868, by the expedient of holding the crucial meeting in

Norwich,[2] out of the reach of the London-based Anthropologicals
(Chapman 1989, 33; Stocking 1987, 254). In 1871, Lubbock, Pitt-
Rivers, Franks and T. H. Huxley oversaw the amalgamation of the
Ethnological Society and the Anthropological Association into the
Anthropological Institute (Chapman 1989, 34). In 1873, Huxley
nominated Evans for President of the new body, but resurgent and alert
Anthropologicals defeated him. The following year, however, the
Ethnological candidate (George Busk) was successful and four of the six
vice-presidencies fell to Ethnologicals, giving them sufficient influence
to change the rules to wipe out Anthropological representation
altogether (Stocking 1987, 256–7).

As an archaeologist and anthropologist Lubbock acted very much as
the Liberal politician. His Parliamentary concerns are those he brought
to his involvement in scientific institutions and which he worked with
close allies to promote. As a Gladstonian Liberal, he stands opposed to
landed Tory self-interest. As a politician, he sits at the centre of an
extensive network of contacts and interests, all more or less political in
the party-political sense. He is one of Perkin's rising middle-class pro-
fessionals, assisting in the creation of the distinct disciplines of archaeology and anthropology, classifying and defining appropriate behaviour
patterns for these new sciences. By legislating for the protection of
ancient monuments and placing the responsibility for that protection in
the hands of people like himself, Lubbock and his allies would gain
control over that material. This was the aim of Lubbock's attempts at
archaeological legislation from 1872 to 1882.

A political archaeologist

Within archaeology, Lubbock's main interest lies in prehistory, and this
can be related to his political concerns, his network of contacts, and his
efforts at legislation. As a middle-class Liberal, Lubbock can be seen to
be opposed to aristocratic self-interest on the one hand and collectivist
socialism on the other. These political oppositions serve to explain
certain other aspects of the legislation and its passage.

Lubbock's Bill if passed into law would have conveniently met the
terms of Talbot's call for legislation in 1858. It proposed to establish a
National Monuments Commission which would have the power to
acquire rights in ancient monuments by agreement with the owners of
the land on which they stood. In addition, a schedule of monuments
considered sufficiently important to be worthy of protection was
appended to the Bill. It would be a criminal offence deliberately to
damage any monument on the schedule or in which the Commission
had acquired rights. If the landowner wished to injure any such monument, notice would need to be given to the Commission, who had the

right to purchase the monument within three months. The expenses of the Commission would come from Treasury funds (Chippindale 1983a, 9).

Lubbock proposed his Bill each Parliamentary session between 1873 and 1880. As noted by other commentators, these attempts all failed because of the opposition of the landed interests in the House of Commons. But in 1882 he managed to force a vote of the House that committed Gladstone's newly elected government to put through a Bill of their own. This government Bill – drafted by George Shaw Lefevre, the Commissioner for Works (Chippindale 1983a, 17) – became the Ancient Monuments Protection Act of 1882. Other than those covered above, there is one important feature that is common to Lubbock's Bills and the Act as finally passed; and one great difference. The point of identity is that the monuments to be protected under Lubbock's Bills and the Act are prehistoric and only prehistoric (Chippindale 1983a, 9). The difference is that Lubbock's Bills covered the whole of the United Kingdom, including Ireland; while the Act as passed covered only Great Britain.

The limitation of the Bill to prehistoric monuments is generally taken to be a tactical measure to ensure passage. Medieval monuments, which were specifically excluded (Chippindale 1983a, 9), were argued out on the basis that they would be expensive to preserve, and that they were too well known to be in any particular danger (Chippindale 1983a, 9; Murray 1990, 63). More revealing is the suggestion – voiced by Lubbock alone – that extension of the Bill to medieval remains would involve 'contentious issues in aesthetics' (Chippindale 1983a, 9) or, as Lubbock himself put it, 'aesthetic questions, with reference to which there are great differences of opinion' (quoted by Murray 1990, 63). What was the basis for these differences of opinion over aesthetics as they relate to medieval material?

Earlier in the 1850s, when Talbot de Malahide was endeavouring to appropriate Treasure Trove, British archaeology was 'only beginning to stir from the doldrums of antiquarianism . . . [and] focusing primarily on the relics of the medieval period' (Stocking 1987, 71). This antiquarian-ism was related to an older 'Anglo-Saxon radicalism' when scholars searched for native English precedents to justify the break with Rome and then the defence of Parliamentary power against royalist pretension (Stocking 1987, 62). This connection between religion, politics and cultural taste was reflected in the world of art, where a nascent German art-historical tradition had 'rediscovered' Renaissance Northern primitive art (Haskell 1980). This process was particularly fascinating to an English audience because 'it demonstrated . . . how an ideology (nationalism) and a religious belief (Roman Catholicism) could be given visual expression through a private collection' of paintings (Haskell 1980, 79–81). The emergence of the Pre-Raphaelite brotherhood as a group hostile to English salon art (ibid., 87) was reflected in hostility to the Italian 'primitive' style they favoured (ibid., 98). The popular vogue at this time was for artists who could exemplify the qualities of 'faith and progress' (ibid., 104) – what the Pre-Raphaelites castigated as 'slosh' (ibid., 87).

The point of this apparent digression is that an interest in things medieval belonged to groups to which Lubbock and his like were opposed politically. Medievalist antiquarians – and the kind of 'Anthropologicals' Lubbock, Pitt-Rivers, Franks and the rest had fought in the Ethnological Society and Anthropological Association – were mostly aristocratic Tories. Talbot de Malahide, an ally and possible mentor of Lubbock, was particularly concerned with Roman and Irish Celtic remains. Lubbock and his colleagues were prehistorians. As Haskell makes clear, however, as early as 1860 the perceived threat to English art from the Continental interest in the primitive was over (Haskell 1980, 106). Accordingly, Lubbock's reference to aesthetic controversy is to old battles which are now finished. Why bother with them in the 1870s? The answer may be that – although aesthetic disputes have been finished with – others over the same material are not.

Chippindale (1983a, 9) notes that Lubbock was a founder member of William Morris's '"anti-scrape" Society for the Protection of Ancient Buildings' (SPAB) while the Conservative Pitt-Rivers (in particular) was not. SPAB was founded in 1877 (Kennet 1972; Countryside Commission 1989). Its particular concern was the protection of buildings in use – especially ecclesiastical ones – from damage during renovation. The members of SPAB – inspired by Morris's own concerns – were particularly keen to protect medieval structures from damage. Morris, a socialist, was opposed to any form of state authority (Yeo 1986, 353). In the 1880s he would found the Arts and Crafts Movement and write his novel *News from Nowhere*, both of which looked back to a vision of a libertarian Middle Ages as the model for a new society (Morris 1891; Woodcock 1975). He and his friend Peter Kropotkin, the Russian anarchist émigré, shared an understanding of medieval craft guilds as organizations of free individuals who worked in common, a view which contributed much to late nineteenth-century socialist thought (Kropotkin 1972, 141–93, 267–72; Woodcock 1975). Morris's concern for medieval artefacts and art was as politically based as it was a matter of personal taste. It represented his opposition to current politics. Against this can be ranged Lubbock's own Liberalism, which exemplified English freedom in Parliament, and an increasingly interventionist credo as 'society' became associated with 'nation' and 'state' (Collis 1986).

In opposing the legal protection of medieval monuments while proposing the protection of prehistoric monuments, Lubbock was supporting the growth of a privileged professional science of prehistory in opposition simultaneously to aristocratic antiquarianism and socialist libertarianism, both of which favoured medieval material. The arguments that raged over the Bill's passage – which largely concerned the effect of the Bill on private property – may have had more to them than the simple self-interest of the landed classes. What was at stake was not only the fate of certain ancient features but visions of the future of Britain. Alongside Lubbock stood the rising professional middle class whose interests were served by the Liberal party under Gladstone. Their programme – of electoral reform, of widening access to education, and of the maintenance of 'legitimacy' in government – would be supported by the success of Lubbock's Bill since it would promote the scientific study of a past defined in Darwinian terms (Lubbock 1900) and the dissemination of knowledge about that past. Against Lubbock stood the Tory landowning aristocracy whose interests would be harmed by the victory of the new professional middle class represented by Lubbock and his allies. The dispute over preservation was ultimately less to do with the relative merits and demerits of the protection to be afforded to ancient monuments by the law on the one hand and private landowners on the other (Chippindale 1983a, 12–14; Murray 1990, 63), than simple and rather brute power politics.

The cultural activity of the late nineteenth century was deeply implicated in the politics of that time, with the inevitable result that political disputes were fought over cultural issues. This explains why resistance to Lubbock's Bill was so strong. The Bill was possible because it was part of a much wider process of cultural politics, involving the separating out of distinct fields of study into modern disciplines, the rise of a professional middle class, and the privileging of the fields of study dominated by that professional middle class (in particular by granting them legal status). The Bill was firmly resisted because its specifics established the science of prehistory in opposition to other political visions which depended on an appeal to the medieval period.

Lubbock's Bill as originally drafted encompassed the entire United Kingdom, which at this time included southern Ireland. From the point of view of prehistory, Britain could be seen as a single entity: the major monuments of earth and stone are similar types of monument (ringforts, stone circles, large burial chambers) which can be found in Ireland as well as on the British mainland. In emphasizing prehistory at the expense of other periods it made sense for Ireland to be included in the Bill. The fly in the ointment was that in the 1880s the issue of Irish Home Rule was the major political controversy. In 1886 the Liberal

Unionists led by Joseph Chamberlain – who were opposed to Home Rule – left the Liberal Party and forced a general election. Lubbock was also opposed to Irish Home Rule, which is why in the 1890s he reappears in political life as a Conservative.

Lubbock's Irish connections predate his membership of the House of Commons. As Chapman (1989, 27) points out, in the 1860s the London archaeological societies were largely dominated by Irish peers, including Talbot de Malahide. These Anglo-Irish Tories were not likely to favour a policy of Irish Home Rule, and Lubbock's close connection to them would encourage him to support such a position. Indeed, his archaeological understanding also led him to it. Supporters of Home Rule argued their case in part on the premise that there were four distinct nationalities incorporated within the United Kingdom, that the Irish were one of these four and this difference justified a degree of self-determination for Ireland (Boyce 1986, 235). In 1886, the year of the Liberal split, Lubbock wrote a letter to *The Times* in support of the anti-Home Rule group by arguing that any attempt to justify Ireland's status as a separate nation by reference to the racial origins of its people was fallacious. Instead there was 'a Saxon division that covered most of east England, the east of Ireland and Scotland, and a Celtic division that comprised most of west Ireland and west Scotland together with Wales and Cornwall' (Lubbock *et al.* 1887). For Lubbock not only was the racial mix identical throughout the British Isles, but also identically distributed through it. In other words, on the Irish issue as elsewhere, his politics inform his archaeological aims, and his archaeology supports his political beliefs. The Act as finally passed reflected Lubbock's concerns for prehistory, but his opposition to Irish Home Rule met a temporary setback.

Definitive evidence that the debates about the legal protection of ancient monuments were at least in part 'really' about Irish policy is impossible to obtain – not least because an open and public admission by those involved would have ruined their chances of success. Accordingly, a strict reliance on the contents of *Hansard* is misplaced. There is nevertheless at least one indication in the debates of the House of Commons of a direct connection between the politics of Ireland and those of archaeology. On the evening of Friday 11 March into the early morning of Saturday 12 March 1881, the House debated the Peace Preservation (Ireland) Bill (*Hansard (JHC)* CXXXVI, 1881, 122). This measure had a controversial history, having been originally introduced as urgent government business (*Hansard (JHC)* CXXXVI, 1881, 100) but subsequently becoming the object of attempts to delay its reading (*Hansard (JHC)* CXXXVI, 1881, 101–2). The votes of early Saturday 12 March 1881 resulted in its amendment and third reading but only after a further attempt to delay the Bill had been defeated (*Hansard (JHC)* CXXXVI, 1881, 122). Immediately after this vote was taken, the House considered the motion to resolve itself into the Committee of Supply and for the Speaker to leave the Chair. This motion was met by an amendment to delete the words 'That Mr Speaker do now leave the Chair' and their replacement with:

> That in the opinion of this House, it is desirable that Her Majesty's Government should take steps to provide for the protection of Ancient Monuments. (*Hansard (JHC)* CXXXVI, 1881, 122)

The vote was then taken on the formal motion that 'The words to be left out stand part of the question' – in other words, that the original motion (that the Speaker stand down) should be put. The vote was lost by a vote of 79 to 56. Accordingly the replacement motion was put to the House and this led ultimately to the Ancient Monuments Protection Act of 1882.

The significant thing so far as the connection with Ireland is concerned, however, is the names of the Tellers for this vote. Since 1859, the rule has been that 'a Member [of the House] is bound to act as Teller for that side of the question with which he has declared himself when appointed by the Speaker' (*Erskine May* 1989, 344). Lubbock and a Mr Stanhope were appointed the Tellers for the Noes, in favour of Government legislation on ancient monuments. The Tellers for the Yeas – against this – were Lords Grosvenor and Kensington, who had previously acted as the Tellers in favour of the vote to delay the Peace Preservation (Ireland) Bill. This coincidence is, of course, by no means conclusive, but it is strongly suggestive of a close link between a direct interest in Government action on Irish politics and an interest in Government protection of ancient monuments. It thus serves to support the other connections made in this chapter.

SUMMARY AND CONCLUSIONS

The purpose of this chapter has been to seek to understand how the Ancient Monuments Protection Act of 1882 came into being. The success of Talbot de Malahide in appropriating the law of Treasure Trove for the service of the nascent discipline of archaeology led to a concern for visible landscape and townscape features.

In constructing a contextual history for what followed it has been necessary to explore the nature of the cultural politics of the later nineteenth century, and in particular the conditions which allowed the separation out from formerly wide fields of study of the discrete discipline, the professionalization of that discipline at the expense of amateur involvement, and the way in which ideological and party political battles were fought out over cultural issues. The expansion of the public domain – which was in part the cause and in part the result of the increasing professionalization of many areas of life in the 1860s and 1870s – provided a *raison d'être* for bodies of legislation in a wide range of fields. Archaeology was subject to the same forces at this time as any other discipline, and it was therefore appropriate to legislate in order to gain control over the use of archaeological material.

Those that sought to achieve this legislative control were also those engaged in other areas of cultural politics – and especially Sir John Lubbock, the promoter of the first Bill to protect ancient monuments. Lubbock's Gladstonian Liberalism supported his views on the purpose and use of archaeology and his archaeology was of use in legitimizing his political vision of Britain. His interest in prehistory reflected his political opposition to both aristocratic Tories and radical socialists, both of whom looked to a vision of the Middle Ages to confirm their political beliefs. In drafting a Bill to cover Ireland, Lubbock acted in support of his allies in archaeological and ethnographical circles as well as in support of his own position on the issue of Irish Home Rule. All of these aspects of his life were implicated in his archaeological work and in his efforts to pass the Bill.

His efforts were partly successful. The Act passed in 1882 confirmed the importance of prehistory by retaining the schedule to Lubbock's Bill. Unlike the Bill, however, it did not cover Ireland, reflecting deep divisions over the Home Rule issue.

The battles over Lubbock's Bill accordingly reflect more general concerns within late nineteenth-century Britain. The attempts to pass the Bill and the passage of the Act of 1882 were the product of complex and wide-ranging historical and social factors. There was quite clearly no consensus on the value of protecting archaeological material by law; the drive for such protection was as much the product of other political concerns as a reflection of the care shown by certain individuals for the archaeological heritage. The attempts to legislate were deeply involved with other issues of weight at the time and a cynic could see them as mere tactical ploys to achieve other – quite different – ends. Such a view, however, ignores the centrality of cultural concerns within the politics of this age. As an important part of cultural life in the late nineteenth century, archaeology was central to political activity and politics was central to archaeology. The political activity associated with the attempts to legislate for ancient monuments served to promote a science of prehistory, and the science of prehistory thus promoted served to support a particular political ideology.

Chapter 5 will briefly chart the fortunes of the 1882 Act and how it became – to all intents and purposes – defunct by the turn of the century and will then trace the development of such legislation to the present. The preceding Interlude will consider how and why the idea of legislation remained so powerful despite the ultimate failure of the Act of 1882.

NOTES
1. The Bank Holiday was one of Lubbock's early Parliamentary achievements.
2. The Norwich meeting was also subject to disputes over its legality, since the holding of meetings outside London was not specifically allowed by the Society's Rules.

Theoretical Interlude
Political cultures and legislating for archaeology

THE PURPOSE OF LEGISLATION

Drawing on Cultural Theory (Schwarz and Thompson 1990; Thompson *et al.* 1990) and Rubbish Theory (Thompson 1979), I have argued in Chapters 2 and 3 that the law acts to give a value to the material to which it is applied, and that this value is ascribed as the final stage of a three-part process of selection, categorization and finally valuation. The appropriation of Treasure Trove and attempts to legislate the protection of prehistoric remains were closely tied to the process of the development of the discipline of archaeology itself during the latter part of the nineteenth century. The form of the laws chosen for appropriation or enactment reflected the particular interests of those aiming to apply law to their field of archaeology, and this goes far to explain the particular content of legal provisions (Chapter 4). Over and above the provision of value to specific items, however, the law also gives an overarching value to the general class of material to which that item belongs. By privileging specifically prehistoric monuments, therefore, all ancient monuments (Roman, Anglo-Saxon, medieval and post-medieval) were to an extent given the potential for similar prominence.

The political scientist Murray Edelman (1967, 1971) argues the important symbolic role of political action. He recognizes that laws constitute 'symbols against threat (even though repealed in effect by administrative policy, budget starvation or other means)' (1967, 37–8) rather than useful 'predictions of future actions' (1967, 104). He points out that 'to formulate a law is essentially a job of constituting a setting in the sense of building background assumptions and limits that will persist over time [and accordingly a] statute may state norms . . . to which everyone will agree' (1967, 103). This description fits the case of the 1882 Act very well. The success in passing the Act was not matched in its operation, and it was indeed 'repealed in effect' by a combination of administrative policy (attaching the Inspector to the Office of Works rather than giving Pitt-Rivers his own department) and budget starvation (making only very limited finances available to the Inspector) (see Chapter 5). Nevertheless, it did build 'background assumptions . . . that persist over time' in that the idea of legislating the protection of ancient material was given practical effect by the Act.

As Edelman puts it, 'groups which present claims upon resources may be rendered quiescent by their success in securing nontangible values' (1967, 40) and 'legislation . . . signalling that a group aspiring to a valued status has achieved it reassures the group that in the future its adversaries will be limited in their use of private bargaining tactics and other resources' (1971, 10). In other words, the achievement of the passage of legislation was to promote prehistoric archaeology to a special status – as a discipline with legal authority, over and above that of other disciplines. As argued in Chapter 4, this was always one of Lubbock's aims in promoting his Bills, but the eventual passage of the Act signalled both to other archaeologists and to members of other disciplines the success of this project regardless of the effectiveness of the legislation itself. The significance of the Act of 1882 lay accordingly in its capacity to change the expectations and demands of those involved in the new scientific disciplines. This reflects Edelman's view of the ultimate purpose of politics:

> Government affects behaviour chiefly by shaping the cognitions of large numbers of people in ambiguous situations. It helps create their beliefs about what is proper; the perceptions of what is fact; and their expectations of what is to come. . . . *Political actions chiefly arouse or satisfy people not by granting their substantive demands, but rather by changing the demands and expectations.* (Edelman 1971, 7; original emphasis)

With the passage of the 1882 Act, prehistoric archaeology became a field of significance with Parliamentary approval. The decades that followed would see other disciplines with comparable material achieve the same status and other branches of archaeology extend legal coverage to their material (see Chapter 5).

NETWORKS AND BOUNDARIES

The actions of Talbot and Lubbock in the fields of Treasure Trove and ancient monuments legislation respectively were essentially political actions. Edelman makes it clear that it is groups that are the beneficiaries of political action, and this encourages the investigation of the actions of Talbot, Lubbock and their colleagues as group-building exercises. This is because in order to understand fully the relationship between the development of the discipline of archaeology and the political actions of archaeologists in the late nineteenth century, it is necessary to understand the relationship between political action and the construction of groups.

Cultural Theory and political action

In an effort to model social and political action, Michael Thompson (1979, 155–83) draws largely on Basil Bernstein's (1971, 1972, 1973) work in the sociology of education to construct a dynamic model of the 'curriculum cycle' whereby the hierarchical 'collection curriculum' is transformed into the more open and flexible 'integrated curriculum'. The crucial factor he identifies is the degree of erosion of the boundary between disciplines which can be described by a three-dimensional catastrophe theory model. Along the x axis he measures those new research projects approved by the collection ideology (and thus recognized as 'within the discipline'); along the y axis those new research projects undertaken despite the collection ideology (which classes them as 'outside the discipline'); and vertically along the z axis the ratio between the two, expressed as an 'index of boundary maintenance' (Thompson 1979, 174). This model can be refined and made more broadly applicable by relabelling the x axis as the measure of force acting to uphold the boundary and relabelling the y axis as the measure of force acting to erode the boundary, while the z axis remains the ratio between them. The model can now be made to describe the statics and dynamics of any situation where a boundary exists, whatever form it may take.

Thompson's (1982) application of this model to individual social action identifies three processes at work, two of which correspond to the axes of the Cultural Theory model (Chapter 2). Along the grid dimension, the individual is engaged in a process of involvement in networks: to move 'up-grid' is to become increasingly marginalized and unable to control events – to be placed on the periphery of the network; to move 'down-grid' is to become increasingly involved in the network and more able to control events – to be placed near the centre of things (Thompson 1982, 38–9). Along the group dimension, the individual is engaged in a process of inclusion or exclusion from definable clusters of individuals: to move 'up-group' is to become more intensively included – to be increasingly reliant on one's group membership; to move 'down-group' is to become more intensively excluded – to have group support increasingly withdrawn from one (Thompson 1982, 39–40). The third axis is that of manipulation, that is 'doing things, wittingly or unwittingly, to yourself and having things done, wittingly or unwittingly, to you by others' (Thompson 1982, 40); it is defined as 'power made manifest', exhibiting itself individualistically in the network context and collectivistically in the group context (Thompson 1982, 41).

Networks are extensive – they cross boundaries – and as 'grid' (prescriptions on action) seek to encompass all within them; they therefore correspond to the forces seeking to erode boundaries along the y axis. Groups are tightly bounded – they are defined in terms of opposition to other groups – and aim to include us while excluding them; the group dimension thus corresponds to the forces acting to uphold the boundary along the x axis. Manipulation is measured in terms of grid and group, and so corresponds to the index of boundary maintenance vertically along the z axis.

Political action thus contains three processes: networking; boundary construction; and manipulation between them.

Nineteenth-century networking

Chapman (1989) has charted the interdisciplinary connections between archaeologists in the archaeological and anthropological societies of the 1860s. Other more extensive networks were also in place. Despite his political opposition to socialism, Lubbock was a founder member of William Morris's Society for the Protection of Ancient Buildings (SPAB), formed in 1877. The concern of Morris and his associates was primarily with the preservation of medieval structures, and specially ecclesiastical buildings. This network of medievalists has as one important node John Ruskin, who influenced Morris very strongly and has been described as 'a violent Tory of the old school [and] the reddest also of the red' (quoted in Shannon 1976, 490). Ruskin also influenced other late nineteenth-century conservationists, in particular Octavia Hill, H. D. Rawnsley (alias Hardie) and Robert Hunter, three of the founders of the National Trust in 1896 and all Christian Socialists. Like Lubbock – and H. L. Grosvenor, Duke of Westminster, the fourth founder of the National Trust – all were concerned with issues of social welfare and education (Gaze 1988, 12–22). Hunter was linked directly to Lubbock as the lawyer responsible for drafting the Bills presented in 1872 to 1879 (Gaze 1988, 78). Lubbock's involvement in this network is, however, limited: far from being central, he occupies a position on the periphery, connected only via his membership of SPAB and his legal association with Hunter. In Thompson's (1982) terms, he operates 'up-grid' in this network, with limited control over the activities of SPAB and the socialist medievalists.

Political groups

Groups are about exclusivity, and Lubbock's record supports this. His exclusive X-Club 'devoted enormous energy to gaining power' (Barton

1990, 72), as did he and his allies in the Anthropological Institute (Stocking 1987, 245–73; Chapter 4). As Chapman (1989) demonstrates, there were close ties between Talbot, Lubbock, Pitt-Rivers, A. W. Franks and others in the 1860s which persisted into later decades. Similarly, Bradley (1983, 7) and Hudson (1987, 33) demonstrate how Pitt-Rivers' politics informed his archaeology and vice versa in a manner similar to that of Lubbock (1900; Chapter 4). These individuals formed a close band of allies who separated themselves out from others, and indeed actively sought to deny to others access to their field of operations in archaeology and ethnology. In Thompson's (1982) terms, they engaged in strict boundary maintenance – they operated highly 'up-group'.

Manipulation
The benefits of the efforts of Lubbock and his associates accrued very strongly to the discipline of prehistoric archaeology as associated with ethnology (Chapter 4). This is exactly what one would expect from Thompson's (1982) model, since the exercise of power is expressed individualistically in the grid context, but collectivistically in the group context. Lubbock operates in a weak grid context but a very strong group context. Accordingly, the benefits accrue to the group rather than the individual, and in this case the group is the discipline. Murray (1990, 58) in particular recognizes 'the importance of preservation as a context of archaeological theory-building and legitimation [and that] preservationism is an important stimulus to the development of theory and method in prehistoric archaeology'. The reverse is also true: specific forms of archaeological activity (such as a concentration on prehistory) give rise to preservationist activities. This dialectical relationship between disciplinary development and the preservation of its material provides the driving force behind yet further preservationist efforts on the part of others.

SUMMARY
In Cultural Theory terms (Chapter 2), the combination of high grid and high group locates Lubbock in the 'hierarchy' space where 'legal authority' applies (cf. Weber 1968, 216–17). The discipline of prehistoric archaeology is very largely the creation of Lubbock and his allies; accordingly, the application of a legal regime over its material of study is his chosen form for its regulation. By working to provide such a legal regime, Lubbock sought to promote the study of prehistory and the related field of ethnology over other periods and styles of study. This promotion followed from the work of others – particularly Talbot de Malahide – in promoting the study of things over the study of oral traditions and written material.

5
A proliferation of laws

The Ancient Monuments Protection Act of 1882 contained a schedule of prehistoric monuments considered sufficiently important by the main archaeological societies that their owners could, if they wished, place them under the guardianship of the state. There was provision for additional monuments to be placed on the schedule by Order in Council. Once it was placed in guardianship, anyone who damaged the monument would be subject to a fine of £5. In addition, one or more Inspectors were to be appointed under the Act, whose task it would be to report to the newly established Commissioners for Works (a government department) on the condition of the monuments listed in the schedule and suggest the manner in which they could best be preserved.

This legislation was very weak. Inclusion in the schedule was no guarantee of protection under the law for a monument, since this constituted only an invitation to the owner to seek such protection for it. The Inspector(s) had no powers other than to report and advise on the condition of those monuments specifically listed in the schedule, and their recommendations would need the agreement of the Commissioners for Works (Chippindale 1983a, 17–19; Saunders 1983, 11–12).

In 1883 John Lubbock's associate and ally, Augustus Henry Lane Fox Pitt-Rivers, was appointed the first Inspector. Pitt-Rivers was not afraid to exceed his legal authority, whether by instituting surveys of non-guardian and non-scheduled monuments; by excavating monuments; by inviting suggestions for monuments to be added to the schedule; or by arranging the private protection of sites (Chippindale 1983a, 23; Saunders 1983, 13). Much of this was necessary because state funding was also limited: Pitt-Rivers' annual salary as Inspector was only £250, and any assistants he employed he paid for himself; a mere £100 was set aside annually for other costs, an amount subsequently raised to £200 (Chippindale 1983a, 19–21). Despite the Inspector's hard work, by the time of Pitt-Rivers' retirement in 1890 the Act of 1882 was effectively defunct in that no more monuments were taken into state care after that date, and on Pitt-Rivers' death in 1900, the post of Inspector was left vacant (Chippindale 1983a, 30–1; Saunders 1983, 14).

As early as 1883, Lord Carnarvon had referred to the Act as 'crippled in its powers and limited in its scope' (quoted in Saunders 1983, 11) and by the time of its demise only 43 monuments had been taken into state guardianship, none in the ten years up to 1900, and only 20 of these in England, the Isle of Man and Wales, about half as many as listed on Lubbock's original schedule of 1872 (Chippindale 1983a, 29). To a large extent the late Victorian project of legislating the state protection of archaeological material must be counted as a failure.

THE LEGACY OF 1882

Given the original lack of success of the preservationist project, however, the question arises: if first attempts at legislating state control of archaeological remains were ultimately failures, how did the idea that this was an appropriate method of preservation persist? Chapter 4 has demonstrated that the concept of state protection was by no means 'natural' and self-affirming, but was the result of political action by certain individuals in the pursuit of political goals. With the passing of those politically motivated individuals, it might be expected that the drive for legislation might also expire. However, further legislation on ancient monuments was enacted in 1892 (although limited to Ireland), 1900, 1910 and 1913, followed by periodic further legislation up to 1979 and 1983. In addition, the idea that government action – usually in the form of legislation – is the appropriate means for the protection of ancient remains has persisted and penetrated into all areas of environmental preservation, both cultural and natural. The story is told in outline in Tables 5.1 and 5.2, which when read together chart the main developments in legislation to protect aspects of the cultural and natural heritage in England.

The passage into abeyance of the 1882 Act should have marked the defeat of its promoters in at least one area of political action. Despite the weakness of the legislation that was finally put in place and its ultimate failure, the fact of legislation itself had an effect on attitudes towards all archaeological material of all periods. By promoting prehistoric remains, the Act also promoted the material of other periods and brought it too into the public domain. Thereafter it would be possible to legislate the protection of other such material on the same basis as that of prehistoric remains. Accordingly, the proponents of all material that was comparable to prehistoric remains would seek to have such material given legal status. The next section of this chapter briefly charts the growth and spread of such legislation to the present.

Table 5.1   DEVELOPMENTS IN ENVIRONMENTAL PRESERVATION

1872	Lubbock enters Parliament.
1873	Lubbock Bills (to 1879).
1877	Society for the Protection of Ancient Buildings (SPAB) founded.
1882	*Ancient Monuments Protection Act*: schedule, guardianship.
1883	Pitt-Rivers appointed first Inspector of Ancient Monuments.
1889	Royal Society for the Protection of Birds founded.
1890	Pitt-Rivers retires.
1894	*Merchant Shipping Act*: salvage law codified.
1895	National Trust founded.
1900	*Ancient Monuments Act*: 'monument' defined; public access; local authority guardianship; monuments to be uninhabited.
1904	British Vegetation Committee founded.
1907	*National Trust Act*: legal recognition; power to hold land inalienably.
1908	Royal Commissions for Historic Monuments founded: national survey instituted. Access to Mountains Bill.
1910	*Finance Act*: artworks to state for tax ('gifts for the public benefit').
1911	Tattershall Castle sale.
1912	Society for the Promotion of Nature Reserves founded.
1913	*Ancient Monuments Act*: pre-emptive purchase; preservation orders; extension of protection to medieval remains. British Ecological Society founded.
1914	Outbreak of First World War (to 1918).
1924	British Coordinating Committee (for nature conservation) founded.
1926	Access to Mountains Bill. Council for the Protection of Rural England founded.
1927	Access to Mountains Bill. National Trust empowered to acquire great houses.
1928	Access to Mountains Bill.
1929	Addison Committee (into National Parks, etc.).
1931	Preservation Orders to be automatically approved unless objections. Access to Mountains Bill.
1932	*Planning Act*: preservation orders by local authorities. Mass trespass.
1933	Objections to preservation orders to be heard by public enquiry.
1935	Ramblers' Association founded.
1936	Standing Committee for National Parks founded.
1937	Access to Mountains Bill. Georgian Group founded.
1938	*Faculty Jurisdiction Measure*. Access to Mountains Bill.
1939	*Access to Mountains Act* (not implemented). Outbreak of Second World War (to 1945). Export controls.
1944	*Town and Country Planning Act*: listed buildings.
1945	National Land Fund (state aid for the National Trust).
1947	*Town and Country Planning Act*: intervention powers to local authorities.
1949	*National Parks and Access to the Countryside Act*: areas of outstanding natural beauty; national parks; nature reserves; sites of special scientific interest.
1953	*Historic Buildings and Ancient Monuments Act*: grants for maintenance of historic buildings; Historic Buildings Councils established.
1955	*Inspection of Churches Measure*.
1957	Civic Trust founded.
1962	*Local Authority (Civic Buildings) Act*: local authority funds for maintenance of historic buildings.

Continued overleaf

Table 5.1   Continued

1967	*Civic Amenities Act*: conservation areas. *Faculty Jurisdiction Measure* and *Rules*.
1968	*Town and Country Planning Act*: group listing; statutory consultees; express permission required to alter listed building. *Pastoral Measure*: Redundant Churches Fund.
1969	*Redundant Churches Act*. *Housing Act*: General Improvement Areas (to encourage re-use of existing dwellings).
1971	*Town and Country Planning Act*: no demolition in conservation areas.
1973	*Protection of Wrecks Act*.
1974	*Town and Country Planning Amenities Act*: administration of conservation areas; support for historic preservation.
1975	*Faculty Jurisdiction* (revised) *Rules*.
1979	*Ancient Monuments and Archaeological Areas Act*: areas of archaeological importance; ban on the use of metal detectors on scheduled monuments.
1980	*National Heritage Act*: National Heritage Memorial Fund (replaces National Land Fund).
1983	*National Heritage Act*: Historic Buildings and Monuments Commission for England (English Heritage).
1986	*Agriculture Act*: environmental impact assessments.
1989	*Water Act*: water companies responsible for historic 'water environment'.
1990	*Environmental Protection Act*: environmentally sensitive area; landscape conservation order. *Cathedrals Measure*.

Sources: Countryside Commission (1989); Kennet (1972); Newcombe (1979)

THE PROLIFERATION OF LEGISLATIVE FIELDS

A survey of *British Archaeological News* – the bi-monthly newspaper of the Council for British Archaeology – for the years 1986 to 1990 revealed the key legal categories as they apply to archaeology in England. These are listed in Table 5.2 by year of first appearance as they relate to components of either the cultural or natural environment or both. As Newcombe (1979, 92) notes, these categories are 'accretional' – that is, rather than replacing one another over time, each new category is added to the others. A glance at Table 5.1 – which charts developments in preservationist legislation and the foundation of certain key preservationist societies since 1882 – indicates the extent to which the rate of addition of new categories of relevance to archaeology increases as one approaches the present.

The latter years of the nineteenth century and the very early years of the twentieth are punctuated by a very few developments. There is a small rash in the years prior to the First World War and a further rash in the fifteen years up to the Second World War; the war years themselves are quiescent. Thereafter, to the 1980s, virtually every year sees some kind of development taking place. The 1980s are relatively quiescent, although the privatization of public utilities and the passage of major

Table 5.2   FIRST APPEARANCE OF KEY LEGAL CATEGORIES AS THEY RELATE TO CLASSES OF MATERIAL

Date	Cultural	Intermediate	Natural
Imm.	Royal palace		
	Salvage		
	Treasure Trove		
1252	Faculty jurisdiction		
1882	Schedule		
	Guardianship		
1900	Ancient monument		
1907			National Trust land rights
1910	Gifts for public benefit		
1913	National importance		
	Pre-emptive purchase		
	Preservation order		
	'Scheduling'		
1932	Planning		
1939	Export controls		
1944	Listed building		
1949			AONB
			National Park
			Nature Reserve
			SSSI
1963	Group listing		
1967	Conservation areas		
1969	Redundant church		
1973	Protected wreck		
1979	AAI		
1980		National Heritage	
		Environmental impact	
1986		Environmentally Sensitive Area	
1990		LCO	

Notes:
AAI   = Area of Archaeological Importance
AONB = Area of Outstanding Natural Beauty
Imm.   = From time immemorial (date unrecorded)
LCO   = Landscape Conservation Order
SSSI   = Site of Special Scientific Interest

consolidating legislation have been significant developments. The relatively slow growth of the field up to the middle of the twentieth century is also evident from Table 5.2. Of the few concepts which predate 1882, only one has a firm date to it. The year 1913 sees four new concepts introduced into the sphere of the cultural heritage, and a further three only up to the Second World War. The significant terms that relate to the natural heritage are introduced in 1949, and the 1960s and 1970s see several further terms of importance to the cultural heritage. The most recent development has been the conflation of the cultural and natural heritages under single rubrics, very much in line with the current thinking of international law (Batisse 1980). It is apparent from this Table that the majority of precise concepts apply to cultural materials of various kinds, reflecting to a large extent the range of applicable types of law in this field; by comparison, laws relating to the natural heritage are more unified.

This combined increase in protective coverage and range of terminology derives from Lubbock's original success in passing the Act of 1882. By the simple fact of passing this Act, the conditions were created in which pressure groups could justly expect the material in which they were primarily interested to be made at some time subject to some form of legal control.

A national conservation body: the National Trust

The foundation of the National Trust in 1895 has already been alluded to. It was formed by people predominantly of socialist leanings who had been influenced by John Ruskin, the great mid-Victorian medievalist. The Trust was formed initially as a pressure group to preserve ancient rights of access to the countryside, building on the work of the Commons Preservation Society formed in 1865. As listed by Gaze (1988, 5), the organization has many interests of concern to archaeology: landscapes; ancient monuments and historic buildings; country houses; historic gardens; industrial sites and features; stretches of coastline; and historic interpretation.

It is not the purpose of this book to discuss the history of this organization in detail, but three developments of legal import are worthy of note. In 1907 the National Trust Act gave state recognition to the body and empowered it to hold land inalienably. In an Act of 1927, the Trust was empowered to take into its care historic houses rather than just land; this represented a shift in the Trust's activities towards the promotion of the great country house as opposed to the countryside. In 1945 further status was granted by the establishment of the National Land Fund for the purchase of tracts of land by the Trust on behalf of the people of Britain as a reward for their efforts during two devastating World Wars.

Lubbock's battle lost and won: Ancient Monuments continued

Lubbock's bid to accord special status to prehistoric monuments was undone by the Ancient Monuments Protection Act of 1900. In an effort to ensure the coverage of Eleanor Crosses, and rather than relying on the uncertain inclusion of items on a schedule, this Act legally defined the term 'ancient monument' for the first time as 'any structure, erection of historic or architectural interest or the remains thereof' (Saunders 1983, 15) but excluded from coverage any inhabited structure. The Act also included the power of local authorities to accept monuments into guardianship.

In an Act of 1910, the right of public access to guardianship monuments was introduced. Public education was always part of Lubbock's and Pitt-Rivers' programme and the provision of public access to ancient monuments is a logical consequence of this aim. At the same time, the introduction of this right some time after the initial provision of legal protection is an indication of the extent to which public interest is created by legal protection, rather than providing the spur for such protection. The drive for protection had come from bodies to which membership was limited; once protected by law, ancient monuments only then became a matter of general public concern.

In 1908 the Royal Commissions for Historic Monuments were established, charged with responsibility for a national inventory. Shortly after, in 1910–11, the work of the Office of Works in relation to ancient structures was put on a professional footing (Saunders 1983, 15–19). The scandal of the impending sale (and wholesale transportation) of Tattershall Castle to the United States in 1912 led to the consolidating and amending Ancient Monuments Act of 1913, a much stronger piece of legislation than those previously passed.

The 1913 Act was guided through Parliament and actively supported by Lord Curzon, the responsible Minister, recently returned from the Governorship of India, a 'proconsular imperialist, notorious for his pomposity and aristocratic hauteur' (Shannon 1976, 481). Curzon was the kind of aristocratic Tory, although not born to it (Shannon 1976, 481), to whom Lubbock's politics were opposed. During his term in India, Curzon had come to admire the architecture of Hindu temples and had been active in their preservation (Thapar 1984, 65). On his return to England, Curzon sought to extend similar protection to England's medieval remains, which he saw as comparable. He was largely responsible for the (unsuccessful) efforts to include ecclesiastical buildings under the terms of the Act (see below). To this extent, Curzon was responsible for the defeat of Lubbock's project of privileging prehistoric remains over those of other periods; he did so, however, not by defeating the project of preserving ancient remains, but by extending that preservation to all other periods.

The 1913 Act is also significant in other ways, since it has formed the basis of the approach taken in ancient monuments legislation ever since. First, the Act separated the concept of guardianship introduced in the

1882 Act from the schedule listing monuments considered important. Hereafter, guardianship monuments were those which had been taken specifically into state care, to which there was a right of public access. In addition, the Schedule to the Act listed monuments accorded automatic state protection on the basis of their 'National Importance', and to which penalties accrued if damaged. In this connection, the Act provided for the granting of preservation orders and the right of pre-emptive purchase by the state in the case of impending destruction of a monument deemed worthy of preservation.

Subsequent legislation would modify and extend the principles enshrined in the provisions of the 1913 Act rather than alter them substantively. From 1931, preservation orders under the 1913 Act were to be automatically approved by Parliament unless objections were received. From 1933, the hearing of objections to preservation orders was to be at public enquiries. In 1953, the Historic Buildings and Ancient Monuments Act provided state grants for the maintenance of historic buildings in private ownership, and established the Historic Buildings Councils to advise on appropriate action in relation to historic buildings under the legislation. In 1962, the Local Authority (Historic Buildings) Act provided for local authorities to give grants for the maintenance of historic buildings in their area.

In 1979 the legislation was consolidated and replaced by the Ancient Monuments and Archaeological Areas Act, the bulk of which is still in force. The main addition brought in by this Act was the power to designate areas of archaeological importance rather than merely single sites and monuments as before. In addition, it made the use of metal detectors on scheduled sites a criminal offence. The 1980 National Heritage Act replaced the National Land Fund with the National Heritage Memorial Fund and widened the scope of the organizations which could benefit from it. The 1983 National Heritage Act did away with the direct responsibility of the Department of the Environment (which had absorbed the Office of Works) for the day-to-day management of ancient monuments law and passed this to a new quasi-autonomous non-government organization, the Historic Buildings and Monuments Commission for England (otherwise known as English Heritage); responsibility for the designation of scheduled monuments and areas of archaeological importance remained with the responsible Secretary of State (most recently, the Heritage Secretary).

Spiritual versus temporal power: faculty jurisdiction and ecclesiastical exemption

In 1252 the Papal Legate Otho forbade any work to be carried out on churches except with the prior grant of a faculty (or licence) by the

Bishop (Binney and Burman 1977, 62). His aim was to prevent the unauthorized demolition of places of worship by Lords of the Manor, an exercise of temporal power over the spiritual which no medieval churchman could let pass. Church property was thereby removed from the sphere of secular control and law and became subject only to ecclesiastical law.

Over time, the grant of faculties for church repair and restoration was delegated, first to the Bishop's Chancellor and subsequently to his Archdeacon. Use of the faculty declined during the eighteenth and nineteenth centuries but was revived as a result of Curzon's intention to include Anglican church property within the terms of the 1913 Ancient Monuments Act (see above). The usual explanation for this intention is the demise of widespread nineteenth-century amateur archaeological interest in English churches, thus requiring active state intervention instead (Rodwell 1977, 19; 1981, 26). Since the idea of such state intervention was still quite new, however, a truer reason may be simply Curzon's desire to extend to medieval structures (of which Church property constitutes a large part) the importance accorded to prehistoric remains under existing legislation.

During the Parliamentary debate on the 1913 Bill, Sir Lewis Dibdin justified ecclesiastical exemption by arguing that 'control [of church buildings] by the Office of Works . . . would cut clear across the whole ecclesiastical administration'. In the House of Lords, Archbishop Randall Davidson undertook to revive the system of faculty control (Binney and Burman 1977, 63). Accordingly, in the 1920s, Diocesan Advisory Committees for the Welfare of Churches were established and the structure formalized by the Faculty Jurisdiction Measure of 1938 which allowed minor works to be carried out on the grant of an Archdeacon's Certificate so long as there was no change in external appearance. The procedure was tightened up in the Faculty Jurisdiction Measure of 1967, and Rules governing the procedure were propagated in that year and revised Rules in 1975.

Twentieth-century developments have led to further ecclesiastical laws on the treatment of church buildings. The decline of the role of the local squirearchy in the maintenance of churches following the First World War led in 1955 to the Inspection of Churches Measure (Binney and Burman 1977, 73). This requires all churches in use to be inspected at least once every five years by a qualified architect. In parallel with this, declining church attendance has resulted in churches falling into disuse. The 1968 Pastoral Measure provided for a procedure whereby decisions could be taken on the future of churches no longer in use as places of worship: an initial 'declaration of redundancy' (regarded by the Church authorities as recognition of an existing state rather than the creation of a new status for the building affected) (Binney and Burman 1977, 165) is followed by a waiting period of up to three years while a new use is sought, at the end of which time a 'redundancy scheme' is put into effect.

The principle of ecclesiastical exemption has led to some peculiarities when it meets other legislation. The Deans and Chapters who administer cathedrals are largely independent, but must obtain both Planning and Listed Buildings consents for structural alterations. By contrast, churches and chapels are exempt from Listed Building consents. A problem here is that the system of listing for church buildings is different from that of other kinds of structures and cannot easily be reconciled with it (Binney and Burman 1977, 208). Where demolition is the chosen solution for a redundant church, the 1969 Redundant Churches Act provides exemption from Listed Building consent but not ancient monuments legislation if the structure is also scheduled.

Complete exemption for cathedrals came to an end in 1990 with the Care of Cathedrals Measure. This requires all cathedrals to appoint an archaeological consultant and a Fabric Advisory Committee (Tatton-Brown 1991, 74). In return, Deans and Chapters become eligible for state aid for the maintenance of cathedral buildings.

In exchange: finance and taxation

The 1910 Finance Bill provided an alternative to the payment of Death Duties in cash. Hereafter, by allowing those with property to give 'gifts' to the state in the form of works of art and other significant 'heritage' items (provided they had a measurable money value), Death Duties otherwise payable in cash would be limited. Many of these 'gifts' consist of items of historic interest.

The origins of this provision lie in Liberal politics. By the early years of the twentieth century, Liberalism had completed its nineteenth-century programme and provided for state protection for the very young and the very old with a number of measures, including the introduction of old-age pensions. A second phase would take Liberals in the direction of a system of National Insurance for the great mass of the working population (Shannon 1976, 393). Such programmes cost a great deal of money, however, and required a reformed tax system to achieve them. The budget of 1909 proposed such a reformed system, simultaneously increasing the tax burden by £16 million and relieving the government of the need to apply the increased revenue to the repayment of the national debt (Shannon 1976, 396). As well as some completely new taxes, Death Duties were sharply increased, and it was partly to offset this damage to the landed gentry, although the Liberals' political enemies (Shannon 1976, 396), that this provision was introduced (Kennet 1972, 40).

The Finance Bill containing this provision became part of a much more significant political dispute when the House of Lords attempted to prevent its passage. Prime Minister Asquith threatened the creation of a mass of Liberal peers to ensure the passage of his government's measures, and the Lords finally backed down and passed the measure as part of the Finance Act in April 1910 (Shannon 1976, 404).

Originally intended as a 'sop' to the landed gentry in a time of political trial, this provision has passed down the years as a contribution to the state protection of the cultural heritage. The power of the Treasury to accept 'gifts for the public benefit' as part-payment of inheritance tax was restated as recently as 1984 in the Inheritance Tax Act of that year.

(Re)Construction: planning law

The origins of planning law again look back to the Liberal programme of the late nineteenth century. A concern for public health and proper housing was evident from mid-century on (Chapter 4). In 1909, the Housing Act gave local authorities the power to clear existing sub-standard housing and to build new houses. It also gave the power in Section 54 to prepare schemes:

> as respects any land which is in the course of development or appears likely to be used for building purposes, with the general object of securing proper sanitary conditions, *amenity*, and con-venience in connection with the laying out and use of the land, and of any neighbouring lands. (emphasis added)

'Here', says lawyer Victor Moore (1990, 1), 'was the beginning of planning law.' However, it was not until the massive needs of post-war reconstruction imposed themselves on the government agenda that planning law became of major significance.

From an archaeological point of view, the first important devel-opment was the introduction of the Listed Building in the 1944 Town and Country Planning Act. The great Town and Country Planning Act of 1947 gave further powers to local authorities to intervene in proposed developments and required them to draw up development plans for their area. Their powers in relation to Listed Buildings were also strengthened.

Significant changes in the details of planning law have taken place in the years since 1947 (see Moore 1990, 4–6) but the principles remain largely the same. The subsequent legislation has nevertheless introduced certain key concepts which still apply. The 1967 Civic Amenities Act introduced the idea of the conservation area in addition to the protection of individual structures. The Town and Country Planning Act of 1968 extended the listing provisions to allow the listing of groups of buildings and established statutory consultees to advise on the application of the legislation. The 1969 Housing Act introduced the general improvement area, encouraging the re-use of existing housing rather than demolition (a reversal of the intentions of the Act of 1909). The 1971 Town and Country Planning Act banned demolition within conservation areas, and the Town and Country Planning Amenities Act of 1974 provided for the administration of conservation areas. In 1990 planning legislation was consolidated into four related Acts: Town and Country Planning Act 1990, Planning (Listed Buildings and Conservation Areas) Act 1990, Planning (Hazardous Substances) Act 1990 and Planning (Consequential Provisions) Act 1990 (Moore 1990, 6–7).

Outdoor pursuits: environmental protection and countryside management

The story of the development of the legal preservation of the natural environment has been well covered elsewhere (see Countryside Commission 1989; and references cited therein). It is not the concern of this book to go over this well-trodden ground once more except to indicate its relevance to the history of the law as it affects archaeological material.

With the exception of the Commons Preservation Society formed in 1865, the founding of all the main societies concerned with the preservation of the natural environment post-date the passage of the 1882 Ancient Monuments Protection Act – another indication that public interest is created by legislation rather than the passage of legislation being the result of manifest public concern. The societies represent two sets of distinct and contradictory aims. Organizations such as the Royal Society for the Protection of Birds (formed in 1889) and the Society for the Promotion of Nature Reserves (formed in 1912) were almost exclusively concerned with the legal protection of species and their habitats at the expense of public access (Countryside Commission 1989, 13). By contrast, the Commons Preservation Society, the National Trust (formed in 1895) and the Ramblers' Association (formed in 1935) were primarily concerned with public access to the countryside as part of a programme of mass education and health (Countryside Commission 1989, 29). These two contradictory aims would ultimately both be enshrined in the legislation. The high point came in the 1930s, with the first mass trespass on the privately owned Kinder Scout in 1932. A series of Access to Mountains Bills were put forward, requiring free public access to upland regions in private ownership. The passage of the 1939 Access to Mountains Act was a significant victory but rendered empty by the outbreak of war later that year.

A general policy on land use became a post-war priority as a result of the emphasis on post-war reconstruction, reflected in the growth of planning regulation. A necessary component of this policy was the provision and protection of areas of natural landscape for recreational purposes. The 1949 National Parks and Access to the Countryside Act created four categories of natural material for legal protection. The National Park was intended for mass public access, with controls on the uses to which land within areas so designated could be put. The Area of Outstanding Natural Beauty was also subject to protection, specifically to maintain its amenity value as a place to visit. Nature Reserves were established to preserve specific types of habitat and the species occupying them. The Site of Special Scientific Interest was protected because of its importance for scientific study. The land comprising all or any of these categories may contain evidence for − or be the result of − human activity in the past and accordingly relevant to archaeology. Nevertheless, the prime aim of this legislation was to protect the natural environment and to make it available for public access rather than the service of archaeology. Subsequent legislation has served to amend and extend the provisions of the 1949 Act but has not substantially altered the structure of such protection or the relevant categories.

In 1990 the legislation was consolidated and amended to meet additional requirements of EU environmental policy. In addition, as part of the privatization programme of the 1980s certain preservation responsibilities were passed to newly established bodies. New categories introduced were those of the environmental impact assessment, the environmentally sensitive area and the landscape conservation order, all of which have both a cultural and natural dimension to them. This reflects the holistic vision of 'heritage' in current international thinking (Batisse 1980).

(Re)Movable property: export controls

The wartime crisis had more effects than to cancel the provisions of the Access to Mountains Act of 1939. In the same year a series of emergency defence measures were passed, among them the Import, Export and Customs Powers (Defence) Act 'to provide for controlling the importation, exportation and carriage . . . of goods'. Under Section 1 it gave to the Board of Trade swingeing powers to 'make such provisions as the Board thinks expedient for . . . regulating . . . the . . . exportation from, the United Kingdom . . . of all goods or goods of any specified description'. Section 9(3) provides that the Act will continue in force 'until such date as His Majesty [*sic*] may by Order in Council declare to be the date on which the emergency that was the occasion of the passing of this Act came to an end'. Despite its introduction as a wartime measure, and despite the actual cessation of hostilities in 1945, legally this legislation still has effect since the emergency that brought it into being has not yet been officially – and for the purpose of export control – declared to be over.

The use of the Act since 1945 has been to regulate the importation and exportation of certain classes of material for a number of purposes. The 1987 Export of Goods (Control) Order limits the export of live animals, organic materials, coins and industrial waste containing valuable metals as well as photographic material, antiques, and collector's items. This remains its purpose, although a declaration by the Heritage Secretary suggests that it may cease to apply to 'heritage' objects (*British Archaeological News* 7.5, 58).

Spoil from the sea: salvage and wrecks

It was not until the development of the aqualung during and after the Second World War that archaeologists could take a serious interest in items of historic interest under the sea (Muckelroy 1978, vii). Indeed, the first historic wreck site to be positively identified in Britain was as late as 1965 (Muckelroy 1978, 18). Accordingly, until this time the law of salvage and wreck cannot be said to form part of archaeological heritage law, although from then on it must.

Until the late nineteenth century the law concerning offshore wrecks and the salvage of material from the sea was part of the Common Law of England: based upon agreed principles set down by the courts but not written down in Parliamentary statute. The 1894 Merchant Shipping Act codified such law in favour of the retrieval of such material by providing for a reward based upon the value of the items recovered (which could include entire vessels and their cargo). Such an approach resulted in the plundering of wrecks for their contents. The recognition of the disservice this did to archaeology led in 1973 to the Protection of Wrecks Act which aims to protect certain designated offshore wrecks from such damage but without repealing the previous legislation.

The responsibility for both pieces of legislation lies with the Department of Transport and in particular the Receiver of Wrecks. As *British Archaeological News* (4.4, 49) acerbically stated in 1989: 'the Merchant Shipping Act 1894 actually encouraged the destruction of the heritage by providing financial rewards to salvors for raising archaeological material, whilst the Protection of Wrecks Act 1973 protected only the handful of designated wrecks and not the material within them. Thus the Department of Transport was responsible for the administration of two statutes that were diametrically opposed in their effects!'

As noted by O'Keefe and Prott (1984, 122–3) 'salvage law is designed to promote the rescue of goods and vessels which are in peril of the sea.

. . . The emphasis is on the fact and achievement of rescue using economic reward as motivation for the salvage act . . . [Thus there is] an emphasis on speedy removal of objects from the site and on the priority of those objects which have the highest commercial value [and this] is directly incompatible [with the aims of archaeology].'

WHERE WE ARE NOW

The aim of this part of the book, and especially the first part of Chapter 3, the whole of Chapter 4 and this chapter, has been to understand the current state of law in England as it affects archaeology by examining the processes by which it came into being. The underlying philosophy of this approach is that one way to know where you are is to see how you arrived there. A different approach – that of looking around after one has arrived – will be taken up in the next part of the book. The final part of this chapter, therefore, will be devoted to a summary of the results of this examination of the historical trajectory of English law as it relates to archaeology.

The increase of legal privilege

The first attempt at legislating for archaeology was the appropriation of Treasure Trove in the 1850s by Baron Talbot de Malahide and other archaeologists who were concerned to build a collection of British antiquities in the British Museum (Chapter 3). This limited success was built upon by the next generation of archaeologists – the protégés of Talbot led by John Lubbock – who followed up Talbot's call in 1859 for the protection by law of landscape monuments. This effort culminated in the Act of 1882 (Chapter 4). This chapter has charted the ultimate expansion of legal protection to archaeological material from all periods and to other classes of material which may also be of concern to archaeologists.

This review of the process reveals that the legal protection of material is not a natural and inevitable fact of life, but is instead a consequence of the drive by certain individuals to privilege material in which they have an interest over other classes of material. This in turn drives others to seek comparable status for material in which they have an interest. Once legal protection is granted to one class of material in a category (in this instance, prehistoric monuments) then other material in that category is given a similar status and efforts will result in its protection also (as in this case with all other archaeological material). The change in expectations brought about by the political success in acquiring legal protection for one class of material then encourages others to include their own favoured material in the range of protected materials, and the process continues. The range of materials thus brought into the public domain is constantly expanding as new groups vie for the same status as has already been granted to others. The process is also necessarily additive: in the terminology of the theory of games (Luce and Raiffa 1957; Ordeshook 1986), this process is not a zero-sum game (in which one privileged class of material would drive out another) but a positive-sum game (in which new additions increase the total value available to all players).

It is normal to explain this 'accretional aspect of British preservation legislation' either in terms of 'a failure to do the job correctly the first time' or as evidence that British legislators learnt through experience and showed a willingness 'to adapt as conditions changed' (Newcombe 1979, 92–3). A case can perhaps be made for the partial influence of both these factors, but the real reason is simply the effect of the political process involved in legislating the protection of material which culminates in this ongoing positive-sum game.

The acquisition of laws

The pre-existing doctrine of Treasure Trove – as seen in Chapter 3 – was deliberately appropriated for the benefit of archaeology by Talbot and his associates. By contrast, Lubbock specifically legislated the protection of prehistoric monuments. All of the bodies of law concerned with preservation as covered in this chapter were brought into effect either by legislation or by appropriation and, in a few cases, a combination of both.

Laws appropriated

The ecclesiastical law of the faculty and exemption from civil jurisdiction was not intended to preserve church buildings as historic monuments, but originally to prevent their destruction by temporal authority in the thirteenth century. The 1913 concession to the Church authorities to allow them to use their existing procedures to preserve their historic buildings represents a significant victory by the preservationist lobby. Similarly, the capacity to donate items of value to the state in part payment of Death Duties was not intended to benefit museums but rather to prevent the non-payment of taxes. Nevertheless, this is one means whereby state museums are today enriched. Export controls were introduced as wartime emergency measures, but today may be used to prevent the export from the country of valued 'heritage items'.

Laws created

The laws protecting ancient monuments have been the result of a continuous process of creation. Prior to 1882 no such laws existed, and there is no pre-existing body of law to which they are related. In many ways they act as the model for other such laws, although (as argued in Chapter 3 and will be demonstrated in the following chapters) the underlying structure is identical to that of Treasure Trove. Nevertheless, the laws relating to town and country planning, environmental protection and the protection of wrecks owe much to the concepts contained in ancient monuments law. These three – planning, environmental protection, and the protection of wrecks – are the 'children' of ancient monuments law to the extent that the possibility of their own passage derives from the passage of Lubbock's 1882 Act; and the concepts on which they are based derive closely from ancient monuments law in general.

Hybrid acquisition
There is a sense in which the laws concerning planning, environmental protection and wreck are hybrid. Originally, none were intended directly to concern archaeology. Environmental protection legislation was about the preservation of specifically natural resources – either for science or for public access. It is only 'accidentally' archaeological since 'natural' sites and resources are so often the product of human activity. Planning law (as seen above) derives first from the public health programmes and housing regulation of the nineteenth century. By regulating land use and seeking to preserve elements of the historic environment, planning law became of concern to archaeologists and others interested in the material remains of the past. The ancient right of salvage relates to preservation only in the sense that its object – items of commercial value – would otherwise be lost to the sea. Accordingly, it has its part to play in maritime archaeology, but it is less preservationist legislation than a licence to retrieve specific types of material. From this perspective, the protection of wrecks legislation is a mere amendment to an older doctrine which otherwise remains unchanged and has partially been appropriated for archaeological purposes.

Underlying values
The preceding discussion has revealed the original intent of the bodies of law discussed in this chapter. Those of Treasure Trove, finance legislation, salvage, and export controls relate primarily to questions of money value. Those of certain portions of ancient monuments, planning, environmental protection and ecclesiastical law relate to questions of amenity and use value. Those of other portions of ancient monuments, planning and environmental protection together with the protection of wrecks law relate to scientific value. Each of these kinds of value – money, amenity/use and scientific – and their specific application in each case will be discussed in more detail in Chapter 8. The

point to be made here is that these original intents remain in place even after amendment by statute or appropriation for use by archaeology. In Thompson's (1990, 125; Chapters 2 and 3) term, each of these underlying concerns represents a different value gradient along which an item may be placed. These gradients exist in opposition to one another and the application of law mediates between them and serves to place items on the appropriate gradient.

Money value
In the case of Treasure Trove, placement is disputed between a money value (where the item is declared not to be Treasure Trove and is likely to be placed in an auction room) and an amenity value – specifically as a display item in a museum. In the case of a 'heritage item' subject to export controls, it is its money value which is taken into account in the decision to grant or withhold a licence for export. It is the money value of an item that makes it worthwhile as a 'gift' to the state for the payment of Inheritance Tax. In the case of salvage, the purpose of retrieval is to realize the money value of an item.

Amenity and use value
An object on display has amenity value in the sense that its mere presence enhances human existence. In the case of Treasure Trove, the declaration destines the object for the museum case where it will excite interest. Similarly, the preservation of single historic buildings or a conservation area provide a focus for the gaze in a city, the area of outstanding natural beauty a pleasant outlook in the countryside, and the maintenance of a guardianship site an item of historic interest in a landscape. Medieval churches are a centre of interest in most communities, and their continuance in use (as places of worship or otherwise) additionally gives them use value.

Scientific value
Objects and structures otherwise in use are unavailable for scientific examination. Accordingly, the preservation of items in an unchanged state and without public access makes them potentially available for scientific study (now or in the future), as in the case of the scheduled ancient monument, the site of special scientific interest and the protected wreck.

The valuation process
All of the descriptions cited above are those of legal categories rather than 'real' items. The categorization of an object under the law has consequences for it in terms of its subsequent usage and the value placed

upon it. The placement of a value on an item is not an accidental side effect of the application of law to that object, but rather its intention. The whole point of the law is to give items a value sufficiently high that they become worthy of preservation. As argued in Chapters 2 and 3 it is law that places values on material, rather than any inherent value in the material that requires its legal protection. Accordingly, archaeological material is not protected because it is valued, but rather it is valued because it is protected. In addition, as argued in the Interlude and this chapter, the very fact of preservation for a class of material encourages the search for the preservation of other classes of material.

Since the category in which an item is placed determines its value, then its preliminary selection for categorization becomes a matter for consideration. This is the three-stage process identified in Chapters 2 and 3 – selection, categorization, and finally valuation – which provides the structure for the next part of the book.

Part Three
The effects of laws

6
Selection under the law

There is currently a plethora of laws affecting archaeological material in England. These laws are conventionally divided into a number of separate fields. There are eight of these as listed in Chapter 2, with occasional outliers in other branches of law, including military law (here included for convenience with ancient monuments legislation), administrative law (which touches on planning regulation) and the 'law of finders' (which has connections with Treasure Trove: Palmer 1989, 185–6). Each separate branch of law covers – as it was designed to – a specific body of material, as described in Chapters 4 and 5. The processes involved in the growth of this legislation have been outlined in Part Two of the book and the origins of the drive to legislate traced to the political activities of the proponents of these various classes of material.

An examination of ideas on the social process of valuation (Chapter 2) followed by an enquiry into the workings of Treasure Trove (Chapter 3) led to the construction of a model of the tripartite manner in which the law works on archaeological remains: first selection, then categorization and finally valuation. The detailed examination of this overarching structure is the purpose of this part of the book.

LEGAL PATHWAYS

As outlined in Chapter 2, analysis of the law in England has been conducted by the identification of the key terms and concepts employed in the law in its treatment of archaeology. Such terms are treated independently of the specific branch of law to which they relate unless there are strong reasons for doing otherwise (such as inapplicability). The aim is to demonstrate the manner in which the law works on archaeology as a discipline and as the object of study of that discipline. This manner is common to all the relevant branches of law and it is therefore inappropriate to separate them out from one another.

The ultimate purpose of analysing the law in this way is to chart the path of material that is of concern to archaeologists through the law via the tripartite process of transformation already identified. Each key term

Table 6.1   THE SELECTION PHASE OF THE LEGAL PROCESS:
ORGANIZATION OF KEY LEGAL TERMS

Organization of terms	*Legal terms*
Components of the archaeological heritage	
Wholes	Cave, excavation (noun), vehicle/vessel, wreck, garden, building, human remains, object, group/collection of objects, coin, photograph, postage stamp, aircraft, document, goods, remains, dwelling house, [monument], [ancient monument], man-made object, structure
Parts	Exterior of building, feature, machinery, hatch, opening, ship's stores
Attributes	Age, crashed, sunk, stranded, military service, precious (of metal)
Contexts of components	
	Group of buildings, group of monuments, land adjoining monuments, associated land, seabed, sea, site, area, distance, high-water mark, Scilly Isles, United Kingdom waters, international waters
Ancillary items	
	Vehicle/vessel (used for conveyance), equipment

Note: Items in [square brackets] are also legal categories (Table 7.1)

identified in the analysis belongs to a particular stage of this process, each of which can be broken down into convenient fields. After initial selection for treatment on the basis of physical description, the process of categorization consists of a number of relevant fields charting a 'route' through the legal provisions. Categorization (Chapter 7) involves the ascription to the item of a specific legally defined description or name from which follow certain consequences: allocation to a particular legally empowered body which is responsible for its treatment and which is limited by its legal duties and functions; actual physical changes in the material, wrought by the responsible authority; potential physical changes wrought by others; actual moral changes in the material wrought by the authority; and potential moral changes wrought by others. Valuation (Chapter 8) – constituting a moral change of a special kind – consists of two fields: the ascription of a type of value, equivalent to placement on a particular value gradient (Chapter 2); and the ascription of a level or quantity of value (equivalent to placement at a particular point along that value gradient). The detailed analysis of the selection process is contained in Appendix 1: Material Protected by Law. Table 6.1 summarizes the organization of the analysis and lists the key terms.

SELECTION BY LAW

In examining the manner in which the law selects material for treatment, a problem is immediately encountered. In the search for the key terms and concepts through which the law operates and is applied, it is difficult to separate out the definitions of legal categories into which the material is put (the subject of Chapter 7) from descriptions and definitions of material to be so categorized (the concern of this chapter). Any distinction to be drawn will be arbitrary, but the attempt must nevertheless be made if only to test the degree to which the law seeks to define its object.

For the purposes of this chapter, the distinction between actual material and legal categories is made on the basis of whether or not an item named in the law has an objective physical existence in the world. A category, by contrast, is distinguished: (a) by its primarily conceptual nature; and (b) its direct relation to the consequences for material of categorization. Descriptions and definitions are thus static while categories always look forward to what happens next. There are also hybrid terms (partly physical description, partly conceptual and consequential) which will reappear in the following chapter as legal categories.

The terms relating to the selection of material for legal coverage fall into two broad groupings: those that describe or relate directly to components of the archaeological heritage; and those that describe contexts for that heritage or materials ancillary to its legal treatment. The former can be subdivided into terms descriptive of an entire component of the heritage, a part of any such component or an attribute of any such component (Table 6.1). These divisions conveniently provide the structure for this section of the chapter.

It will be clear from Table 6.1 and the analysis contained in Appendix 1 that the law does not provide an all-inclusive list of material to be covered by it. To some extent this is because of the problem mentioned above: that of separating out legal categories (into which material will be placed) from its initial definitions. Appendix 1 illustrates the extent to which categorization is a part of the selection process: of the 41 legal terms which have some physical correlate, 20 (virtually all of those representing components of the archaeological heritage) look forward to the categorization process and its consequences for some part of their definition. These comprise: aircraft, ancient monument, building, coin, exterior of a building, feature, goods, machinery, man-made object, monument, objects generally, photograph, precious metal, remains, ship's stores, stamp, structure, vehicle/vessel (terms which are used interchangeably and together), and wreck. To this extent categorization and selection merge together as the first phase of the legal transformation process.

Monuments and sites

At first glance, the term 'monument' as used in the law is a useful catch-all term for any kind of archaeological remains, but the use of the terms 'building', 'structure' and 'work' limit its application to digging into or under or construction on the land surface. The term thus definitively excludes such surface deposits as flint scatters and domestic refuse spread on fields as fertilizer. On the other hand, because of the lack of restriction on the age of the 'work', the modern archaeological excavation of such a scatter or deposition would render the term applicable to such a feature.

The lack of an age restriction is additionally of interest since it might be assumed that those monuments that are classed as 'ancient' should be identifiable on the basis of their age, but as the analysis in Appendix 1 shows the term 'ancient' has two quite distinct meanings. The more limited of these (applying to the functions of the Secretary of State) carries with it the limitations on the definition of 'monument', since it is no more than a recategorization of those things that can be classed as monuments (AMAA79, s. 61[7–11]). The more closely defined and wider meaning, however, only applies to the functions of the HBMCE (NH83, s. 33[8]). As will be further discussed and shown in Chapter 7 and Appendix 2, these terms are not interchangeable, and the later (wider) definition does not replace the earlier (more restricted) one. They apply in different circumstances and for quite different purposes. Here we see the additive process outlined in Chapter 5 in operation. Rather than the incorporation of a new definition bringing about an alteration in the way the law works, it merely adds a new component into the legal canon.

Where it does seek to define its object, the law also places boundaries around it. Both monuments and sites are understood as clearly demarcated spaces which have hard edges that can be identified. A monument must be a physical feature, deliberately placed where it stands or penetrates the earth together with the land on which it stands or which is penetrated by the feature. A site is the site of such a feature and any land allowing it to remain in place (the ground under a built structure, the roof and walls of a digging or cave). Intuitively and by observation, we all know that objects have hard edges, buildings and churches have walls and so on. It is not so clear that a site or a monument has such well-defined boundaries and yet the law treats them as if this is the case. The same applies to the site of a crashed, stranded or sunk aircraft, vehicle or vessel.

In addition – and deriving from this ascription of a quality of boundedness – there is a circularity in the legal understanding of these terms. A monument can include its site, but at the same time the site of a monument can comprise the monument, and a site may indeed constitute an ancient monument in its own right. In other words, the site is the monument and the monument is the site. To talk of one is to encompass the other – and in so doing to increase the degree of ascribed boundedness possessed by each. This has implications for archaeology, since the archaeological use of the concept of 'the site' is increasingly fluid, and indeed may one day result in the abandonment of the concept altogether.

Sites and landscapes

'Off-site' or 'non-site' archaeology (Dunnell and Dancey 1983; Foley 1981) consists of an approach

> that takes into account the full range of archaeological material on or in a landscape, treating the material that is distributed across it as a spatially continuous variable [and subsuming] within it the information contained in a site [which is defined as] a concentration of humanly modified materials. (Foley 1981, 11)

Accordingly,

> it is predicted that a landscape should contain . . . a continuously distributed scatter of artefacts, exhibiting properties of differential spatial densities [and] these density distributions may be expected to conform to the distribution and frequency of prehistoric human activities. (Foley 1981, 32)

This approach thus merges two quite distinct understandings of the concept of 'site'. First, sites may be understood as places where relatively more archaeological material is found than in the landscape surrounding them, although such material is scattered all over that landscape. Second, they may represent nodes of more concentrated activity within a larger area over which activities were conducted. Both of these ideas of the nature of the site are reflected to some extent in the understandings of the concept of site enshrined in English legislation, although the former is dominant.

The first idea – as a relatively dense concentration of archaeological material – represents the site as a contemporary phenomenon that is the concern of the archaeologist. This is the understanding contained within the definitions of monument (AMAA79, s. 61[7–11]) and ancient monument (NH83, s. 33[8]) – timeless, related to form as identifiable now (as upstanding, earth penetrating, or by geographical extent), dependent on a specifically ascribed historic, architectural, traditional or archaeological interest to make it 'ancient' (AMAA79, s. 61[12]). The second idea – that of a locus of past human activity – is specifically reflected in the wider definition of ancient monument as a particular form of material, specifically and originally created as such – the garden (NH83, s. 33[8]).

To the extent that the legislation relies on bounded single features (sites, monuments) it lags somewhat behind archaeological thought. As off-site archaeology develops, the concept of 'site-based' archaeology loses importance. At the same time, the concept of site as defined in terms of past activity is giving way to the alternative of the 'activity area'. This is 'a place within a site where a relatively limited set of tasks was performed with a limited set of artifacts' (Rigaud and Simek 1991, 200), and such areas are always intrasite phenomena (Kent 1990, 1; Kroll and Price 1991, 1–3). In terms of archaeological practice, as the site is replaced by the landscape as the focus of archaeological attention, with the site relegated to no more than a nodal concentration within an artefact distribution, these now less important sites themselves become no more than bundles of 'activity areas' which become the new focus for remaining archaeological attention. Accordingly, while at one ('macro') level the site merges into the landscape, at another ('micro') level, it is broken down into a number of activity areas. The result is the simultaneous shift 'upscale' away from the site to the landscape and 'downscale' from the site to the activity area.

The 'activity area' – defined as a relatively bounded and discrete phenomenon – is capable of recategorization for legal purposes as a site. The problem lies in moving upscale towards the landscape, for which the law makes no similar provision (Startin 1995). The legislative response to this gap in coverage – the area of archaeological importance – is treated in Appendix 2, although it has to be noted here that few such areas have been designated in favour of treatment under planning procedures. The wider definition of 'ancient monument' (NH83, s. 33[8]) allows the inclusion of areas of unspecified extent, but again it has to be emphasized that this definition does not relate to items that can be given protection under the scheduling provisions, which first have to meet the conditions for classification as a monument (AMAA79, s. 61[7–11]).

Of course, landscapes, monuments, sites and activity areas are all things that are conceptual in nature rather than items with an objective physical existence. They are focuses for the attention of archaeologists constituting various categories into which material is put rather than the material itself to be so categorized. The problem remains of understanding how archaeologists recognize the actual things with which they are concerned.

UNDERSTANDING SELECTION
The study of the manner in which phenomena are accepted by archaeologists and others as lying within the realm of their concern is in its infancy. For instance, in adopting a 'constructivist' approach, Joan Gero (1990, 1991) has examined the ways in which archaeological 'facts' are negotiated into being and are accepted by the discipline. She takes as her start-point for discussion the identification of objects and sites which by common disciplinary consent are already agreed to exist. Accordingly, she does not address directly the question of how they became recognized as 'archaeological' in the first instance.

The 'ethnography of archaeology' usefully takes one step further back to examine how archaeologists in the field perform the initial 'act of discovery' of artefacts. Here,

> objects emerge and take form, in our perception only as we *give* form to them, by *acting* upon the material field in various ways, through the application of material and cognitive tools. (Edgeworth 1990, 243–4; original emphasis)

The act of discovery itself is described as '*the practical meeting-ground of an expectation and its material conditions of satisfaction*' (Edgeworth 1990, 247; original emphasis). In other words, what is 'newly' discovered is what was already expected to be found, and accordingly 'the act of discovery reproduces existing knowledge' (ibid.). What follows from this insight is that the so-called act of 'discovery' is never the finding of something totally new, but is instead the product of (1) the deliberate seeking of objects within a class already known or suspected by the seeker to exist; and (2) the recognition by the seeker of a specific object as belonging to that class.

However, 'the object [so recognized] may surprise or contradict the practical schemes that are brought to bear on it, so that these schemes are modified . . . to take account of the object' (Edgeworth 1990, 249). Thus, what was initially thought to be one thing by the discoverer may on further investigation turn out to differ slightly – or possibly significantly – from the initial expectation. This suggests that the initial recognition is not absolute, but – especially when made in the field, where such judgements are quick and intuitive – a provisional estimate or a probabilistic judgement that what has been seen belongs to the class sought for.

In his major study *Intuition*, Bastick considers the phenomenon of 'intuitive recognition', defined as 'to know [something] again as experienced before' (1982, 239). Throughout the book, the importance of context in providing the framework for the intuitive process is emphasized, and particularly so in the case of intuitive recognition, where one important element is the 'emotional set' (Bastick 1982, 242) which also constitutes the usual context for a particular stimulus (ibid., 239). 'A stimulus [such as an object] is recognised when it evokes an emotional set. When a percept is part of this response the stimulus is literally re-cognised, i.e. its perception is put into mind' (ibid., 114). Since 'external stimuli are intuitively recognised when they evoke an emotional set rather than a discordant emotional state' then 'the lack of tension afforded by the responses is the feeling of recognition' and 'this intuitive recognition allows us to accept a novel stimulus, for which we have no emotional set, by presenting it with stimuli for which we do have emotional sets' (ibid., 136). Emotional sets thus condition the circumstances in which objects can be recognized, and reinforcement of these emotional sets invokes the factor of redundancy since 'recognition of a stimulus . . . further conditions that stimulus to the emotional set and probably introduces new associations, making later recognition more likely' (ibid., 241). Accordingly, it is 'possible for a novel stimulus, e.g. a stimulus not previously experienced in a specific context, to be mistakenly intuitively recognised as belonging to that context under circumstances of great redundancy' (ibid., 241).

Bastick's 'intuitive recognition' is essentially the same process as that described by Edgeworth (1990). Since the law cannot act alone but must be put into operation by people, this has implications for our understanding of the selection process. In particular, the part played by necessary preconditions in creating the circumstances in which recognition can take place (expectation from Edgeworth, emotional set and context from Bastick) must be taken into account.

Implications

The selection process for the legal treatment of archaeological material was first introduced in this work as if it were a unity – a discrete, bounded, single action which, once it has taken place, has then passed – to be replaced by the following similarly unitary phase of categorization (Chapters 2 and 3). However, the idea underlying Rubbish Theory (Thompson 1979), the latter part of Chapter 3 and all of Chapters 4 and 5 has been the alternative and more sophisticated notion that the entire tripartite process is not one of the creation of a new phenomenon from nothing, but rather the transformation of an extant phenomenon into something new. In Rubbish Theory an object passes from one region of fixed assumptions (the transient category) into another such region (the durable category) by passing through the intervening stage of rubbish, in which it is deemed to be invisible and thus capable of cognitive manipulation. In Treasure Trove, objects of gold and silver are changed from items of private ownership into items of public ownership. In Chapters 4 and 5, previously unregarded landscape features were shown to have been transformed into publicly valued phenomena by the political actions of groups of individuals with particular interests in their promotion. This concept of the transformative role of law is much closer to the identical processes of 'discovery' described by Edgeworth (1990) and intuitive recognition described by Bastick (1982).

The initial selection of material for treatment is an obvious and necessary part of this transformation process. This initial selection consists in the identification or recognition of material as belonging to a relevant class of material — an earthen bank and ditch or mound as a product of past human activity, or a style of building as deriving from a particular historical period, for instance. As suggested by the analysis conducted here, however, it also assumes two latent capacities for that material: first, the capacity to carry the relevant new categorization to be applied in phase two (as 'treasure', as an 'ancient monument', as a 'historic building'); and second — in part deriving from the first — the capacity to carry any new value to be placed upon it.

The selection process is thus not simple but is instead a complex of subsidiary stages. Rather than the entire valuation function of law being, as suggested in Chapter 2, a straightforward three-part process:

$$\text{selection} \longrightarrow \text{categorization} \longrightarrow \text{valuation}$$

it involves an additional preliminary stage of provisional valuation:

$$\text{identification of things with [value]} \longrightarrow \text{selection from things with [value]}$$
$$\longrightarrow \text{categorization} \longrightarrow \text{valuation}$$

where [value] = identification as belonging to a relevant class + potential capacity to be recategorized appropriately + potential capacity to carry any new value to be ascribed. It is the purpose of the second and third phases of the transformation process (categorization and valuation) to proceed to actual recategorization and the ascription of a new value.

It has been noted above that the selection and categorization phases to some extent merge into one another. In like manner, the selection phase looks forward to the third phase in the legal process — the ascription of a final 'official' and legally sanctioned value. This merging of the phases is also reflected in AHM practice: the 'discrimination' stage of the Monuments Protection Programme seeks to 'differentiate those sites among the total population of known examples of a particular class which are of national importance from those which are of regional or local importance' (Darvill *et al.* 1987, 397). The most important and first aspect of [value] in the sense in which that term is understood and used here, however (and thus both primary and central to its understanding and use), is the recognition (in Bastick's (1982) sense) of the object as belonging to a relevant class of objects which is defined by law. This is a more specific equivalent of the broader historical process of legislating for preservation noted in Chapter 5.

Chapter 5 introduced the idea that by passing laws relating to certain bodies of material, other material potentially falling within the same broad category would become similarly eligible for legislative protection. The result was an ongoing non-zero-sum game in which it pays all players to introduce new material to the legislative framework. At the level of individual provisions, however, while only individual examples of specific types of material may be selected for specific forms of legal protection, nevertheless the entire class to which those individuals belong is identified by law as provisionally eligible for such legal coverage. Thus, while not all ancient monuments will be scheduled or taken into guardianship, nevertheless all the things which are included in that category – all the structures and features legally defined as monuments – are taken note of at this preliminary stage. Out of all the things which are thus available, some will proceed to the subsequent stages of specific categorization and valuation. It is this selection from the entire range of available items which begins the process of transformation noted in Part Two of the book and identified from the consideration of Rubbish Theory.

The selection phase in time

The selection phase is the first phase of the legal process as it relates to specific objects within the entire range of ancient material. This phase is more than the simple definition of those objects which are covered by law, since those not ultimately selected for preservation are nevertheless involved in the process. In this way the selection phase reflects the larger scale workings of the legal process as a whole discussed in Chapter 5. The entire selection phase consists of two sub-phases, each of them a process of selection from a greater range of objects.

The first – preliminary – sub-phase serves to separate out classes of material to which the law relates, excluding those that are not legally defined. By so doing it marks all the components of these classes as having what is referred to here as [value] – a potential (but no more) for legal coverage and a capacity to proceed to the subsequent legal phases of categorization and valuation. It is this preliminary phase of selection which acts as the driving force for the larger scale process identified earlier in the book. It does so by 'marking' certain specific types of material (rather than individual items) as worthy of legal coverage, excluding other types however similar in form but which do not meet the specific terms of legislation in force. The potential for value thus created 'spills out' towards that other non-legally recognized material, creating the conditions under which its proponents can argue for its privileging under new laws. The result is the non-zero-sum game which has operated at this larger historical scale for the past century and more in Britain.

Here we glimpse the role of the law as a social 'institution' in the sense in which Giddens uses the term – '[those] practices which have the greatest time–space extension . . . the more enduring features of social life' (Giddens 1984, 17). Institutions such as the law exist in 'reversible time' (ibid., 35), the *longue durée* of which exceeds the lifetime of individual human beings and which thus provides a measure of consistency and certainty over time. Institutional time (here referred to as 'historical') is reversible in that 'events and routines do not have a one-way flow to them' but are constantly repeated, recursive and reproduced (ibid., 35). The time of heritage laws is reversible in the manner in which it constantly acquires new components and in which the acquisition of those components encourages the further inclusion of yet new components.

The second sub-phase of selection for legal coverage concerns the selection of specific objects from the class marked out in the preliminary sub-phase. These individual objects – monuments, buildings, movables – will be recategorized in the law's terms and proceed to the phase of valuation by being treated in a particular way as the law determines for their category. This second sub-phase is limited to the workings of an individual law on individual items and is not reflected in the larger scale processes which represent the law as an institution operating in the *longue durée*. Instead, it serves to remove items from the more generalized historical process of potential valuation and to begin the process of specific valuation which is the ultimate product of such laws.

The institutional, historical process of potential valuation is the same as the process referred to above and identified in Chapter 5: that of the constant addition of new material for coverage. The removal of items from this large-scale process of potential valuation for specific treatment under individual legal provisions is a different process: one of reduction. Thus, at one (institutional, historical) level the law is constantly increasing in scope and size, while simultaneously at another local and specific level it is reducing its coverage to individual items. This apparent (but only apparent) paradox gives a clue to the manner in which the law in England operates on heritage items, and will be further addressed in Chapters 7 and 8. Overall, at the 'macro' scale – that of historical time and the law as social institution – the law is additive and incorporative.

At the 'micro' scale — that of individual components of the heritage and individual laws and as will be seen in Chapters 7 and 8 — the law acts as a reductive and homogenizing value system.

SUMMARY

In its two sub-phases, the selection process — the first phase of the workings of law on ancient material — serves to link the larger scale process operating in historical time with the smaller scale process acting on individual components of the archaeological record. The first sub-phase serves to 'mark' those types of material worthy of legal coverage — and thus to create the conditions for increasing the range of legal coverage to other types of material. The second sub-phase selects those specific items which will be recategorized and given specific value under the law. In thus merging with the subsequent categorization phase of the process the second sub-phase 'extracts' specific items out of the realm of potential for legal treatment to insert them into the more specific process of individual treatment culminating in recategorization and the ascription of new value. In so doing, the overall workings of the law as a social institution are revealed — at once additive and reductive.

These workings become clearer with the analysis of the subsequent phases of recategorization and valuation. It is to these subsequent phases that we now turn.

7
Categorization under the law

Rooms are spaces which one can enter, move around inside and then exit, frequently by a different route from which one entered. This metaphor is perhaps appropriate for a discussion of the manner in which archaeological material is processed by law. The initial selection described in Chapter 6 brings bodies of archaeological material into the realm of law where they can be transformed into matters of public concern. Once it encounters law, such material ceases to be solely 'archaeological' and is cognitively manipulated to re-emerge with a new label – no longer just a landscape feature from the distant past, but an ancient monument; no longer just gold or silver jewellery hidden many years ago but treasure; no longer just an old house but a historic building. Chapter 5 charted not only the extension of English law to new classes of material but also the growth of legal categories in which to place them.

Like the selection procedure, however, the categorization process is not a unity but is made up of subsidiary elements. The new categories to be applied to the material selected for legal treatment are themselves defined by law. Accordingly, they are limited in number and even more limited in relevance to any particular body of material. Once a category has been selected for application, all other possible categories are denied. By categorizing, the route of the material through the transformation process is delineated. Depending on the categorization, it will be allocated to a particular legally empowered body for treatment in accordance with prescribed rules. The valuation with which it will then finally exit (treated in Chapter 8) will also ultimately depend on this categorization.

The categorization phase of the tripartite transformation process operates like a funnel – collecting the material that has successfully passed through the selection phase, and directing it along the appropriate channel for processing.

LEGAL CATEGORIZATION AND ITS CONSEQUENCES
The concern in Chapter 6 was with items that had some objective existence. Appendix 1 shows that some items are closely defined in

terms of their physical attributes, while others are assumed to be readily identifiable without any need for description. Here, the concern is with the legal categories into which these items are placed. These categories do not reflect the physical attributes of an item so much as an understanding of it. The categories look forward to what will happen to the item as it passes along the legal pathway deemed to be appropriate for it: its allocation to a particular agency which will have responsibility for it; the physical and cognitive ('moral') changes that will or may be wrought on it; and the valuation with which it will ultimately emerge.

The detailed analysis of the categorization process is contained in Appendix 2: Legal Categories. Table 7.1 summarizes the organization of the analysis and lists the key terms. The immediate consequence of categorization is that the item in question becomes the concern of a specific, legally empowered agency or organization. The duties and functions of these bodies are defined and limited by the applicable law and this in turn limits the future of the item to particular paths. Once categorized and placed under the responsibility of a particular institution, two kinds of things can happen to a component of the archaeological heritage under the law. It may face a physical change of some sort, or the way it is thought about and understood may change. These changes may be wrought by the institution responsible for it, or by others. Certain of these changes are mandatory – the inevitable consequence of legal categorization. Others are merely possible, and of these some are allowed while others are prohibited.

Physical consequences
Changes which affect the fabric of the item may be wrought by the responsible institution or by others. Those wrought by institutions include various forms of investigation into or of the item, the removal of part or all of it, entry on to it, and some form of temporary or permanent prevention of physical change, itself paradoxically constituting such a change. Changes wrought by others may include actual harm to the fabric, works on or around the fabric, transformations of the fabric or interference with the fabric by way of removal, transportation, entry into or access on to the fabric.

Moral consequences
Whereas physical changes alter the fabric of a component of the archaeological record by the removal or addition of some or all of it, a moral change alters the way the item is conceptualized and understood. Like physical changes, these may be the product of actions by the responsible institution or others. Such moral changes include those relating to control over the fortunes of the item (including rights over

Table 7.1 THE CATEGORIZATION PHASE OF THE LEGAL PROCESS: ORGANIZATION OF KEY LEGAL TERMS

Organization of terms	Legal terms
Legal categories	
Monuments	Monument, ancient monument, scheduled monument, protected monument, protected wreck.
Buildings	Listed building, historic building, ecclesiastical property, church.
Movables	Treasure, prohibited goods, scheduled goods.
Locations	Area of archaeological importance, conservation area, restricted area, prohibited area, controlled site, protected place.
Ancillaries	Crown land, curtilage, easement.
Consequences of categorization	
Institutions	
State	Crown, Board of Trade, Treasury, Valuation Office of the Inland Revenue, Secretary of State, Chancellor of the Duchy of Lancaster, Ministers.
Quasi-state	HBMCE, RCHME, NHMF, Coroner, finder, local authority, investigating authority, Church of England, Church Commissioners, Diocesan Synod, parochial church council, churchwardens, advisory committee for the care of churches, architect, statutory undertaker.
Independent	Redundant Churches Fund, Architectural Heritage Fund, person/body with special knowledge or interest, developer, owner, occupier, person with interest, limited owner.
Physical changes	Prohibitions.
By institutions	Archaeological investigation, inspection, observation, archaeological examination, custody, sampling, excavation, power of entry, assistance, survey, search, bore, boarding, seizure, protection, preservation, maintenance, safe-keeping, provision, educational facilities, public use.
By others	Damage, demolition, destruction, obliteration, tipping, depositing, obstruction, flooding, clearance, clearance operations, operations, disturbing the ground, exempt operations, works, excepted works, execution (of works), alteration, extension, addition, affixing, deliberate inclusion, unauthorized interference, tampering, repair, unearthing, removal, salvage services, salvage operations, moving, exportation, conveyance (of prohibited goods), diving (use of), metal detector, public access, public display.

Continued overleaf

Table 7.1   Continued

Moral changes

By institutions	Control, regulation, restricting use, superintendence, acquisition, gift, devise, purchase, ownership, agreement, trust, guardianship, scheme, right of way, disposal, knowledge, information, instruction, educational services, inquiries, guidance, advice, survey, reports, records, recording, publishing, schedule of monuments, designation order, building preservation notice, scheduled monument consent, class order, planning permission, certificate of non-listing, certificate, licence, export licence, conditions, notice to excavate, operations notice, financial contribution, voluntary contribution, grant, loan (of money), repayment, investment, salvage, valuation, payment, compensation, penalty.
By anyone	Development, finding, hiding, danger, false statement/ information/document, interest, public inspection, insurance, loan (of object), bequest, forfeit, defences.

it, ownership and so on), the availability of information concerning the item, administrative procedures applied to the item, and financial arrangements.

The content of Appendix 2 indicates the degree to which legal regulation in the field of heritage is concerned with categorization and its consequences. These cover the allocation to specific categories of the components of the heritage selected for legal treatment (see Chapter 6); the legally empowered institutions to which categories of material are allocated and their powers, duties and functions; other categories of persons subject to the authority of these institutions; the physical changes that may be wrought on components of the heritage; and the moral changes that may be wrought on such material. All of these chart the path of the material through the law, culminating in the ascription of a particular value to that material, the subject of Chapter 8. Since it is not the purpose of this book to provide a manual for managers of the archaeological heritage but an insight into the workings of these laws and their effect on archaeological material, the specific paths available to specific components will not be delineated: these may be derived from the law itself or from published works relating to the practicalities of legal regulation (see Chapter 2). Instead, the focus here is on the categorization phase of the legal process in order to indicate its power of heritage law over the material which is its object.

Appendix 2 and Table 7.1 identify 21 categories into which material can be placed, and 24 institutions legally empowered to deal with them.

Chapter 6 covered 29 classes of material identified by law. The coincidence of the near equality of these numbers is in fact meaningless. Of the 24 institutions, some are subsidiary elements of others: the Church of England, for example, comprises the Church itself, the Church Commissioners, Diocesan Synods, parochial church councils, advisory committees for the care of churches, churchwardens and archdeacons. At the same time, identically named components may be categorized differently: a building, for example, may constitute a monument and by derivation via the more limited definition (AMAA79, s. 61[12]) an ancient monument or via the wider definition (NH83, s. 33[8]) an ancient monument in its own right, a redundant building, a historic building or a listed building; it may accordingly become the responsibility of various institutions for various forms of treatment. The powers of these institutions – including their duties and functions – are many and wide. By contrast, the nine types of other persons identified are very much subject to the authority of these institutions.

Physical changes to material which are sanctioned by law belong entirely to the empowered institutions. These cover investigations of various kinds, access, protection and the provision of items or services. Physical changes which are mostly prohibited by law are the province of other persons, and cover damage, removal, alterations, uncovering, and entry. The 21 types of physical change allowed to institutions are met by 35 mostly non-sanctioned such changes by others.

Moral changes which are the province of legally empowered institutions comprise those relating to control, acquisition, ownership and legal rights, information, the placing on lists of various kinds, the grant of various forms of consents, the service of various forms of notice, and finance. Those which are the province of other persons comprise the making of plans, giving false information and finance. The 51 types of moral change belonging to institutions heavily outnumber the 14 belonging to others.

CATEGORIZATION: CHANGING THINGS CONCEPTUALLY
The categorization process outlined above and more fully described in Appendix 2 comprises the following subsidiary phases: (re)categorization itself, allocation to a specific legally empowered institution, and the making or prohibiting of physical and moral changes to items thus treated. The number of moral changes that can and must be made significantly exceeds the physical changes that can and must be made, and does so even when those physical changes that are prohibited are added in. Since valuation is itself only a special kind of moral change, the law can be envisaged simply as a machine for making moral (that is, conceptual) changes to heritage items.

As argued in Part Two of the book, the drive for legislation derived from a desire to promote certain kinds of archaeological material to a special status, leading to a positive-sum game in which all players seek to obtain such status for particular bodies of material in which they have an interest. This status is achieved by the application of specific laws to these specific bodies of material. Both at the overarching level of legal provision as a whole and at the level of specific laws, the aim is thus to bring about moral changes to material in which their proponents have an interest. In this sense all such laws are identical. At another level, however, there are similarities between specific categories which suggest this identity of purpose is matched by an identity of form and content.

Relationships between categories

The detailed review of categories provided in Appendix 2 suggests that certain categories are closely related in meaning. In particular, the categories 'monument' and the two senses of the term 'ancient monument' are related. The term protected place is applied in two different circumstances; the processes of investigation, observation and examination are very similar; as are those of preservation, maintenance, protection, safe keeping and custody; and so are clearance, operations and works.

One sense of the term ancient monument (AMAA79, s. 61[12][b]) derives from that of monument, whereas the other is more precise (NH83, s. 33[8]) (see Chapter 6). A monument that is not first redefined as ancient can only be scheduled (that is, placed on the schedule of monuments of national importance [AMAA79, s. 1]), whereupon it becomes an ancient monument. A monument that is redefined as an ancient monument under the narrower definition (that is, because the Secretary of State has scheduled it [AMAA79, s. 61(12)(a)] or deems it to be of public interest [AMAA79, s. 61(12)(b)]) can be taken into guardianship or acquired by the state or a local authority or become subject to a management agreement (AMAA79, s. 17). The possible trajectories of monuments through the legal system are thus determined by their categorization. There is, however, no reason why the same monument should not be both scheduled and taken into guardianship, which would require it to be divided conceptually into two. It will thus acquire two distinct moral statuses in the sense in which that term is used here.

Any problems that arise are compounded by the third element in this complex equation: the wider definition of ancient monument, which does not require prior categorization as a monument (NH83, s. 33[8]). This only applies to the functions of the HBMCE and not to those of the Secretary of State or local authorities. Accordingly, if not already categorized as a monument (as a site [other than the site of a monument

– AMAA79, s. 61(10)], a garden or an area may not be [compare AMAA79, s. 61(7) with NH83, s. 33(8)]), then it cannot be scheduled, taken into guardianship or ownership or become subject to a management agreement, and can only have educational facilities and services provided, advice given, money spent and records kept in respect of it. Problems may thus arise in attempting to treat certain items as ancient monuments – in particular gardens, which may not be capable of categorization as a 'work' and are not a 'building' or a 'structure'; advice given previously in this area may thus be seriously at fault (e.g. Priddy 1991, 190).

Protected places comprise either scheduled monuments, ancient monuments owned or in guardianship and any place inside an AAI (AMAA79, s. 42[2]) or the remains of aircraft and designated vessels lost while in military service (PMR86, s. 42[2]). The two usages of this term overlap since a monument can comprise the site of the remains of a vessel or aircraft (AMAA79, s. 61[7][c]). However, they are not synonymous since each carries certain consequences which distinguish it from the other: in particular, under AMAA79, only the use of a metal detector is prohibited (AMAA79, s. 42[1]); under PMR86, any tampering, damage, removal, unearthing or entry is prohibited (PMR86, s. 2[1–2]).

Archaeological examinations and investigations are distinguished from one another (AMAA79, s. 61[4] and 61[5]) and yet either may apply as a condition of scheduled monument consent (AMAA79, s. 2[5]), and both include the right to remove samples (AMAA79, s. 44[5]). They are distinguished to the extent that investigations but not examinations may be authorized by the Secretary of State in respect of any ancient monument under the narrower definition (AMAA79, s. 26[1]), specifically include excavation (AMAA79, s. 26[2]) and may be published (AMAA79, s. 45[3]); whereas examinations but not investigations may be authorized in respect of guardianship monuments (AMAA79, s. 13[4][a–b]) and include the power to take objects into custody (AMAA79, s. 54[1]). The power to take objects into custody is shared by observations on operations in AAIs (AMAA79, s. 54[1]), which perhaps implies that examination is limited to visual examination and the power of custody only applies to objects discovered during the course of other people's work. However, the power to take samples is shared with investigation, and suggests a limited capacity to excavate, even if only in *sondages*. These terms are accordingly very close in meaning. A limited investigation may in practice constitute an examination, while an extensive examination may become in practice identical to an investigation, and an observation may turn in practice into an examination without any breach of legal limitation.

Of the terms preservation, protection, maintenance, safe keeping and custody, only maintenance is given a definition. As 'repairing . . . or protecting . . . from decay or injury' (AMAA79, s. 13[7]) maintenance incorporates protection, which in everyday usage is synonymous with safe keeping and preservation. All of these terms contain the idea of maintaining the current state of something and preventing or prohibiting physical change in perpetuity. These five terms are, however, distinguished in that they apply in different contexts – protection to wrecks and controlled sites (PW73, s. 1 and PMR86, s. 1[5]); safe keeping to objects subject to NHMF grants and loans (NH80, 3[4]); custody to objects retrieved as part of archaeological examinations and investigations (AMAA79, s. 54[1]); maintenance to ancient monuments (AMAA79), items subject to NHMF grants or loans (NH80, s. 3) and former places of public worship (RC69, s. 5); and preservation to scheduled and guardianship monuments (AMAA79), objects and amenities subject to NHMF grants and loans (NH80, s. 3), historic buildings and conservation areas (NH83, s. 33 and PLBC90, s. 1[3]) and aircraft and vessels lost on military service (PMR86, s. 1[5]). Preservation therefore not only has the widest coverage but also overlaps with all the others except custody, which nevertheless has an affinity to safe keeping. All of these concepts relate to keeping the object of law in the same state in which it was first encountered and limiting the amount of physical change possible. Thus they all fall into the single category of preservation despite the differences in terminology.

However, these laws make only limited provision for the lifting of the preservation provisions. A guardianship monument may be subject to examination but not investigation (AMAA79, s. 13[4][a–b]) which rules out very extensive excavation since this is only allowed in investigation (AMAA79, s. 26[2]). Similarly, a scheduled monument (as an ancient monument under the narrower definition) may be subject to investigation (AMAA79, s. 26[1]) but this requires the specific authority of the Secretary of State and will amount to a grant of scheduled monument consent. In all cases, however, the injunction to preserve is very strong. For example, preservation is the purpose behind the compulsory acquisition of ancient monuments (AMAA79, s. 10), the only reason for the relocation of a guardianship monument (AMAA79, s. 13[4][c]), must be provided for on terminating guardianship (AMAA79, s. 14[3]), and is the only justification for urgent works on a scheduled monument (AMAA79, s. 5); while the maintenance of guardianship monuments is an overriding duty of the Secretary of State and local authorities (AMAA79, s. 13[1]) and the safe keeping of objects a justification for an NHMF grant or loan (NH80, s. 3[4][a][ii]). Accordingly, unless there are very powerful reasons to the contrary, preservation from physical alteration is not likely to be removed to allow scientific investigation, and in practice, in the case of scheduled monuments, scheduled monument consent is more likely to be granted for development than research.

Works include 'operations of any description' (AMAA79, s. 61[1]), and operations are those that disturb the ground or involve flooding or tipping (AMAA79, s. 35[2]) without any limit being placed upon the extent of the definition. Accordingly, works comprise operations and operations are automatically works. Clearance operations are those that involve 'the demolition and removal of any existing building [or] structure and the removal of any other materials . . . to clear the surface of the land (but do not include the levelling of the surface or the removal of materials from below the surface)' (AMAA79, s. 41[1][d]). Clearance is thus an operation and accordingly also constitutes works. This neat hierarchy, however, has little practical relevance since the three terms only apply to one another in the case of AAIs, none of which have been designated. More importantly from the point of view of the general principles enshrined in law, while works and operations are subject to limitation, clearance is not: it is perfectly allowed to destroy the above-ground remains of ancient features so long as the below-ground components are untouched; in addition, while levelling of the site and digging below the surface are not allowed, the question of what precisely constitutes the surface of the land is left unaddressed. There is thus a strong case for redesignating clearance as no more than another work or operation and subjecting it to similar controls, rather than separating it out and privileging it.

Here, categorization and its consequences are revealed as essentially reductive and homogenizing, the 'micro'-scale process identified in Chapter 6. Where a number of similar terms are used, they can be shown not only to overlap in meaning and application, but also to be capable of reduction to a single concept which comprises them all. Accordingly, the two kinds of protected places are given protection from the kinds of damage likely to be inflicted upon them; investigations, examinations and observations comprise identical sets of actions; protection, maintenance, safe keeping and custody are all forms of preservation. The exceptions are the two meanings of ancient monument and monument, but the purpose of these is to allow the incorporation into law of different bodies of material; they thus fall under the heading of addition and incorporation.

Additions and incorporations
The complex, overlapping and duplicatory nature of the relationships between categories outlined above derives directly from the way in

which these laws were constructed. As outlined in Chapter 5, the process was an additive one: as the body of material favoured by one group of people was given legal status, other groups also vied for it in respect of other material; the result was the constant creation of new legal categories in which to fit new bodies of material. This ongoing process has created a corpus of laws which are incorporative, in the sense that they seek to include within their coverage all types of relevant material, and they aim to achieve this by a process of constant addition. This in turn gives rise to a tinkering approach to changes in the law: old laws are not scrapped and totally new ones created to meet new situations, but instead existing laws are altered by the addition of new categories to include the new circumstances and material in the existing framework. Thus, sites and gardens were added to the definition of ancient monument but only for certain purposes (NH83, s. 33[8]).

This is also what has happened in the case of Planning Policy Guidance Note 16 (PPG16) (Department of the Environment 1990). AAIs (a new category brought in by AMAA79) were intended to cover the new archaeological interest in landscapes which could not be incorporated in the existing site-based approach (Chapter 6). As a result of problems with the legislation – including the likely consequences for archaeology of the distinctions between works, operations and clearance discussed above – and opposition to the law from both archaeologists and developers, together with the simultaneous emergence of a policy in favour of developer funding in British archaeology (*British Archaeological News* 3.9, 85), proposals to designate AAIs were abandoned (*British Archaeological News* 5.5, 59). Instead, PPG16 was drafted to place the protection of archaeological landscapes within the field of planning regulation, and therefore make it a responsibility of local rather than national government, although the HBMCE would retain a strong advisory role and the Secretary of State ultimate authority. In other words, the failure of one legislative policy begat an alternative, but that alternative would not have come into being without the prior attempt at legislation.

In this respect it is also worth noting that while the legislation relating to AAIs was designed to operate in a manner that was complementary but different to that covering discrete sites (allowing for archaeological investigation as part of the development process rather than protection in opposition to development), PPG16 specifically includes as part of its advice the criteria used by the Secretary of State for scheduling monuments (see Chapter 1 on 'significance'). Indeed, the emphasis throughout PPG16 is on 'preservation *in situ* of archaeological remains' (Department of the Environment 1990, para. 25) rather than investigation (Department of the Environment 1990, paras 6, 12, 13, 16, 18, 21) and 'preservation by record' (Department of the Environment 1990, paras 24–6) is relegated to the second-best option. Accordingly, the treatment of landscapes is made to match more closely that for the treatment of discrete sites, and planning provision that for ancient monuments legislation.

The process of addition was also at work in the case of legislating the protection of wrecks. The Merchant Shipping Act of 1894 provides for the acquisition for the Crown of the rights to wrecks by purchase out of the proceeds of salvage generally (MS94, s. 528). Any such purchase would need to be made by the Board of Trade with the consent of the Treasury which requires these two Government Departments to agree, but this is not an insoluble problem if the Government as a whole considers the purchase worthwhile. This provision lays down no specific justifications for such purchases, and accordingly commercial or cultural reasons will do as well as each other. Taking wrecks into the ownership of the Crown has a close affinity with the guardianship provisions for ancient monuments or their purchase by the state or local authorities. Accordingly, when maritime archaeology became a concern this provision (MS94, s. 528) could have been used to ensure the protection of wrecks by acquiring them for the Crown. This did not happen. Instead, the Protection of Wrecks Act of 1973 was passed making alternative arrangements. One justification may simply be the cost involved in applying MS94 since PW73 does not involve purchase. Another and equally likely reason for this, however, is the promotion of the idea of protecting wrecks, which would not have the same force if it entailed only the resurrection of an obscure, probably forgotten and rarely exercised provision from legislation passed in the previous century. By legislating anew, the importance of preservation was stated and marked, as was that of the material to be preserved. This is the same point as was made in Chapter 5, which concerned the wider discussion of the history of this legislative process, and demonstrated the additive process by which 'heritage' legislation developed.

This additive, incorporative, tinkering process of making laws continues today. Treasure Trove has been subject to a number of attempts to modify it by legislation since Talbot de Malahide's abortive Bill of 1859 (see Chapter 3). One such attempt in the early 1980s was 'effectively sabotaged' and another delayed pending review by the Department of the Environment (*British Archaeological News* 2.8, 77); the latter attempt ultimately resulted in no action being taken (*British Archaeological News* 6.1, 3). The most recent attempt has been an effort by members of the Surrey Archaeological Society, which gained the support of such diverse interest groups as the British Museum and the Country Landowners' Association as well as the archaeological community in general (*British Archaeological News* 6.6, 70). In January

1993, the Parliamentary Heritage Group (composed of MPs of all parties) also expressed its support for the initiative. Despite successfully passing through all stages in the House of Lords, even without Government support, the Bill was effectively 'killed' in the House of Commons. Instead, the Government accepted the case for reform of Treasure Trove and announced that a consultation paper on these issues would be produced after discussions between Lord Perth (promoter of the Bill in the House of Lords) and the Department of National Heritage (*The Times* 10.3.94; *British Archaeological News New Series* 12, 4). Plans to reintroduce the Bill when Parliament reconvened in November 1994 (*British Archaeological News New Series* 12, 4) were not fulfilled. However, the formation of the Standing Conference on Portable Antiquities promoted by the Council for British Archaeology at a meeting in London on 24 May 1995 resolved to urge the Government to proceed urgently with the passage of the Bill and on 7 June 1995, in reply to a question from Lord Perth in the House of Lords, Baroness Trumpington confirmed the intention to reintroduce the Bill with Government support in the next session of Parliament.

The changes to Treasure Trove that are planned in the Perth Bill (as it has become known) are several, and derive in part from the reconfirmation from the case of *R v. Hancock* that total reliance cannot be placed on a Coroner's jury verdict (see Chapter 3). The coverage of the law is to be extended to include all treasure, whether hidden, lost, abandoned or placed in a grave. Treasure is to be redefined as comprising coins or other items containing specified amounts of gold or silver, their containers or other objects forming a series with or found in association with the treasure, and any class of material specified by the Secretary of State; all with the exception of Treasure Trove which will remain a separate category. Coroners would retain responsibility for deciding whether items constitute Treasure Trove, and this responsibility is extended to deciding what constitutes treasure as defined in the Bill, but in both cases the Coroner alone is empowered to do so without a jury. Pending any such decision on specific material, all such items would be vested in the Crown (thus overcoming the problem exposed in *R v. Hancock*). Reporting of finds is to be made within four weeks to a Coroner, and failure to report a find would be a criminal offence. The Secretary of State would be empowered to publish appropriate Codes of Practice in respect of Treasure Trove procedure. The Bill's exclusion of Treasure Trove ensures that neither the Crown's prerogative powers nor the making of *ex gratia* payments to finders would be affected by its provisions; accordingly, Treasure Trove items would still revert to the Crown and honest finders be rewarded for reporting the find and the same privilege may be extended to finders of all treasure.

The effects of the Bill if passed in that form would be twofold. First, Treasure Trove itself would remain untouched and, unlike as in the case of the Talbot Bill of 1859, would remain independent of statute law. The new law would, however, bring all objects of gold and silver and associated and other designated objects within the same procedure. Second, the law would extend Crown ownership to all such additional material. Overall, the laws relating to Treasure Trove and treasure would remain anomalous in that they place the emphasis on ownership of items rather than on controls on their use (which is the case with scheduling, guardianship, export control and planning regulation, for example). It does serve, however, potentially to extend heritage law to all movable antiquities.

The point of this discussion is that such a change as the Perth Bill proposes will incorporate entirely new material within the coverage of heritage law. This will have been achieved by a relatively small change to the law as it stands, but the structure of the law – in terms of the way it operates – will remain unaltered. The form and structure of Treasure Trove will thus remain intact but effectively able to incorporate new bodies of material. A small change in the law ('tinkering') thus has a significant effect on the range of material covered by law without altering the mode of operation of law as a whole.

In similar manner, the Hedgerow Protection Bill began its progress through Parliament in 1993. The aim of this unsuccessful legislation was to 'protect hedges of special importance for landscape, wildlife or historical reasons' (*British Archaeological News New Series* 2, 9). Here again, a new category of material – the hedgerow – was to be specifically incorporated into the coverage provided by law by the mechanism of creating new law. Accordingly, rather than attempting to reinterpret the existing law to allow incorporation of the new category under existing provisions, new legislation was proposed – as in the case of wrecks.

Institutions and (re)interpretations
The bodies responsible for the application of the law are also those given power to interpret it. Many of these bodies, however, also have the law to thank for their very existence. The HBMCE (NH83), the NHMF, its Ministers and Trustees (NH80), statutory undertakers (AMAA79, s. 61[2]), the Redundant Churches Fund (RC69), local authorities (Shannon 1976, 236–7) and investigating authorities (AMAA79) are all the direct children of statute. While the first emergence of the Crown, the Secretary of State, the Duchy of Lancaster, the Treasury, the Board of Trade, the Inland Revenue, Coroners and the Church of England all predate the origin of 'heritage' laws, their powers and duties in this respect are the product of legislation, the only exception being the

jurisdiction of Coroners over Treasure Trove although this needed to be restated in legislation in 1988 (CA88, s. 30). The RCHME is not, as a Royal Commission, the child of statute, but its powers of entry in relation to AAIs derive specifically from legislation.

The situation is, then, that those institutions charged with implementing the law also interpret it, but they and their powers in relation to the heritage are themselves the product of that law. They are as closely bound by it as any other object of that law and accordingly, when interpreting it, do not stand 'outside' of it but do so from 'within'. The result is that while the law is constantly subject to reinterpretation on a day-to-day basis, the relationship with the law of those whose task it is to conduct that reinterpretation binds them to do it always the same way. The consequence is that reinterpretation reinforces existing understandings and is thus not able to generate significant change.

THE LAW AS PROCEDURE

The reduction of the law into its component parts by the analysis conducted here indicates the intense concentration of the law, first, on the empowerment of certain institutions, and second, on the law's role as a vector of moral changes in the material which is its object. The physical changes allowed are relatively few in number, while those that are prohibited exceed them. In the field of moral changes, however, the opposite is the case: moral changes that are prescribed or allowed exceed those that are prohibited by at least a factor of three. Since these moral changes are those belonging to the empowered institutions, such moral changes are given even greater force.

Accordingly, the power given by the law to specific institutions to affect the material which is the object of heritage laws far outweighs the power given to others. This places the focus of the categorization phase of the legal process on the workings of those institutions. The law itself was described in Chapter 6 as an 'institution' in the sense used by Giddens (1984), that is as a feature of society which operates over the long term. By contrast, the term as used in this chapter refers to those specific named organizations which operate under legal authority. These are perhaps more conveniently labelled 'bureaucracies', although without the pejorative overtones which frequently accompany use of this term. These institutions, organizations, bureaucracies each operate their own schemes which are themselves forms of bureaucracy.

Evaluation as an example of archaeological bureaucracy

The discussion of evaluation in Chapter 1 can be criticized on the grounds that, in arguing against the 'objectivity' of evaluation as applied in practice, it takes no account of the expertise of individual archaeologists drawing on a collective disciplinary body of knowledge and skill. Instead, it can be argued, the developed form of evaluation represented by, for example, the MPP should be seen as an expression of that collective knowledge and skill, and a device for systematizing that knowledge and skill and making it widely applicable (Darvill 1995; Startin 1993, 186–8, 194). Seen from this perspective, evaluation in general – and the MPP in particular – is intended to support decisions made by individual experts rather than being the sole basis on which such decisions are made (and thus the opposite of the criticism made above). As a form of collective decision-making, evaluation becomes an 'organization' – 'a social system which is able to "bracket time–space", and which does so via the reflexive monitoring of system reproduction and the articulation of discursive "history"' (Giddens 1987, 153).

Evaluation is able to bracket time–space in that it requires the repetitive application of identical procedures and criteria to different objects. It serves to allow the monitoring of system reproduction by requiring the recording of the results of the application of its procedures and criteria and their reduction to a common format. It articulates discursive history by the production of records which can be used for comparison with other similar records as they are produced. Evaluation displays the distinctive characteristics of modern systems since its whole purpose is to intensify 'surveillance as information collation and retrieval' (Giddens 1987, 155), is inevitably associated with 'specifically designed locales' (the offices of English Heritage; and ancient monuments [Antony Firth, pers. comm.]) (Giddens 1987, 157) and has much to do with 'the relation between locales and the timing and spacing of activities' (ibid., 160).

Evaluation also displays the characteristics of the modern bureaucracy, the purpose of which is to impose 'rational controls over the material universe' (Berger 1973, 202). The limitation of evaluation to measuring 'national importance' constitutes the phenomenon of limited compe-tence encountered in bureaucratic systems, which in turn requires the capacity to refer other questions elsewhere for coverage by an appropriate but different agency (ibid., 46). Here, the extension of the evaluation criteria to decisions concerning the grant-aiding of rescue projects and the planning process reflect this aspect of bureaucracy. In approach, evaluation – and the MPP in particular – is orderly (ibid., 50) in that it requires the application of a set of criteria previously agreed. Because these criteria are always available to be applied, regardless of the individual assessor, the evaluation thus demonstrates 'general and auton-omous organisability' (ibid., 53). The constant application of the same criteria creates an impression (however flawed) of system predictability (ibid., 52) and consistency, equivalent to a 'general expectation of justice' (ibid., 52). Because it does not matter who applies the criteria – and because the same result is always to be expected (whatever the actual outcome) in each individual case – evaluation displays 'moralised anonymity', the sum of all these qualities (ibid., 53) and akin to the 'otherworldly morality' of 'the [corporate] group [which] outlives its members' (Douglas and Isherwood 1979, 37).

This designation of evaluation – including the MPP – as a 'bureaucracy' should not, however, be taken as pejorative. Rather, it is an attempt to describe the qualities and effects of evaluation in more generalized and more widely applicable terms than those typically applied in critical discussions. The purpose of the application of evaluation criteria – and especially the MPP – is to make a vague and previously unassessable 'quantity' (that of 'national importance') assessable, and to do so in a way that can be repeated across all the various classes of archaeological remains consistently and (in some sense) meaningfully. In this it shows a measure of success, and it does so because of the bureaucratic 'style' it adopts. In so doing, it reflects its times in which technology and its social equivalent bureaucracy have become the prime agents of social change (Berger 1973, 15–16). As a bureaucracy in this specific sense it also constitutes an organization – a device for the bracketing of time–space to allow repeatable practice in the realm of AHM.

Legal categorization as administration: the case of the Rose Theatre
The rediscovery of the remains of Shakespeare's first theatre in Southwark, London, was a major *cause célèbre* of 1989 (for coverage of the story, see Biddle 1989; Chippindale 1989; Gurr 1994; Orrell and Gurr 1989; Wainwright 1989). There was common agreement as to the archaeological and historic importance of the site:

> The unique status of the Rose's remains is, by a stroke of quite extraordinary good luck, matched by the equally unique survival of its written records.
> The Rose is a unique phenomenon. Its dates put it . . . at the height of the evolution of Elizabethan playhouse design. . . . The Rose gave Marlowe his early chance, and he gave it the first great stage successes of the London theatre. It may well have been Shakespeare's training ground. . . . To lose it would be a new kind of Shakespearean tragedy. (Orrell and Gurr 1989, 421, 428–9)

> [These] things are not matters of objective knowledge alone. They are to do with a sense of place, and the emotions that a sense of place rightly stirs. (Chippindale 1989, 413)

The problem was that the remains had been discovered during the redevelopment of a site for office building and the extent of preservation came as a surprise to all those involved. There was a delay in construction while new plans were produced with the aim of preserving the remains beneath the new structure to be built. Thus, 'on 15th June [1989], the Secretary of State accepted that the remains of the Rose Theatre are of national importance within the terms of his non-statutory criteria [see Chapter 1] but declined to schedule them at the present time' (Wainwright 1989, 434). In the meantime, concerned individuals (many of them well known and eminent) formed an association to work for the preservation of the remains and endeavoured to force the Secretary of State to schedule them. The judgement upheld the Secretary of State's right to make the decision on a number of grounds. First, that the relevant legislative provision (AMAA79, 1[3]) gives the Secretary of State a broad discretion in deciding to schedule (*R v. Secretary of State for the Environment, ex parte Rose Theatre Trust Co.* in *All England Law Reports* 1, 1990, 761). In so doing, the Secretary of State is entitled to take into account any likelihood of compensation to be paid, competing pressures on the parties involved, the degree of cooperation of the developer, the degree of immediate threat to the monument, and the usefulness of keeping future options open (*All England Law Reports* 1, 1990, 763–5). The judgement also ruled that the Rose Theatre Trust Co. and its individual members had no standing in law to ask for the decision to be overturned. As the judgement put it, 'The ordinary citizen does not have a sufficient interest [in the decision not to schedule a monument] to entitle him [*sic*] to obtain leave for a judicial review' (*All England Law Reports* 1, 1990, 767).

Whether the Rose Theatre was 'of national importance' as a monument was not an issue in the case: all concerned considered that it was. The question was accordingly not 'how valuable is this monument?' but simply whether the Secretary of State had carried out his duties properly in refusing to schedule the remains and if the complainants had a legal right to question the decision. In reaching judgement, the judge in the case treated scheduling as a purely administrative function: the question of 'national importance' never entered into the case.

This is of some importance to the argument of this book for it has two implications. First, in ruling that the Secretary of State has a discretion in questions of scheduling, the question of the value of the monument is detached from the procedure available to be followed. By not being scheduled, the Rose Theatre did not become 'of national importance', even though the Secretary of State considered that it deserved that status. Instead, the remains were left at the preliminary stage of the selection process outlined in Chapter 6: as something that could be given a legally sanctioned value but which was not yet so privileged. Second, in going on to rule that the complainants had no legal standing, the judge confirmed that scheduling is purely a matter of administration and not of valuation. If the question of 'national importance' had been at issue, it would have been open for the complainants to claim that – simply by virtue of being citizens of the country – they had a direct interest in the matter and thus were legally entitled to challenge the Secretary of State's decision. In fact they had no such right because it was not a question of 'national importance' but instead simply of procedure. By being rediscovered and identified, the Rose Theatre entered the realm of heritage law, but by not being scheduled it remained only potentially valued. The decision on its future has yet – at the time of writing – to be made: whether to excavate and repair it for public display; or to preserve it and schedule the site, and thus to mark it definitively as 'of national importance' (Gurr 1994).

The Rose Theatre case thus confirms that the valuation of material is the third and final phase of the legal process as it applies to the components of the historic environment. Valuation is itself, however, no more than a very specific kind of moral change and is therefore deeply implicated in the categorization process.

SUMMARY

The law as a long-term social institution operates as a body of procedure – as a bureaucracy in a non-pejorative sense of that term. As such, the categorization phase is concerned with the powers of the specific institutions to which the law allocates specific components of the heritage. At the same time, however, the law remains a device for changing the moral status of those components, and is reductive and homogenizing in the way it treats them. This reductive and homogenizing manner of treatment is complementary to the additive and incorporative system which operates at the 'institutional' or 'historical' scale identified in Chapter 6. Valuation – the end result of the legal process and its ultimate aim – is one more moral change to the material process by law, but a very special one and so worthy of separate treatment in the next chapter.

8
Valuation under the law

Conventional readings of the legislation suggest that archaeological material is protected by law because of some inherent value it possesses. In fact, the law provides no means to measure the value of components of the archaeological heritage. Rather, instead of responding to a value the material already supposedly possesses, applying the processes of law to material results in the ascription of a specific value to that material. This is the same process as was demonstrated for the material subject to Treasure Trove discussed in Chapter 3.

The ascription of a specific kind and quantity of value to components of the archaeological heritage is the third and final stage in the application of law to ancient remains. It is also the ultimate purpose of the application of law, which – as argued in Chapters 2, 3, 4 and 5 – serves to transform archaeological material by promoting it into the public domain. In seeking to provide public protection for one particular class of material (prehistoric field monuments – Chapter 4), the proponents of such material created the political conditions in which the proponents of other classes of material could argue for the extension of legal protection to those other classes of material (Chapter 5). The result has been an ongoing positive-sum game in which it serves the advantage of all players to continue to seek legal protection for new classes of material.

VALUE GRADIENTS
The values the law ascribes to material depend on the previous two phases of the transformation into the realm of public concern. By categorizing the material in a certain way (Chapter 7) alternative options for the treatment of the material are closed. But – as we have seen in Chapter 6 – the first phase of selection included the assumption that the material selected would be able to carry any valuation finally ascribed.

This final value ascription consists of two elements. First, it consists of a type of value – location of the item on a particular legally defined value gradient (Chapter 2). Second, it consists of a measure or quantity of value – location at a particular point along that value gradient.

Table 8.1   THE VALUATION PHASE OF THE LEGAL PROCESS:
ORGANIZATION OF KEY LEGAL TERMS

Organization of terms	*Legal terms*
Types of value	
Amenity/use value	Treasure Trove, national importance, importance to the national heritage, memorial, died for the United Kingdom, public interest, public benefit, amenity, public knowledge, public enjoyment, scenic interest, character.
Scientific value	Aesthetic, artistic, architectural, archaeological, historical, historic, traditional, scientific, nature conservation.
Levels of value	National, importance, interest, outstanding, special, contribute, substantial amount, affect, enhancement, restoration.

   The detailed analysis of the values ascribed by law is contained in Appendix 3: Ascribed Values. Table 8.1 summarizes the organization of the analysis and lists the key terms.

Types of value
At the end of Chapter 5 it was suggested that material affected by the law could be placed on one of three broad value gradients which stand in opposition to one another – that of money value, that of amenity/ use value or that of scientific value. Each of these broad bands can be further resolved into a number of discrete gradients as demonstrated in Appendix 3. Accordingly, the law specifies certain types of amenity and scientific values, but eschews money value since this is the kind of value an item will be ascribed if it remains untreated by law. Accordingly, from the point of view of the law money value is a residual category – it lies outside the realm of 'heritage' law and is instead to be found in the economics of the marketplace, where other principles apply. Accordingly, while the market sets money values, the law sets only amenity and scientific values.
   A money value is described in financial terms, related to the exchangeability of an item and equivalent to its 'commodity situation' (Appadurai 1986a, 13). Scientific value is measured in terms of the 'knowledge content' of an item for the purposes of a particular discipline, a particular and very special type of use value (T. Darvill, pers. comm. on Lipe 1984, 3). Amenity value relates to the value an item is ascribed simply by its existence – perhaps as something pleasant to look at or walk over.

Levels of value – 'quantifying' legal valuation
In addition to specifying types of value, the law imposes a stiff gradation
of levels of value, from the 'national' down through 'importance' to
'interest'. There are also terms which qualify others and allow a degree
of movement up and down the value scales.

Component values
The law serves to direct certain components of the archaeological
heritage towards certain specific types and quantities of value. These
specific values are only capable of ascription to particular components of
the archaeological heritage – those which have been selected for the
purpose, linking the system back to its start-point at selection, the
subject of Chapter 6.

- *Land, buildings* and *structures* may be of national status, historic,
  archaeological, aesthetic, artistic, architectural, scenic, traditional,
  scientific and of public interest.
- *Works* may be of national status, historic, archaeological, artistic,
  architectural, traditional and of public interest.
- *Caves, excavations, vehicles, aircraft, machinery* may be of national status,
  historic, archaeological, artistic, architectural, traditional and of
  public interest.
- *Vessels* may be of national status, historic, historical, archaeological,
  artistic, architectural, traditional and of public interest.
- *Objects* may be of national status, historical, archaeological, artistic
  and scientific.
- *Collections and groups of objects* may be of national status, artistic or
  scientific.
- *Coins* may only be treasure.
- *Sites, gardens* and *areas* may be historic, archaeological, artistic,
  architectural or traditional.
- *Features external to a building* and the *exterior of a building* may be
  historic or architectural.
- *Matters* which are the subject of inspections may be historical or
  archaeological.

This summary of the values ascribed by law to material 'closes the circle'
and returns us to the beginning of the analysis of English 'heritage'
legislation by relating these values directly to specific components of the
archaeological heritage. These components were the subject of Chapter
6, which concerned the process of the selection of such material for legal
treatment.

VALUATION AS A MORAL CHANGE

The various legally ascribed values were organized above into those which represent amenity values and those representing scientific values. These distinctions are justified on the grounds of their dictionary definitions, since none of the value ascriptions contained in the law are defined in the legislation except in terms of other value ascriptions. While very few amenity values are defined in anything other than general dictionaries, scientific values are also defined in scientific dictionaries and encyclopaedias (e.g. Kuper and Kuper 1985; Sills 1968).

Amenity

Amenity is the 'quality of being pleasant or agreeable' and by extension amenities are 'pleasant places or scenes' (*Oxford English Dictionary* 1971) which thus require the quality of 'visibility' (ibid.). Scenic qualities consist of 'abounding in fine scenery [or] affording landscape views' (ibid.). Character consists of 'the aggregate of the distinctive features of any thing; [its] essential peculiarity' (ibid.). A memorial 'preserves the memory of a person or thing', is equivalent to a commemoration, and is 'something by which the memory of a person, thing or event is preserved' (ibid.).

What the NHMF preserves is the memory of those who died for the United Kingdom, and this is clearly intended as a closed category. It does not include all those who have died in the United Kingdom nor necessarily those who have merely died while in the service of the United Kingdom (as holders of some public office). Those intended to be commemorated must have died in the performance of some act or acts specifically related to the good of the United Kingdom, and this means the United Kingdom as a whole rather than any of its parts. In practice, what is meant is those persons who have died in wars in which the United Kingdom as such was engaged as a combatant, and thus to no one who died and no act prior to the Act of Union (of the Crowns of England and Scotland, which created the United Kingdom) of 1707. This creates a connection with national value which consists of things 'of or belonging to the nation [as a whole]' (*Oxford English Dictionary* 1971) – the relevant nation in the case of the NHMF being the United Kingdom and in the case of the HBMCE, England. What belongs to the nation is the heritage, 'that which may be inherited' (ibid.) or passed down from generation to generation. What is passed down is something 'pertaining to the people of a country or locality as a whole' and 'open to general observation, sight or cognizance' (ibid.) – that is, it is public – and as public interest it is something 'normative rather than analytical', concerning 'the safety of the state and the welfare of the community [or being] the objective of the duly authorised organs of government' (Sills 1968, Vol. 13, 170).

Scientific values
These relate directly to fields of study – 'science' in the broad sense of any 'branch of knowledge' (*Oxford English Dictionary* 1971). Aesthetics is 'generalised enquiry relevant to the arts . . . in creating art, in perceiving and understanding art, and in being influenced by art' (Sills 1968, Vol. 1, 116) or the study concerned with 'the creation and appreciation of beauty' (Kuper and Kuper 1985, 9), and accordingly aesthetic value pertains to 'the appreciation or criticism of beauty' (*Oxford English Dictionary* 1971). Artistic value pertains to 'art . . . or artists', the latter being those who 'cultivate . . . one of the fine arts, in which the object is mainly to gratify the aesthetic emotions' (ibid.). Architecture is 'the art' or 'the science of building' (*Oxford English Dictionary* 1971; Sills 1968, Vol. 1, 392). Archaeological, historic and historical values all relate to the study of the past.

Two hybrid values remain – both counted as scientific so far but also related to amenity values. Traditional value, which relates to 'the action of . . . the transmission of . . . customs and the like, esp. [*sic*] by word of mouth or in practice without writing' (*Oxford English Dictionary* 1971), in one sense constitutes a study of the past through folklore and the archaeological study of technology (Schlanger and Sinclair 1990), while in another sense it relates to inheritance and thus 'heritage'. Nature conservation, the 'preservation from destructive influence' of 'the features and products of the earth itself, as contrasted with those of human civilisation' (*Oxford English Dictionary* 1971), is also a hybrid form of value, concerned with the creation of amenity but requiring an input from the natural sciences (cf. Cox *et al.* 1995).

Matched pairs
The particular differences between aesthetic and artistic value and between historic and historical value are perhaps worth addressing. All four terms have been placed in the scientific value set, and are paired – aesthetic with artistic, historic with historical. Used loosely, the members of each pair can be taken as synonymous, but the use in the law of both terms in each pair indicates that they should be distinguished.

Aesthetic value is applied only to three items, while artistic applies to fifteen; those to which aesthetic value apply are the same as those to which scenic value apply, while artistic value also applies to these three. Accordingly, all three terms need to be distinguished. While aesthetics is concerned with the quality of beauty, and scenic requires the quality of fine scenery or the presence of landscape views, artistic relates to the manufacture of beauty by human work. The differences can thus be resolved by treating aesthetic and scenic items as those which are judged to be beautiful or scenic merely by presence. In contrast, artistic items are those which constitute, contain or are the subject of artworks – that is, items of beauty made by human endeavour. The degree of overlap in coverage may be explained as an attempt by the legislators to ensure as broad a coverage as possible – if something is not quite 'aesthetic', it may count as 'artistic' or 'scenic', and vice versa. Nevertheless, both amenity and scientific values are mixed here.

Historical value applies to three items, and historic to fourteen; there is a strong overlap, except that matters which are the subject of investigation are only historical and not historic. The dictionary definitions of historical and historic are of assistance here: historical means 'of or pertaining to history' (*Oxford English Dictionary* 1971) as does historic, but historic also carries the current particular meaning of 'having an interest or importance due in connexion with historical events' (ibid.). In other words, while historical means related to history in general, historic means a connection with specific events in history. Accordingly, vessels, matters and objects are of relevance for legal coverage if historical in general, while other items (caves, excavations, vehicles, machinery, land, structures, works, buildings and their exteriors and exterior features, sites, gardens and areas) need to be related directly to particular events in history. This may present problems in respect of certain specific items, but only if the idea of 'historical event' is read narrowly to mean events in the short term (*événements*) rather than in terms of historical period or the *longue durée* (cf. Hodder 1987). Either way, both historic and historical relate to scientific value.

This discussion has confirmed the division of specific value ascriptions into those of amenity (to be enjoyed) or science (a branch of knowledge or research). Most specific value ascriptions fit comfortably and without problem into one or other of these categories. Even where some doubt arises – either through the 'hybrid' nature of the value type (traditional, nature conservation) or distinguishing similar ascriptions (aesthetic, scenic, artistic; historic, historical) – the value ascriptions will still fit the broad areas of science or amenity. Accordingly, at base the law is only concerned with two kinds of value – amenity and scientific.

A reductive and homogenizing value system

The two fields of value ascription 'amenity' and 'science' relate closely to the purposes to which the material is to be put. Amenity values relate to use now, while scientific values relate to current preservation (or 'storage') against some future use. To some extent this is inevitable, since if amenity value represents 'the quality of being pleasant or agreeable' (*Oxford English Dictionary* 1971) then it carries the capacity to be enjoyed immediately, while the needs of science demand a measure of forward planning to ensure appropriate use ('appropriate' being understood here in terms of the knowledge to be extracted from the item). In the case of archaeology, use (investigation, excavation) implies destruction – what an economist would recognize as 'consumption'. This gives rise in economic terms to a direct consumptive value (Brown 1990, 213), that is, utility[1] accruing directly to the consumer (in this case, the archaeologist). However, the law does not seek the immediate use of the item, but its preservation for future use. Similarly, amenity values – which relate to both current and future availability for enjoyment – do not imply destruction, but rather that amenities 'fall to the class of undepletable externalities [so that] your visiting or photographing [them] does not keep me from viewing them. . . . [and studies] . . . carried out by one group does not deny the opportunity [for study] to another [group]' (Brown 1990, 214).[2]

In applying economic analysis to 'heritage' sites, Greffe (1990, 32–45) characterizes with some agreement to English law the various values of such sites as aesthetic, artistic, historic, cognitive (of knowledge), economic, amenity (*l'image de marque*) and social. He classes all these as the 'services' provided by heritage sites for which consumer demand exists (ibid., 5, 41–5). Consumption of these services does not exhaust the site, but instead calls for the supply of 'support' to the enjoyment of these services (ibid., 5, 41–5). This 'support' is what is purchased, consisting of an option value (ibid., 53–7), which has been defined as a willingness 'to pay to preserve the option of purchasing [the right to visit] the site in the future' (Brown 1990, 214). Such a 'future uncertain nonconsumptive value' (ibid., 214) may derive from three sources: existence (the utility mere existence of a thing provides); bequest to a future generation, so that one's descendants may derive utility from enjoying a thing at some unspecified point in the future; and scientific value, in the sense of 'the public knowledge [to be provided] in the future' (ibid., 215). Such an economic value is future in that it relates to future (rather than current) use, uncertain in that what is 'bought' is not actual use but the possibility of use whether that possibility is realized or not, and nonconsumptive because such use does not deny use to others.

An exception to the nonconsumptive principle may be scientific value, predicated on the need for research which in the case of archaeology will be destructive. Two factors, however, override this. First, not all research will be destructive – non-invasive survey (Clark 1990; Scollar *et al.* 1990); 'vertical archaeology' on buildings (Hutton 1986; ICOMOS 1990). Second, the law provides for the preservation of items while awaiting such research. One ultimate result of valuation under law is that while the various types of value defined fall into only two broad value classes, these may also be merged into a single class of economic value which subsumes them both.

This single future uncertain nonconsumptive value can be envisaged as a unitary realm of value divided into two distinct value gradients. Here, the clearer the identity with either science or amenity, the higher the item is to be placed on the relevant value gradient and the further from the 'fuzzy' area that divides them. Conversely, the more hybrid the valuation, the closer it is to the 'fuzzy' area and the lower the value. Thus, traditional interest (a very hybrid value) is relatively low on the scale of both science and amenity, along with nature conservation (which is low on the list of priorities for loans or grants from the NHMF [NH80, s. 3(6)]). Other, more clearly defined values, lie higher on the relevant gradient.

The argument made here and in Chapter 7 as to the reductive and homogenizing nature of the legal process on components of the archaeological heritage is supported by the relatively few value ascriptions given by law. The 29 items covered by Chapter 6 have only 21 value ascriptions given to them, and these reduce to two broad types and then (as argued above) to one only. Moreover, of the 21, one is self-referencing: 'public interest' is defined in terms of historic, architectural, traditional, artistic and archaeological interest (AMAA79, s. 61[12]). This gives rise to an alternative way of looking at the realm of future uncertain nonconsumptive value, which is to see it as a continuum stretching from 'pure' amenity value at one extreme to 'pure' scientific value at the other. At ninety degrees to this axis lies another along which value can be measured from lesser to greater. Within this two-dimensional space all the values ascribed by law can be located (Figure 8.1).

All legal value ascriptions are now seen to exist in a hierarchical relationship with one another. What follows from this is that the paths through the legal process available to different components of the heritage are also in a hierarchical relationship to one another. Thus, because scheduled monuments are ascribed 'national importance', scheduling is a more powerful device than placing into guardianship, acquisition or management agreements which relate to components which are of 'public interest'. In other words, in any dispute between the requirements of scheduling and those of, say, guardianship, the requirements of scheduling will always have to outweigh those of guardianship regardless of specific circumstances. This implies very strongly that preservation for future scientific use is more important to the law than other factors, such as public access.

What precisely is valued and how?
The values ascribed by law have been related back to individual components of the heritage. In the law itself, however, what is ascribed

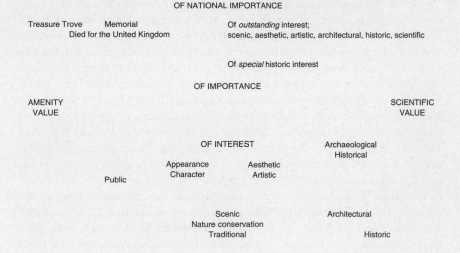

Figure 8.1   The space of legally ascribed values

value is the category into which the item falls: monuments, ancient monuments, historic buildings, sites, conservation areas, and so on, as described above under types of value. What is in fact ascribed a specific value by the law is not the item itself but the capacity of that item to be categorized in a particular way.

This finding should not be a surprise because, as pointed out in Chapter 7, the valuation phase is merely a special form of moral change to components of the heritage. To that extent, it derives directly from the categorization process and in a sense belongs to it. The three phases of the legal process – selection, categorization and valuation – thus link together in a manner in which the later ones are dependent on and succeed the former, but are nevertheless implicated from the very beginning of the process.

HERITAGE LAW AS A HIGH-ENERGY FUNNEL

By derivation from the preceding discussion, the law in England relating to the heritage can be considered to be in essence a machine for changing the way people think about material from the past. As suggested by the discussions in Chapters 6 and 7, it is in its mode of operation additive, incorporative, reductive and homogenizing. It is additive because it is altered by adding new categories to the law rather than cancelling the existing ones and constructing an entirely new body of law. It is incorporative because each addition extends the range of the law while leaving existing coverage unaffected, rather than old categories 'dropping out' of the system. It is reductive because as an item passes through the legal system, the range of categories relevant to it reduce in number until it reaches the final valuation stage from where it re-enters the world with a new meaning. This new meaning is either one of amenity or scientific, and in either case is a future uncertain non-consumptive value. It is homogenizing because the treatment given to all bodies of material is essentially identical and the end result and final valuations the same. This is always the case because those bodies responsible for applying and interpreting the law are those created by or given authority under that same law.

Chapters 3, 4 and 5 indicated the manner in which the law in this field developed. Individuals with particular interests sought to promote specific bodies of material which in some manner represented their political philosophy. Success in gaining legal recognition for archaeological material (first through the appropriation of Treasure Trove and subsequently through legislation on prehistoric field monuments) led to the drive by others to gain similar recognition for other types of material – medieval monuments, natural landscapes, wrecks, military remains. This is a positive-sum game in which it serves the interests of all players to continue to add new material to the law since the total value available to players increases as the game continues. The product of this history is the additive and incorporative nature of such law.

The reductive and homogenizing nature of such law is also a product of this history. To be part of the game, material must be treated the same way as the other components. Accordingly, all such law works the same way. As described in Chapters 6, 7 and this chapter, all material subject to 'heritage' law – regardless of its type or the specific, legally defined branch of law to which it belongs – is treated the same way. It is first selected for coverage, then recategorized, allocated to a specific body for treatment, made subject to (few) physical and (more) moral changes, and finally given a specific value as either an amenity or an item of scientific value. This scheme is a developed form of the tripartite scheme described for Treasure Trove in Chapter 3: selection, categorization, and valuation.

An important element briefly touched upon above is the power of the law. As Roberts, quoted in Chapter 2, points out, the 'pre-eminent authority of "the law"' as a setter of norms means that 'all other normative systems give way' to it (Roberts 1979, 22). One of the ways this power is expressed is in the transformation of a simple legally defined permission into a binding injunction. The power of local authorities to enter into agreements with developers regarding restrictions on the use of land is given by s. 106 of the Town and Country Planning Act of 1990; such agreements may provide for the provision of archaeological facilities and their funding by the developer. In practice, this simple permission – which does not require or demand the entry into an agreement nor specify its content, but merely allows this to take place – provides the basis for the established and government approved policy of developer funding for archaeological work (*British Archaeological News* 3.9, 85; Department of the Environment 1990, para. 25). In other words, once something is specifically allowed in legislation it soon becomes mandatory.

This power of the law as it relates to heritage derives from two sources. First, the structure of the law provides for its application and interpretation by institutions, many of which only exist by virtue of that law or whose powers are defined by that law. As discussed in Chapter 7, these institutions are very powerful but constrained by their position 'inside' the law; the law is thus subject to constant reinterpretation but always in the same way. Second, the constant addition of new material to the coverage of the law adds energy to the system, promoting still further the positive-sum game in operation.

The law is sometimes considered to be a delicate clock-like mechanism in which small interventions lead to major changes: a slight turn to a tiny screw affects the rate of movement and thus the time shown on the clock face. In the case of heritage law, such an image may be inappropriate. As indicated by the manner in which changes are brought about, a small change does not have a large effect. Rather, change consists in adding new material to the stock of that capable of legal processing while the process itself remains unaltered. A more appropriate image for heritage law may be that of a large mill-wheel which turns to drive the 'heritage' law system. The faster the wheel turns, the more material can be processed by the law; but at the same time this addition of material increases the total power within the system and the speed of rotation of the wheel. The system is a reductive one, and accordingly material is 'funnelled' along a tube the size of which is constantly reducing. As more material is added to the system at the 'selection' end and the wheel turns faster, the greater the pressure further along the funnel. Material is thus propelled through the system at ever greater speed and force.

This analogy with a high-energy flow suggests that tinkering with the law – that is, making small changes in the hope of achieving greater effects – will not work. As argued above, this is supported by the facts: changes result in the addition of new material to the coverage of the law, but not in substantial alterations to the mode of operation of the law on that material. It is still subject to recategorization and valuation in very specific terms, and the law remains what it always was, a device for changing the conception of things. To alter the mode of operation of the law is in effect to divert the high-energy flow from its present course and on to a new one. This will require the application of much energy to overcome the power of the stream (political energy here, since it means dismantling a body of legislation it has taken over a century to develop). Any energy spent in making small changes while waiting to achieve the major aim will only add energy to the system, making it that much more difficult to divert than it is at present. Accordingly, to bring about any major change – if that is what is desired – will mean abandoning any plans for small changes and the diversion of that political energy into the larger project of changing the system overall.

It is not the purpose of this book to suggest whether the current law in England relating to the heritage should be amended or abandoned or not. The point is to highlight the consequences of the laws we have at present and to indicate that if we wish to change them, it will require a great deal of political energy. Diversion of this energy into small 'tinkering' changes will make the process more difficult rather than easier.

The kinds of heritage laws we have in England at present serve to promote certain bodies of material to a particular status, as measured in the values ascribed to that material by law. The law makes changes to the way those bodies of material are thought about and understood. In essence, the law is a machine for changing the way we think about certain things. In so doing, it transforms those items from things that relate to the past to things which take a particular place in the present. Thus formally and by dint of law they become part of the heritage, whatever they may have been before, and pass into the public domain.

TRANSFORMATIONS: FROM ARCHAEOLOGY TO HERITAGE . . .

The first Theoretical Interlude comprised a review of Treasure Trove as a means of transformation from found object to museum treasure. This section will attempt the same for all items covered by heritage law in England. Treasure Trove is a part of this law and, as argued here, provides the foundational structure on which the rest is built. The superstructure thus constructed over the past century is more complex than the relatively simple doctrine of Treasure Trove. Nevertheless, this law can conveniently be divided into the three phases of selection (Chapter 6), categorization and its consequences (Chapter 7) and valuation (this chapter).

Rubbish Theory (Thompson 1979; Chapter 2) requires items to

'cease to exist' for a fractional time before they can re-emerge with a new valuation and meaning. Treasure Trove items are progressively decontextualized in the phases of selection and categorization, to emerge recontextualized with a new meaning in the phase of valuation. While by no means as straightforward as for Treasure Trove, the same process applies to all items that are the object of heritage law.

Selection (Chapter 6)
The definition of items to process under the law effectively removes them from the realm of archaeology or history and places them in the realm of law. Here, whole items, parts of items, attributes of items and contexts for items are specifically picked out in the law for treatment. Having thus become the subject of legal rather than solely archaeological concern, they have clearly demarcated spatial boundaries placed around them (as monuments, sites, buildings, and so on; Chapter 6). They are thus divorced both from their original archaeological conceptual context and from their physical context. The process is complicated by the facts that, first, some definitions of items with an objective physical existence (monument, site) merge into legal categories which have a conceptual rather than physical existence; and, second, that such terms are also subject to a circularity of legal understanding. This, however, together with the overwhelming power of law as a normative system (Roberts 1979, 22), contributes to the decontextualization of the item by embedding it further in the legal process to which it is now subject. This is the first phase of decontextualization, similar to that for Treasure Trove – a focus on the item itself, divorced from any prior context.

Categorization (Chapter 7)
The categorization process both removes from the item and adds back to it. Recategorization in legal terms strips the item of its previous description and gives it a new name – no longer a particular house but a listed building, no longer a round barrow but a monument, no longer a garden but an ancient monument. This is the second phase of decontextualization proper – the removal of any prior identity. But it is also the first stage of a recontextualization – the adding back of a new identity with a new and specific value.

First, as here, it is renamed in terms of a legally defined category; a new name is added. Second, it is allocated to a specific institution for treatment in accordance with the laws relevant for items in its category; a new context is added. Third, it is altered physically as the law provides or is prevented from being so altered as the law prohibits; some form of preservation or facility is added. Fourth, it is changed conceptually – by a change of control or ownership, by becoming subject to an agreement, by having consents granted or withheld in respect of it; a new moral status is added. This is at once the end of decontextualization and the start of recontextualization.

Adding value (Chapter 8)

The final phase is the addition of a new and specific value to the item, as discussed earlier in this chapter. The item is no longer what it was – a 'little bump . . . in a field' (Jocelyn Stevens, Chairman of the HBMCE, quoted in *The Guardian*, 6.11.1992) – but has been allocated by law a very precise scientific or amenity future uncertain nonconsumptive value. As such it is promoted to a special realm – the public domain (Chapter 2). This promotion has been effected by a focus on the item itself, divorced from prior context and with its former identity stripped away, and its treatment in a new context under a specific regime giving it a new meaning and ultimately a new and specific value.

The public domain

The law promotes components of the historic environment into the public domain and ascribes them a precise value. As discussed in Chapter 2, the public domain is the realm in which the heritage resides and in which 'public people', those with cultural capital (Bourdieu 1984) and who are social controllers (Douglas and Isherwood 1979), are at home (Bourdieu 1984; Merriman 1991). The public domain is part of a conceptual framework which organizes action in the modern social environment (Benn and Gaus 1983b, 5) and exists apart from and in tension with the private realm, where the principles of the private accumulation of wealth rule (Giddens 1984, 197). Items in the public domain are non-excludable (Ordeshook 1986, 211) and the important institution of the public domain is the group rather than the individual (Benn and Gaus 1983a, 39). Accordingly, the preservation of heritage items by law constitutes a form of corporate saving (Douglas and Isherwood 1979, 37) and raises them into a position of hyper-visibility in the cultural landscape, the antithesis of rubbish (Thompson 1979).

The overarching value given to heritage items by law is future, uncertain and nonconsumptive. This broad value band stands in opposition to the broad value band of direct consumptive value, in which the consumption of an item provides immediate utility to the consumer and to no one else. While, then, future uncertain nonconsumptive value (FUN) is the appropriate value for things in the public domain, the appropriate value for things in the private domain – the realm of private ownership and the economic marketplace – is direct consumptive (DC) value. Figure 8.2 is thus the more general application of the diagram shown in Chapter 3 (Figure 3.2).

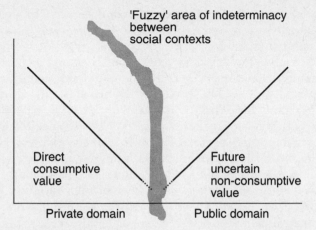

'Fuzzy' area of indeterminacy between social contexts

Direct consumptive value

Future uncertain non-consumptive value

Private domain   Public domain

Figure 8.2   Opposed value systems: the public versus the private domain

Here, FUN value is equivalent to the 'museum' value of items subject to Treasure Trove while DC is equivalent to that of private ownership and the marketplace. When processed by law, items are passed into the public domain where they are ascribed a FUN value. In practice, this means that they are classed either as amenity items and will remain so in perpetuity or as items of scientific concern, in which case they will be 'kept in storage' for the future.

. . . AND BACK AGAIN

FUN and DC values stand in direct opposition to one another – one residing in the public domain, the other in the private (Figure 8.2). Items are passed into the public domain by the action of law. The effect of law on such items is to ascribe them a FUN value so that they are deemed never to become available for consumption – that is, investigation involving damage or destruction. This is what the quality of excludability (the characteristic of items in the public domain such that use by one person does not deny use by another) means. It corresponds to a heightened form of existence in the durable category of Rubbish Theory (Thompson 1979; Figure 2.2).

It is clear, however, that items do pass back into the private domain. Archaeological remains that have been promoted into the public domain – scheduled monuments, museum objects, and so on – can become subject to destructive investigation, vandalism or be stolen or bought and sold. At one level, this is simply a practical legal problem – that of ensuring that the penalties for damaging scheduled monuments and for the theft of items from museums are sufficiently powerful to outweigh the potential benefits to perpetrators, and thus to provide an effective deterrent.

At another level, however, it represents a significant theoretical problem. This is because the scales of value measuring FUN and DC values are completely different. A DC value can be reduced to monetary terms relatively simply. A FUN value – defined in terms of science or amenity – cannot. The 'fuzzy' area between the private and public realms thus defines not only the difference between value gradients but also that between social contexts in which totally different principles apply. The FUN and DC gradients thus occupy not only different places on a two-dimensional diagram, but also different spaces in different but non-exclusive (since both are part of the modern conceptual scheme) 'universes'. Any one item can occupy space in both such 'universes' simultaneously. Thus, to bring the two value gradients into alignment in order to establish some kind of control of this process is the ultimate problem for the future, but to do so in a way that neither promotes DC (market) value to an 'ethical' status it does not deserve, nor reduces FUN value to financial terms (see Chapter 9).

SUMMARY

Linking the values ascribed by law to the components of the heritage that are the objects of that law closes the circle and returns the analysis of law whence it began – with the selection process. In so doing, the operation of heritage law on its object is shown to be reductive, homogenizing, additive and incorporative, and the law itself to be a machine for changing the way in which bodies of material are thought about and understood. The final result of the legal processing of an item is thus established from the outset, implicating the categorization and valuation phases from the beginning. As such, the law can be likened to a high-energy funnel along which material is propelled with great force. As more types of material are added to the legal system, the greater the total energy possessed by the system as a whole and the higher the benefit accruing to players in the positive-sum game this represents.

The law eschews the attribution of monetary values to heritage items, and instead ascribes either a scientific or amenity value. These two types of legally ascribed value are reducible to a single future uncertain nonconsumptive value – the kind of value operative in the public domain – which stands in opposition to a direct consumptive value, which operates in the private domain of economic activity. This corresponds to the opposition of market to museum values operative in the case of Treasure Trove, thus making the model derived from Treasure Trove in Chapter 3 of more general relevance.

NOTES

1. Utility is a 'metaphysical' term (Robinson and Eatwell 1973, 35) describing 'that quality in any object whereby it tends to produce benefit, advance, pleasure, good or happiness' (Bentham 1789, quoted in Douglas and Isherwood 1979, 22). Thus loosely defining this concept, economists avoid the need to consider why people want to buy things, and need only focus on the mechanisms involved in doing so.
2. An externality is the effect of an action by one person on another (Ordeshook 1986, 211). Here (as in the case of all public goods, Chapter 2), to visit and view a site is deemed not to affect another's capacity to do so. Accordingly, the externality is deemed to be incapable of depletion.

Part Four
Consequences

9
Archaeology and the law: a summary and conclusions

This work represents a moment within a new process rather than the culmination of that process. The process is that of transforming AHM from a realm of mere practice (Carman 1991; Chapter 1) into a field of research that is of relevance to archaeologists and students concerned with the social ascription of value. This process has proceeded from a much-needed questioning of the four basic principles of AHM – that the archaeological heritage is finite and non-renewable, that it is of public interest, that it is governed by legislation, and that its components require testing for significance – to show that they are not objective truths but rather unquestioned axioms. Each has some validity, but they can also provide the route whereby further questions may be revealed. The intention of this book has been to open up some of these questions, to provide some initial and provisional answers, and to outline further areas for research. This concluding chapter will outline the fruits of that research so far, the valuable new connections it has made with other disciplines, and the new lines of enquiry it has opened up.

THE RELATIONSHIP OF LAW WITH ARCHAEOLOGY – WHAT WE HAVE LEARNED SO FAR

In **Chapter 1**, the route taken in the course of this research was shown as follows:

the nature of the relationship law $\leftrightarrow$ archaeology $\rightarrow$ history of that relationship $\rightarrow$ history of the development of archaeology $\rightarrow$ how certain materials became the subject of archaeological enquiry $\rightarrow$ how those materials became considered to be valuable $\rightarrow$ the role of law in that process $\rightarrow$ the function of law in archaeology $\rightarrow$ how the law works on archaeological material $\rightarrow$ the values ascribed by law to archaeological material

AHM was revealed as a field of archaeological practice based upon four principles which are subject to criticism (in the popular sense) but not to effective critique. As a consequence, despite the fact that the majority of archaeologists worldwide are engaged in AHM work, AHM is the branch of archaeology that impacts the least on archaeology as an academic discipline. The four basic principles of AHM were examined and shown to be flawed but they were also the basis from which wide-ranging questions – especially concerning the valuation of archaeological material – emerged. These questions formed the basis of the issues at the core of the research leading to this work. In the absence of an existing data-set and methodology for research in AHM, the law in England relating to the archaeological heritage was chosen as the focus for this research. Existing legal and comparative approaches were rejected because of the problems they presented.

Chapter 2 addressed theoretical and methodological issues. In examining the manner in which values are ascribed to things, the work of Bourdieu (1984) and Merriman (1991) was related to that of Douglas and Isherwood (1979). Out of this arose the concept of the public domain, in which the heritage can be said to reside. This realm in turn was associated with the 'upper' part of Thompson's (1979) durable category for objects – the antithesis of rubbish which has (by common consent) no social existence. Thompson's (1979) *Rubbish Theory* was accordingly adopted as a model for the manner in which items pass from one value category to another, and considered to be of particular relevance to archaeological remains by its analogy with Schiffer's (1972) model of N- and C- transforms. In going on to consider the social origins of the ascription of specific values to things, the Cultural Theory model (Schwarz and Thompson 1990) suggested that things are not treated a particular way because they contain a certain value, but are valued in a certain way because in a given social context they are treated in a certain way. This also opened up the possibility of considering the different values to be ascribed to any single object in different social contexts, in terms of both value gradients (Thompson 1990) and quantity. The example of the auction (Smith 1989) demonstrated the importance of social context in this connection and the three phases involved in the valuation process: selection, categorization and (final) value ascription. In using the law to examine these areas, the law was considered as a tool for the achievement of social purposes (Atiyah 1983) and in particular as a setter of social norms (Roberts 1979). In the case of the heritage, it acts as gatekeeper to the public domain. The aim of this research was thus identified as the acquisition of an understanding of how the law in England works in relation to archaeological material, and – by extension – the relationship of such law to archaeology as a discipline. This would be achieved by an examination of the historical relationship between law and archaeology, with the purpose of understanding how such law came into being, and by an analysis of current law by identifying the key terms and phrases contained in such law. Throughout, the law would be treated as a unity rather than breaking it down into separate branches, as a specifically legal approach would require.

The doctrine of Treasure Trove – the most ancient law relating to archaeological material in England – was studied in **Chapter 3**. From a historical perspective, the changes made in the doctrine were charted from the medieval period up to its appropriation for the purposes of the new discipline of archaeology in the mid-nineteenth century. This appropriation was shown to relate both to the drive to increase the amount of specifically British material in the collections of the British Museum, and to attempts within the new discipline of archaeology to force an abandonment of interest in folklore studies and written materials or a focus on the study of objects alone. The doctrine in operation was shown to be concerned exclusively with items of gold or silver, separate from the criminal law but adopting an adversarial approach in its treatment of conflicting claims to such material, treating all such objects in a manner that divorces them from the context in which they were deposited or found, and ultimately concerned with acquiring objects suitable for display in museums. A Theoretical Interlude demonstrated the three-phase process operative in Treasure Trove procedure of progressive decontextualization (two phases) and recontextualization (a single phase) derived from Rubbish Theory, Cultural Theory and the auction, and how this promotes material into the public domain.

The historical approach begun in Chapter 3 was continued in **Chapter 4**, which examined the origins and passage into law of the Ancient Monuments Protection Act of 1882. The legislation of protection for ancient remains was shown to be part of a much wider process of change in nineteenth-century Britain, which promoted many areas of life previously private into the public domain. In drawing on the work of Foucault (1970, 1973, 1977), Levine (1986), Perkin (1989) and Shannon (1976), a contextual framework was constructed within which to comprehend the large-scale processes operative in the late nineteenth century. In particular, the professionalization of many fields of activity and the importance of cultural factors in the politics of the time were emphasized. The promoter of Bills to preserve prehistoric material, Sir John Lubbock, was revealed as both an archaeological politician and a political archaeologist. As an archaeological politician, Lubbock's archaeological interests were related to his Liberal politics and his other legislative efforts in the fields of regulating the new professions, commerce and industry, as well as to his efforts to seize control of archaeological and anthropological societies to promote a particular (and politically informed) theoretical position. As a political archaeologist, Lubbock's concern for prehistoric remains reflected his stance on the major issue of Irish Home Rule and his opposition to groups such as socialists and Tory aristocrats who shared with each other (but not with Lubbock) a concern for medieval material. The passage of the 1882 Act was accordingly as much the product of national politics as it was a 'simple' desire to preserve ancient remains, and the discipline of archaeology itself was deeply implicated and involved in this national politics.

The historical survey of English 'heritage' law continued in **Chapter 5**. The death of Pitt-Rivers left the 1882 Act in a defunct state, and yet the drive to legislate the protection of archaeological material grew. Drawing on Edelman (1967, 1971) and Thompson's (1982) three-dimensional model of Cultural Theory as social action in a second Theoretical Interlude, the effect of the 1882 Act was shown to be that of making the legislative protection of material the appropriate means to promote certain political positions. By successfully legislating, Lubbock and his allies gave a status to prehistoric material that required others who also wished to promote bodies of material similarly to legislate. The result was the beginning of a positive-sum economic game in which the total value accruing to all players increases as new material is added. Accordingly, since 1900, first Roman and medieval remains, then church buildings, movable objects, dwelling houses and urban areas, natural features and landscapes, wrecks and military remains – all became subject to some form of legal protection. These laws were a combination of new laws passed by Parliament and others already existing that were appropriated by interested bodies. All these laws relate, one way or another, either to monetary value, scientific value or amenity value – three broad value gradients standing in opposition to one another.

Turning from the historical development of law to an analytical perspective on current laws, **Chapter 6** reviewed the process of selection of material for legal coverage by identifying and defining key terms used in the law to describe the components of the archaeological heritage. The difficulty of separating descriptions of actual items from legal categories was overcome by limiting coverage in Chapter 6 to those terms relating to things with an objective physical existence in the world. These terms were divided for convenience into actual components (consisting of terms describing their wholes, their parts or their attributes), into contexts for items and into ancillary items. A discussion of the different meanings (legal and archaeological) of terms such as site and monument and their boundedness raised the problem of how archaeologists recognize those items that are their particular concern from those that lie outside it. An approach based on the ethnography of archaeology (Edgeworth 1990) and the study of intuitive recognition (Bastick 1982) indicated that selection for legal treatment is not a unitary process. Instead, it involves first the identification of an item and second the assumption of two latent qualities for that item: the capacity to carry a new categorization and that to carry a new valuation. In recognizing items, the legal process ascribes a provisional value to all items in a particular class, thus creating the conditions for the spread of legal coverage to similar classes (the process identified in Chapter 5). The capacity for specific items to carry a new categorization and value then removes that item from the large–scale 'historical' process of the law and carries it along a highly prescribed path.

Chapter 7 indicated the extent to which the law is concerned with categorization and its consequences. Items are first recategorized in legal terms (as a type of monument, a type of building, a type of movable object, a type of location, or something ancillary to these). They are then allocated to a specific institution for treatment in accordance with legal regulation, these institutions having certain limited powers and duties which provide for or prohibit physical alterations to the item and moral (conceptual) changes to its understanding and status. Since the number of moral changes which are or can be made to items under the law exceed the physical changes that can be made and these moral changes belong to institutions empowered by law, the law should be seen primarily as a vector by which moral changes are made to material – a device for changing people's conception of things.

The discussion of the phase of valuation under the law in **Chapter 8** closed the circle of the argument by linking legally defined value ascriptions to components of the archaeological heritage. The reduction of legally ascribed value to only two value gradients – amenity and scientific – and their subsumption under a single type of economic value (future uncertain nonconsumptive value) – established the law as a reductive and homogenizing process so far as the components of the heritage are concerned. In addition, the additive and incorporative process of the law's development contributed to its reductive and homogenizing nature, in which changes are small and consist of 'tinkering' rather than wholesale reorganization of the legal structure. The law was envisaged as a high–energy funnel the power of which increases as more types of material are added, rendering tinkering changes ineffective in bringing about major transformations. The complexity of the entire corpus of heritage law hides its simple three-stage mode of operation, which remains that of selection, categorization and valuation, although with additional sub-phases contained within it. The amenity and scientific values ascribed by law stand in opposition to one another within the public domain, to which material is promoted by the action of law; and as future uncertain nonconsumptive value both stand together in opposition to a direct consumptive (market) value belonging to the private domain of economic activity.

The **route** taken in this work in presenting the results of this enquiry has been as follows:

The principles of AHM questioned, a focus on law (Chapter 1) → the importance of value, value as a product of social context, the nature of law (Chapter 2) → Treasure Trove, the first 'archaeological law' in England (the relationship law ↔ archaeology 1) (Chapter 3) → the history of the development of 'heritage' law in England (the relationship law ↔ archaeology 2) (Chapters 4 and 5) → the process of law (selection, categorization, valuation) (the relationship law ↔ archaeology 3) (Chapters 6, 7 and 8) → the values ascribed by law and the effect of law on archaeological material (Chapter 8)

The nature of the relationship between law and archaeology and the function of law in archaeology were the themes addressed throughout the work. The history of that relationship, the role of law in that relationship, its connection to the development of archaeology as a discipline and the identification of material considered to be specifically the subject of archaeological enquiry and thus of value – all of these were the issues addressed in Chapters 3, 4 and 5. The way the law works on archaeological material and how it serves to give specific value to that material were the subjects of Chapters 6, 7 and 8.

Alternative routes to the same conclusions

The overall conclusions reached in the two parts of the work – the historical and the analytical – are identical. Lubbock's efforts to promote prehistoric remains over other bodies of material by legislating their protection represent an attempt to use the law as a vector of moral change of that material. This is the same process as can be identified from the analysis of current law – and leads directly to an understanding of the reductive and homogenizing effect of law on material. Similarly, the additive process of creation of the total corpus of law recognized in Chapter 5 (the continuing positive-sum economic game) reflects the 'tinkering' mode of bringing about change in the law identified in the analysis. The historical approach in Chapter 5 also indicated the three opposed value gradients on which material is placed by law – monetary, amenity and scientific – which are the same as those emerging from the analysis in Chapter 8.

For any similar research in the future – whether of English or British law, or the legislation in any other territory – it seems likely that the same conclusions can be achieved either by approaching it from a historical perspective or by way of analysis. Accordingly, by eschewing either history or analysis (as the researcher prefers or conditions dictate) an understanding of a particular corpus of law similar to that presented here can be achieved in far less time. It is, however, essential that any researcher in this field should be made sensitive to the underlying issues. The value of an approach that is both historical and analytical is that the one approach sensitizes the researcher to issues that may emerge out of the other. This sensitivity is not easy to achieve. One certain way to achieve it is to adopt the combined historical and analytical approach taken here.

MAKING LINKS: INTERDISCIPLINARY CONNECTIONS
Elsewhere I have suggested that AHM provides a strong link between archaeology and three other disciplines: law, sociology and economics (Carman 1991, 180–2). This work can add to these three the fields of economic anthropology and sociology, legal anthropology, ethnography, administration, history, the history and philosophy of science, political science, philosophy and psychology. Works in all of these areas have been consulted, and others were read which informed the thought process but did not make a direct and citable contribution to the results of the research. It is, however, perhaps worth re-emphasizing here the underlying belief of this work that AHM is ultimately **archaeology** or it is nothing. The concern of AHM is all the material with which archaeologists deal, whether called the archaeological heritage, the archaeological or cultural resource base, or the archaeological record (Carman in press, Chapter 1). It is also concerned intimately and directly with all areas of archaeological practice (Carman 1991, 178–9). No discipline or field is as concerned with archaeology, whether as material remains from the past or as the study of those remains, as archaeology itself. That concern is – and remains – archaeology, no matter the terminology or language in which it is couched.

The most obvious external connection of this work has been with the field of **law**. In examining the law as it affects archaeological material it is necessary to have some understanding of the nature of law (Atiyah 1983), how to read that law (Cross 1987), Parliamentary practice in passing laws (*Erskine May* 1989) and the content of that law (Hill 1936; Moore 1990; O'Keefe and Prott 1984; Palmer 1981; Purdue *et al.* 1989; Suddards 1988). No lawyer, however, is concerned ultimately with archaeology since the lawyer's job is to interpret the law as it stands and to give advice in the law's own terms. Palmer (1991), for example, has offered advice on issues of legal title as they relate to objects sent to museums; this is a very important practical issue for museum archaeologists in their day-to-day work but does not derive from the archaeological nature of that work. Similarly, lawyers may advise on changes to heritage law but their concern is with maintaining the integrity of law while effecting the change rather than doing archaeology. By contrast, Ian Stead's concern with issues of Treasure Trove at Snettisham (Stead 1991) is no less archaeological for touching on legal concerns. In thus engaging with legal issues, archaeological concerns remain primarily archaeological in AHM.

In looking at the manner by which value is ascribed to things in the contemporary context, a connection was inevitably made with **sociology**. This connection was particularly useful in considering the concept of the public domain where so much of the socially constructed modern world resides (Benn and Gaus 1983c; Giddens 1984), where those with cultural and economic capital freely operate (Bourdieu 1984) and in which perceptual schemes of categorization are negotiated (Douglas 1982, 1). A similar connection was made with **economic anthropology and sociology** where the focus was on the 'social life of things' (Appadurai 1986b), the social ascription of value (Douglas and Isherwood 1979; Thompson 1979) and the social mechanisms by which ascribed values are given legitimacy (Smith 1989); while the field of **legal anthropology** aided an understanding of the nature of law (Moore 1978; Nader 1969; Roberts 1979; Sanday 1976). Such issues were also evident in the field of **ethnography**, especially in understanding the process by which things are categorized (Clifford 1988; Edgeworth 1990).

The field of **economics** is intimately concerned with the values given to things. Brown (1990) and Goldstein (1990) have suggested schemes whereby the nonmarket values of noncommodities can be expressed in terms meaningful to economists, and Greffe (1990) has addressed the specific kinds of utility offered by heritage sites. The notion of the 'public good' plugs directly into the sociological concept of the public domain, while the economic game (Luce and Raiffa 1957; Ordeshook 1986) explains the development of heritage law in the twentieth century.

Law and economics meet to merge into the field of **administration**, a kind of rule-of-thumb applied sociology in the way it meets practical need. Here, legal regulation, financial limitations and economic necessity are addressed in a programme of practical action (Carman 1990b; Cunningham 1979; Scovill *et al.* 1977). This is where we meet the concept of the law as a programme for action in relation to archaeological material (Chapter 2): where the law applies, it requires you to do something, whether in the physical realm (build something, demolish it, enclose it) or in the conceptual one (by having to think about something in a new way). In practice the response to law is administrative.

The study of modern social and political **history** has played a large part in this work, particularly in providing a background to and framework in which to comprehend the development and structure of heritage law (Hobsbawm and Ranger 1983; Perkin 1989; Shannon 1976). At the same time, the **history and philosophy of science** (Foucault 1970, 1973, 1977) – and especially that of archaeology (Levine 1986; Stocking 1987; Trigger 1989) – has provided useful insights into this field. So has **political science**, where the enquiries of Edelman into the political process and its purposes (Edelman 1967, 1971) go some way to support the findings of Cultural Theory (Thompson *et al.* 1990) on the politics of technological development (Schwarz and Thompson 1990) and thus the 'reversed' process of valuation of archaeological material by law introduced in Chapter 2.

The **philosophy** of Peter Berger – especially as it relates to the nature of modernity, the public and private domains, and the pervasiveness of bureaucracy (Berger 1973) – serves to underpin an understanding of archaeological material as a contemporary phenomenon and its treatment under law. Philosophy similarly has its part to play in grasping the nature of categorization and classification (Adams and Adams 1991) and on the problem of the identification of archaeological material from all other classes of material, although this is also a problem addressed through **psychology** (Bastick 1982).

Through AHM archaeology connects with a range of other disciplines, most of which have as their concern contemporary phenomena rather than the study of the past. Other interdisciplinary connections may be urged (Carman 1992, 416) or acted upon (Last 1991) and established connections – with history (Hodder 1986, 77–102; 1987), with ethnology (Davis 1856) and with anthropology (Binford 1962) – maintained. It is doubtful, however, whether a 'pristine' archaeology that 'is archaeology is archaeology is archaeology' (Clarke 1978, 11) or 'a viable and distinctive' archaeology (Hodder 1986, 1) can ever be created, at least in the sense of a discipline that 'stands alone', and indeed such a creation may not be desirable. Rather, what is required is a recognition that archaeology is one discipline among and touching many others. In one direction – by way of palaeoethnobotany (Renfrew 1991) and evolutionary theory (Foley 1987) – lie the biological sciences; in another, by way of ground survey, dating methods and characterization studies (Tite 1972), lie the physical and chemical sciences.

Alternative directions lead to the established links with history, ethnography and anthropology, and through AHM new links are made with those fields discussed above.

TOWARDS A 'SOCIAL ARCHAEOLOGY' OF ARCHAEOLOGY: THE CONTRIBUTION OF AHM RESEARCH

The particular value of research in AHM lies in its concern with one type of material which plays different but simultaneous roles in a number of areas of life. Here is a link back to Rubbish Theory (Thompson 1979): the connection with its origins having been broken by a period of loss or abandonment, archaeological material re-enters the world in a state in which it can be manipulated to suit the conditions of its new context. Because all of its original meanings have been stripped away, any claim on it can be entertained and any use that is sanctioned made of it. In this sense, all archaeological remains are alike, and – as argued here – the homogenizing process of preservation law serves to help make them alike and keep them that way.

Unlike the confusingly broad categories in which many of the disciplines covered above deal, that of 'archaeological material' is kept reasonably narrow and homogeneous. This being the case, its capacity to bear a number of different meanings at the same time is easier to grasp than, for example, the category of 'commodity' with which economists grapple. Archaeological remains are thus ripe for examination from a number of different disciplinary perspectives to understand the social, political and economic processes at work in relation to objects in general. By focusing on one category of material such studies can contribute meaningfully to the broadening of other disciplines. But because the focus is on archaeological material – that is, components of the archaeological record brought to light by archaeological practice – then a specific understanding of archaeology – that is, of the archaeo-logical record and archaeological practice – is fundamental. Any research that thus contributes to neighbouring disciplines necessarily also con-tributes to archaeology. This 'feedback loop' opens up the possibility of a specific understanding of the use made of archaeological material for present purposes, both in terms of the emergence and development of the discipline and the implications of that development for archaeology today. This can perhaps be described as the 'social archaeology' of archaeology.

The social, political and economic history of archaeology

The three areas of the social, the political and the economic are intertwined in the early history of archaeology. Chapters 3, 4 and 5 have opened up tantalizing glimpses of processes at work previously unremarked by historians of archaeology, particularly in relation to the explicitly political role of archaeology in the latter part of the nineteenth century.

Chapman (1989, 27) remarks on the 'surprisingly dominant Irish leadership' of the London archaeological and anthropological societies in the 1860s, but takes this issue no further. However, the close links between such figures as Talbot de Malahide (an Irish peer) and Lubbock, Franks, Pitt-Rivers and their allies (all representatives of the newly emergent professional middle class) suggests some form of political and social alliance between these forces. Using the London societies as a power base (but not the local and county societies) these figures seize control, first of archaeology, which they turn into a discipline concerned exclusively with objects (Chapter 3); then of ethnology, changing its name to anthropology to prevent any alternative strands of this discipline re-emerging to challenge their supremacy; then turn the focus of the combined disciplines of ethnology and archaeology to prehistory, which they promote by legislation; and by so doing help to consolidate the position of the professional class against the interests of aristocratic Tories and socialists who express their politics through an interest in medieval remains (Chapter 4).

While Lubbock, Pitt-Rivers, Franks and others are relatively well-known figures, the importance of those such as Talbot and others yet unnamed may have been severely underestimated. The role of such people in the development of the discipline and the other network connections they had may have contributed much to the way archaeology emerged and accordingly how it has developed – both in the nineteenth century and since. It is equally apparent that archaeology in the nineteenth century is as much about politics as it is about anything else – and overtly so. The question remains as to when archaeology ceased to be political in this overt manner, and how and why (but for a possible answer see Carman 1993). It is also apparent that the cultural associations of London – particularly the archaeological and anthropological ones – provided more than intellectual stimulation to their members; they also provided a base for political action which could be extended to an assault on the institutions of the state itself. Their success in the project of gaining political power is measured in the political importance accorded a figure such as Lubbock, who played a leading role in the Liberal Party split over Ireland and was awarded a peerage on the basis of his work in Parliament. This may have serious implications for the understanding of modern political and social history: these 'cultural' institutions become important places where the 'real' business of government and politics is carried out; it behoves us to understand what is going on there, who is doing it and with what results.

The intense political activity of early archaeology is associated with efforts to concentrate the discipline on certain areas of concern. Folklore and the study of written documents (previous mainstays of the archaeological societies) are driven out in favour of a focus on objects and field monuments alone. The link with ethnology is established and maintained in order to promote prehistory as the 'proper' concern of archaeologists. At the same time, the evolutionary paradigm is adopted as the model for interpreting the past, and by careful promotion through popular literature represents the historical dimension of late nineteenth-century Liberal ideals. By doing all this, other components of the discipline, other bodies of material, other approaches to the past, other modes of interpretation are expelled from the archaeological canon. The question thus arises, what has been forced out and what difference has this made to the development of the discipline? Is any of this retrievable, and if so, can it benefit the understanding of modern archaeology?

The questions posed here remain unanswered for most of the history of archaeology – from the 1840s to today. It seems likely that much of this information is available from a detailed and comprehensive study of the journals and other literature produced by the main London societies in the nineteenth and twentieth centuries. These languish in libraries, largely unread and mostly ignored except as the occasional source of early excavation reports. Their pages, however, contain not only the publication of formal presentations of excavation and research results, but also the records of group meetings, internal policy-making, discussions of group and disciplinary aims and how to achieve them. This **historical** research may be augmented by reference to the private papers and correspondence of the people involved, together with the investigation of those other areas of life in which they were engaged. The biography (as yet unwritten) of figures such as Talbot de Malahide may contribute much to our understanding of the origins and development of archaeology. Overarching all this, we may come to grasp the social, political and economic uses made of ancient material throughout the history of archaeology.

The political economy of archaeology

The characteristics of the public domain, in which the archaeological heritage resides, have been lightly sketched in this work. They may repay more detailed examination for what else they have to tell us about the qualities we ascribe to the archaeological heritage. In particular, since the public domain is defined by and in turn helps to define the private realm, the contents of the public domain – including the archaeological heritage – necessarily affect everyday life by defining the possibilities for social action. This can be approached from two **sociological** directions.

First, by developing the kind of public attitude research undertaken by Merriman (1991) (and in particular by using his results as a starting-point) one can investigate the overt, deliberate, covert and unwitting uses of the past made by people and institutions in their everyday lives. A possible approach here is to construct a more sophisticated question-naire that is not necessarily based on the assumption that respondents reply honestly but 'hides' the point of certain questions behind a plausible 'front', as is done in the case of some **psychological** research; and which does not concern museums and display but focuses instead on aspects of everyday life and attitudes. An alternative approach is to investigate the public and private domains and their interactions at a more generalized conceptual level and then to extrapolate relevant factors to an understanding of the contents of the public domain, including the archaeological record.

The application of **economic** game theory to the study of politics (Luce and Raiffa 1957, 253–8; Ordeshook 1986) is also of relevance to understanding the public domain and thus the archaeological heritage. First, the public domain is the realm in which political activity takes place. Second, political action (such as the passage of legislation) defines the extent of the public domain (as in the late nineteenth century; Chapters 4 and 5). However, game theory depends on the attribution of values to the outcomes of games, and these in turn represent measures of utility. The problem from the point of view of economics is that 'utility' is a 'metaphysical' concept (Robinson and Eatwell 1973, 35) which defies measurement – largely because it is an attribute of the generalized category of 'economic good'. By contrast, this work has identified at least the types of utility ascribed to the narrower category of archaeo-logical remains – amenity, scientific, monetary – which may open up the possibility of a more direct and less vague approach to understanding value. One approach may be through a detailed cross-disciplinary study of the (relatively) simple process of Treasure Trove, in which museum (scientific and amenity) values compete with market (monetary) values and which requires the British Museum to value Treasure Trove items in money terms. Here, the interaction of different value gradients (whereby the ascription of a high museum value may serve to increase the available market value) will come to light and may be made the object of investigation. By thus combining in a single object research in the areas of utility theory and game theory, the breach between micro- and macro-economic concerns (Deane 1978, 205–26) may be closed – a potentially significant contribution to the development of economics, as well as to an area of practical concern to museum archaeologists.

Political action – engaged in the public domain – frequently results in the creation of **law**. The law is thus one of the components of the public domain, and in its capacity as the creator and marker of social norms also serves to prescribe the limits of the public domain. Accordingly, as Edelman's (1967, 1971) **political science** reminded us in the second Theoretical Interlude, political action sets the limits for what is socially possible. By revealing the effect of law on archaeological material, and thus on other bodies of material and other aspects of life as well, the initial and necessary conditions for a questioning and opening up of new possibilities are created. These new possibilities will consist in the creation of new forms of social categorization – not merely to be described as already extant (the job of sociology and **anthropology**) – but also to be created anew, primarily the task of **philosophy**. The creation of any such new categories will also reflect back upon archaeology, leading to the identification and recognition of new classes of archaeological material and new categories in which to place them. Monitoring and understanding such developments in archaeological practice and their consequences will be the task of the **ethnography of archaeology**.

A focus on archaeological practice inevitably encompasses the study of archaeological institutions. Such studies involve the concerns of sociology, law and political science, as reflected in current researches (e.g. papers in Cooper *et al.* 1995; Smith 1993). Such studies can augment the results of this research by going in greater detail into particular areas of law and by concentrating on their application in practice by relevant people and institutions. Such work confirms the inevitably interdisciplinary nature of AHM. By the same token, Smith draws upon sociology and is particularly concerned with 'the role of archaeology in the State, the institutionalisation and structures of power and authority, and the interrelation between the history of archaeological theory and State and bureaucratic apparatus' (Smith 1993, 11). By focusing on AHM in Australia, her work opens up the possibility of useful comparative perspectives.

Comparative approaches
A comparative approach to heritage law across territorial boundaries was eschewed at the outset of this book because of the uncertainty of placing side by side two things that were sufficiently alike to make any comparison meaningful (Chapter 1). However, research which seeks to understand the underlying principles on which such law was and is constructed and how it affects archaeological material – such as is reported here – can be used to compare such law across territorial borders since the results will have been achieved by like means. In such research, factors such as the history of the development of archaeology, the nature of the archaeological record, the theory of law in operation and so on will already have been taken into account.

From a **historical** point of view, the political agenda behind such legislation will have come to light. In England, as shown in Chapters 3, 4 and 5, it concerned the rise of the professional middle class and the promotion of their interests through the adoption of the evolutionary paradigm as exemplified in prehistoric remains and ethnography. In the course of this process, certain elements were expelled from the discipline of archaeology and a particular vision of relevant material given prominence. Similar factors may have influenced developments in other territories, but not necessarily. Differences in the approaches taken to archaeological research between Britain and the countries of the European continent (Hodder 1991), Latin America (Gandara 1990) and perhaps Australia, the United States and elsewhere may well be explained and highlighted by such a focus.

From a **contemporary** perspective, the tripartite process of law – selection, categorization and valuation (Chapters 3, 6, 7 and 8) – may be reflected elsewhere, but again not necessarily. By the same token, the additive, incorporative and reductive, homogenizing effect of such law on archaeological material may be common to other territories, but it may not. The value ascriptions given by law – amenity and scientific, which leave monetary value as a residual category – may not be those given by law in other territories. A comparison on the basis of the principles applied here will thus assist the process of finding alternatives by allowing a degree of selection between legal systems.

Previous attempts at comparative study have been forced to limit themselves to saying, in effect, 'here they do this, there they do that'; and possibly (but rarely) 'this way is better than that'. This limits them either to making no recommendation at all or to the recommendation that a different approach be adopted wholesale, but necessarily including all its limitations and failings. Research that undertakes to reveal the underlying structures and the intended (and possibly unintended) effects of a number of legal systems as they are applied to archaeology, creates the possibility of effecting a more 'mix and match' approach, taking this element from here, that from there, and reworking or reinventing categories to suit particular circumstances. Overall, such future research will serve to open up the range of possibilities for the future of archaeology in Britain and globally.

A ONE-WORLD HEGEMONIC ARCHAEOLOGY? – A CRITIC ANSWERED

Byrne (1991) (see Chapter 1) accuses AHM of levying a 'western hegemony' on archaeology to the detriment of the discipline as a whole, and the narrow application everywhere of the four basic AHM principles listed in Chapter 1 might be likely to achieve just that. The programme of research outlined here, however, is designed specifically to avoid this result.

First, it concerns the detailed investigation of specific archaeologies and their workings within territorial boundaries. The difference of each archaeology from all others, its history and its practice, would thus be exposed to view. Second, because any understanding of individual archaeologies would be produced by like means, these understandings could be compared in a way that is meaningful and the contribution that each may make to others made clear. Where a perceived failing in one archaeology might be answered by a success in another, approaches from one archaeology would become available to be borrowed and applied in that other.

By adopting the research programme in AHM advocated here, differences between archaeologies would remain and can be promoted without detriment. The danger of producing a bland, homogenized, global archaeology by the rigid application of a single approach can thus be avoided.

Part Five

Appendices

Appendix 1
Material protected by law

COMPONENTS OF THE ARCHAEOLOGICAL HERITAGE

Wholes

Certain entire components of the archaeological heritage are deemed sufficiently capable of intuitive recognition that the law does not seek to define them. Of these, some are diagnostic of other components. A cave can be classed as a monument, as can an excavation, the site comprising a vehicle or vessel (so long as it is of 'public interest'), and a work (AMAA79, s. 61[7]). A work and a garden may also constitute an ancient monument (NH83, s. 33[8] and 34[3]). A building can be classed as a monument (AMAA79, s. 61[7]) and listed as a place of special historical or architectural interest but may need to be distinguished from any external features, attachments and related objects (PLBC90, s. 1). A building can also be classed as a place of public religious worship while at the same time any such place must be a building (RC69, s. 4[1]). Human remains constitute part of a crashed, sunk or stranded aircraft or vessel, along with 'any cargo, munitions, apparel, or personal effects which were on board . . . during its final flight or voyage' (PMR86, s. 9[1]), all such terms remaining similarly undefined. An object contained in or near to a wreck may be the factor which renders the wreck as a whole of historical or archaeological importance (PW73, s. 1). Objects may be supplied and maintained for use in a place of public religious worship (RC69, s. 5) while those no longer required may be taken by the authorities (RC69, s. 4[1]) and single objects and groups or collections of objects may be the subject of loans or grants from the NHMF (NH80, s. 3[1]). A vehicle or vessel sunk or stranded while in military service may be designated as a controlled site so long as it was sunk or stranded after 4 August 1914 (the outbreak of World War One), although its location need not be known (PMR86, s. 1[2]–[3]). Access to the site of a wrecked vessel may be restricted because of the vessel's historical or artistic importance, or because it represents a danger to life or property (PW73, s. 1–2).

Coins, photographs (including negatives) and postage stamps are subject to neither definition nor qualification. All coins, photographs and stamps are subject to a ban on export if of a minimum age (EGCO87, Sch. 10), and coins have been held not to be subject to Treasure Trove unless containing a substantial amount of precious metal (Overton82), thus removing copper and nickel coins and tokens from the scope of that law entirely.

Other components are subject to varying degrees of definition. An aircraft 'includes a hovercraft, glider or balloon' (PMR86, s. 9[1]) and those that crash or have crashed while on military service are subject to potential designation as a controlled site (PMR86, s. 1). A document includes 'any record or device by means of which information is recorded or stored' (EGCO87, s. 1[2]), which is a very wide coverage indeed. The term goods is similarly wide and includes ship's stores (IECP39, s. 3[1][a]), the import and export of which are subject to regulation and prohibition, and if of a certain age are banned from export without a licence (EGCO87, Sch. 1). For the purposes of interpreting the ancient monuments legislation, remains 'includes any trace or sign of the previous existence of the thing in question' (AMAA79, s. 61[13]) which appears to assume minimal or slight survival, and the failure to extend this meaning to the Protection of Military Remains Act 1986 may indicate an expectation of the survival of more extensive remains for the purposes of that law. Here, remains are defined as including the contents of the crashed, sunk or stranded aircraft or vessel, including human remains (PMR86, s. 9[1]) but not merely those which allow designation as a controlled site (PMR86, s. 2[9]). Wreck 'includes jetsam, flotsam, lagan and derelict found in or on the shores of the sea' (MS94, s. 510[1]) – ancient seagoing terms otherwise encountered in the common law of salvage and having the same legal meaning as their dictionary definitions. Restrictions on access to a wreck may be placed to secure its protection where it is of historical, archaeological or artistic importance (PW73, s. 1[2][b]) or because of its danger to others (PW73, s. 2[1]).

A dwelling house constitutes a 'negative' component of the archaeological heritage, since they are specifically excluded from inclusion as protected monuments (AMAA79, s. 1[4]). There is no reason, however, why a dwelling cannot legally constitute a monument even though actions that can be taken toward it are limited.

A monument is identifiable as something with an objective physical existence in the form of a large-scale landscape feature, but it also constitutes a legal category towards which actions can be directed. It is defined as:

> (a) any building, structure or work, whether above or below the surface of the land, and any cave or excavation; (b) any site comprising the remains of any such building, structure or work or

of any cave or excavation; and (c) any site comprising, or comprising the remains of, any vehicle, vessel, aircraft or other movable structure or part thereof which neither constitutes nor forms part of any work which is a monument within paragraph (a) above and any machinery attached to a monument shall be regarded as part of the monument if it could not be detached without being dismantled.

Subsection (a) above does not apply to any ecclesiastical building for the time being used for ecclesiastical purposes, and subsection (c) above does not apply – (a) to a site comprising any object or its remains unless the situation of that object or its remains in that particular site is a matter of public interest; (b) to a site comprising, or comprising the remains of, any vessel which is protected by an order under section 1 of the Protection of Wrecks Act 1973 designating an area around the site as a restricted area.

[The] site of a monument includes not only the land in or on which it is situated but also any land comprising or adjoining it which appears to the Secretary of State or a local authority, in the exercise in relation to that monument of any of their functions under [AMAA79], to be essential for the monument's support and preservation.

References . . . to a monument include references – (a) to the site of the monument in question; and (b) to a group of monuments or any part of a monument or group of monuments.

References . . . to the site of a monument – (a) are references to the monument itself where it consists of a site; and (b) in any other case include references to the monument itself. (AMAA79, s. 61[7–11])

The term 'monument' thus includes any kind of interference with the natural land surface regardless of age, plus any land it stands on, except ecclesiastical buildings in use, a 'protected wreck' under other legislation and anything that is movable unless its location in a particular place is of 'public interest'. A 'movable object' (given the size and capacity of much modern lifting gear) is a wide category, and so long as it can be removed without losing its 'public interest' then the object also ceases to be a monument for legal purposes.

An ancient monument is legally two quite separate phenomena. The first is merely a special type of the general class of monument – all scheduled monuments (AMAA79, s. 61[12][a]) and 'any other monument . . . of public interest by reason of the . . . interest attaching to it' (AMAA79, s. 61[12][b]). Limitations on what can legally constitute a monument apply here. The second meaning is at once more precise and wider, being defined as 'any structure, work, site, garden or area which

. . . is of . . . interest' (NH83, s. 33[8] and 34[3]). The limitations on the meaning of monument do not apply here. The first meaning applies in the case of all powers and duties of the Secretary of State towards ancient monuments, including making 'regulations or other instruments of a legislative character' (NH83, s. 34[4][a]) and those relating to royal palaces (NH83, s. 34[4][b]). The second applies only to functions and duties of the HBMCE (NH83, s. 33[8] referring to s. 33[1–2]).

Certain entire components also form parts of others. A man-made object is not defined but can constitute a feature for the purposes of designating a listed building (PLBC90, s. 1[3][b]). A structure is also not specifically defined, but is distinguished from a building by being subject to inspection by authorized persons (AMAA79, s. 40). Like a building it can constitute a monument (AMAA79, s. 1[4]) and an ancient monument (NH83, s. 33[8] and 34[3]) although it is not capable of protection if it is occupied as a dwelling house (AMAA79, s. 1[4]). If affixed to a building, it can constitute a feature for listing purposes (PLBC90, s. 1[3][b]), becomes part of the listed building (PLBC90, s. 1[5][a]) and also becomes part of the listed building if it is part of the land on which the listed building stands so long as the structure is of a certain age (PLBC90, s. 1[5][b]).

Parts

The exterior of a building is capable of contributing to the architectural and historic interest of groups of buildings (PLBC90, s. 1[3][a]). Features external to a building, comprising man-made objects or structures fixed to it or part of the land within the curtilage of the building, may contribute towards the desirability of preserving the building (PLBC90, s. 1[3][b]). Machinery can constitute part of a monument (AMAA79, s. 61[7]). It can be an offence to enter the hatch or opening of an aircraft or vessel (PMR86, s. 2[2][b]). Ship's stores constitute part of goods (IECP39, s. 3[1][a]).

Attributes

The age of an item can be significant for its inclusion in legal coverage. All objects and structures which are part of the land around a listed building are included in the legal protection so long as they have been part of that land since at least 1 July 1948 (PLBC90, s. 1[5][b]). All goods and postage stamps older than 50 years are subject to an export ban, as are photographs over 60 years old. Coins minted prior to 1947 but less than 100 years old are similarly subject to an export ban (EGCO87, Sch. 1). Aircraft that crashed on military service are capable of legal protection (PMR86, s. 1[1]), as are vessels that were sunk or stranded on such service (PMR86, s. 1[2]). Military service covers being 'in service with, or being used for . . . the armed forces' of the United Kingdom or any other country (PMR86, s. 9[2][a]). In the case of aircraft but not ships, it includes delivery for future service with UK forces (PMR86, s. 9[2][b]). There is no specification that the aircraft or ship should have crashed, sunk or been stranded while on active military service – that is, in action against an enemy aircraft or vessel or enemy ground forces. It does, however, exclude civilian aircraft and shipping not in the service of military forces. Precious metal for Treasure Trove is limited to gold and silver, excluding other materials however valuable (Overton82).

CONTEXTS

Certain contexts are immediately recognizable without specific definition and are clearly external to a unitary component of the archaeological heritage. The architectural or historical interest of a group of buildings can be contributed to by the exterior of any one building within the group (PLBC90, s. 1[3][a]). Similarly, a group of monuments clearly comprises more than one single monument (AMAA79, s. 61[10][b]). Land adjoining monuments is included within the site of a monument (AMAA79, s. 61[9]) and may be equivalent to associated land which can be taken into ownership or guardianship along with the monument to which it relates (AMAA79, s. 61[6] and 15[6]).

Land adjoining monuments may include the seabed (AMAA79, s. 53[3]) which is any area submerged at mean high water spring tides (PMR86, s. 9[1]), a definition which will include the seashore but this is specifically excluded for the purposes of the ancient monuments legislation (AMAA79, s. 53[7]). Monuments on the seabed may be protected (AMAA79, s. 53[1]), but the distinction made between the Protection of Military Remains Act and the ancient monuments law prohibits dual coverage of military remains on the seashore. The sea includes the seabed as defined along with creeks, estuaries and 'arms of the sea' (PMR86, s. 9[1] and PW73, s. 3[1]).

Site is a more ambiguous concept. That of a wrecked vessel is included 'within the area to be designated in or on which [the monument] is situated but also any land comprising or adjoining it which appears . . . to be essential for the monument's support and preservation' (AMAA79, s. 61[9]) while at the same time it is included as part of the monument itself and indeed may comprise that monument (AMAA79, s. 61[10]). Accordingly, the site of a component of the archaeological heritage can both contain and be contained within that component, as well as comprising the component itself. A site is usually not a site in itself but is instead the site of something else, except for the purposes of the HBMCE, when it can be an ancient monument (NH83, s. 33[8] and 34[3]). Terms defined in terms of the concept of site are also somewhat ambiguous. The area around a site may be designated a restricted area (PW73, s. 1[1]) and an area of itself can constitute an ancient monument for the HBMCE (NH83, s. 33[8] and 34[3]). A distance from a site measures the extent of any such restricted area (PW73, s. 1[2][a]) while it must be sufficient to ensure the protection of the wreck (PW73, s. 1[2][b]).

Other limits are more easily distinguished. The high water mark of an ordinary spring tide marks the limit of a restricted area (PW73, s. 1[2]), while the ancient monuments legislation is extended to the Scilly Isles, a recognizable geographical location (AMAA79, s. 52). United Kingdom waters comprise those within the seaward limits of the United Kingdom (which is subject to international agreement) (PMR86, s. 9[1] and PW73, s. 3[1]) while international waters comprise those outside the seaward limits of any territory, UK or otherwise (PMR86, s. 9[1]). Only sites within UK waters are capable of designation as restricted areas (PW73, s. 1[1]) while those military remains lying partly in and partly outside UK waters are to have their two parts treated separately (PMR86, s. 9[3]).

ANCILLARIES
Vehicles and vessels used for the conveyance of prohibited goods are outside the definition of the components of the archaeological heritage but nevertheless subject to regulation (IECP39, s. 3[2]). Equipment can be included in a power of entry (AMAA79, s. 44[4]) and is excluded from use in a restricted area (PW73, s. 1[3][b]).

Appendix 2
Legal categories

LEGAL CATEGORIES

Types of monument

A monument is both a physical object and also a legal category which carries legal consequences. In particular, a monument can be included in the schedule of monuments of national importance (AMAA79, s. 1[3]) and be the subject of arrangements for its future well being (AMAA79, s. 30[3]) unless these are no longer practicable (AMAA79, s. 30[4]).

An ancient monument is a special and particular kind of monument, and one of two kinds – either a specific type of feature (NH83, s. 33[8][a] and 34[3]) (the wider definition); or a structure or digging that is deemed to be of historical or archaeological interest (AMAA79, s. 61[12][b]) or one that has been placed on the schedule of monuments of national importance (AMAA79, s. 61[12][a]) (the narrower definition). In other words, a monument (in general) can become specifically an ancient monument by the process of categorization – thus looking forward to a potential value ascription; it does not follow, however, that all ancient monuments as legally defined can be treated alike. The preservation of those more broadly defined (NH83, s. 33[8] and 34[3]) is a duty of the Historic Buildings and Monuments Commission for England (HBMCE) (NH83, s. 33[1][a]), who are also charged with promoting public knowledge and preservation of them (NH83, s. 33[1][c]). The functions of the HBMCE in relation to them cover the provision of educational services, information and advice, and to carry out and pay for research into them, and to maintain appropriate records (NH83, s. 33[2][a–d]). Only ancient monuments in the narrower sense (AMAA79, s. 61[12]) (as opposed to monuments in general) can be taken into guardianship (AMAA79, s. 12), acquired by the state or local authorities for preservation (AMAA79, s. 10–11) or be made the subject of certain agreements concerning land (AMAA79, s. 17). The Secretary of State (through the HBMCE) may advise others concerning them (AMAA79, s. 25[1]), may superintend work on them if invited to do so by the owner (AMAA79, s. 25[2]) and may authorize entry on to land for the purposes of inspecting them (AMAA79, s. 26[1]).

A scheduled monument is one that has been placed on the list of monuments of national importance (AMAA79, s. 1[11]). It is deemed to be an ancient monument (AMAA79, s. 61[12]), constitutes a protected place (AMAA79, s. 42[2]), and may be located on Crown land (AMAA79, s. 50[1][a]) or on the seabed (AMAA79, s. 53[1]), but need be on neither.

A protected monument is any scheduled monument or any monument under state or local authority guardianship (a guardianship monument) or owned by the state or a local authority (AMAA79, s. 28[3]). It is an offence to damage or destroy any such monument (AMAA79, s. 28[1]).

A protected wreck is specifically excluded from inclusion as a monument (AMAA79, s. 61[8]). The purpose of a restricted area order is to protect the wreck so designated from interference (PW73, s. 1[2]).

Buildings

A listed building is any building included in the list compiled by the Secretary of State (PLBC90, s. 1[5]). No such building can be demolished, altered or extended without authorization (PLBC90, s. 7). The list so compiled is one of buildings of special architectural and historic interest in England (PLBC90, s. 1[1–2]), which must be published to various interested authorities (PLBC90, s. 2[1]) and constitutes a legal charge on the land on which the building stands (thus binding all owners and tenants) (PLBC90, s. 2[2]).

A historic building is one to which the HBMCE owes duties and to which the functions of the HBMCE relate. It is otherwise undefined. The HBMCE owe it duties of preservation (NH83, s. 33[1][a]) and of promotion of public knowledge of it and its preservation (PLBC90, s. 33[1][c]). The functions of the HBMCE in relation to it cover the provision of educational services, information and advice, to carry out and pay for research into it and to maintain appropriate records (NH83, s. 33[2][a–d]).

Ecclesiastical property is excluded from being a monument if used for ecclesiastical purposes (AMAA79, s. 61[8]). It includes 'any land belonging to . . . the Church of England, or being or forming part of a church . . . or the site of such a church, or being or forming part of a burial ground' subject to the jurisdiction of the Church of England (AMAA79, s. 51[5]). A place of public religious worship must be a building held in trust for charity and includes a church (RC69, s. 4[1]).

Movable objects

Treasure consists of items constituted of a substantial amount of gold or silver (Overton80 and Overton82). It is the responsibility of the Coroner to inquire into such treasure and the circumstances of its discovery (CA88, s. 30).

Prohibited goods are any goods 'imported, exported, carried . . . or shipped as ship's stores in contravention' of the export controls legislation or any law relating to trade with an enemy, or any goods 'brought to any quay or any other place' for the purpose of such import or export (IECP39, s. 3[1][a–b]). All such goods are subject to forfeiture to the authorities (IECP39, s. 3[1]). Scheduled goods are those currently prohibited from export (ECGO87, s. 1[2]–2).

Locations

An area of archaeological importance (AAI) is one so designated by the Secretary of State (AMAA79, s. 33[1]) or a local authority (AMAA79, s. 33[2] and AMAA79, s. 61[1]). It is a protected place (AMAA79, s. 42[2]) and can only be reduced in size by varying the designation order (AMAA79, s. 33[4]). A conservation area is an area 'of special architectural or historic interest, the character or appearance of which it is desirable to preserve or enhance' and so designated by a local authority (PLBC90, s. 69 and 91[1]). The HBMCE owes them a duty of promoting their preservation and enhancing their character or appearance (NH83, s. 33[1][b]) while the functions of the HBMCE include the provision of education, information and advice concerning them and carrying out and paying for research into them (NH83, s. 33[2][a–c]).

A restricted area is the site of a wreck of historical or archaeological interest so designated by the Secretary of State (PW73, s. 1[1]). Its distance around the wreck must be specified in the designation order (PW73, s. 1[2][a]) and must be sufficient to ensure protection of the wreck from interference (PW73, s. 1[2][b]). The order designating the area can only be revoked if there is no longer a wreck to protect (PW73, s. 3[2]). It is an offence to commit certain acts within such an area without a licence from the Secretary of State (PW73, s. 1[3]). A prohibited area is the site of a wreck that is a danger to life or property so designated by the Secretary of State (PW73, s. 2[1]). It is an offence to enter such an area (PW73, s. 2[3]). A controlled site is one so designated by the Secretary of State containing a vessel or aircraft which was sunk or stranded or which crashed while on military service (PMR86, s. 1[2] and 9[1]). No location can be so designated if it lies outside United Kingdom waters and is either less than 200 years old or an objection is lodged (PMR86, s. 1[4]). It must be no larger than is necessary to protect or preserve the remains (PMR86, s. 1[5]), which is the opposite of the requirement in relation to a restricted area. It is an offence to commit certain acts within such an area (PMR86, s. 2). A protected place is both (a) 'any place which is . . . the site of a scheduled monument or any monument under the guardianship of the . . . State or a local authority . . . or situated in an area of archaeological importance' (AMAA79, s. 42[2]) and (b) the location of the remains contained within a controlled site so long as it is within United Kingdom waters (PMR86, s. 1[6]). It is an offence to use a metal detector at such a place (AMAA79, s. 42[1]) and to commit certain other acts therein (PMR86, s. 2).

Ancillary categories
Crown land means any land owned by the monarch or the Duchy of Lancaster or the Duchy of Cornwall, or any land owned or held by a Government department (AMAA79, s. 50[4]). Monuments on Crown land may be scheduled (AMAA79, s. 50[1][a]) and accordingly all restrictions or powers applicable to scheduled monuments shall apply (which is against the normal practice of Crown exemption) (AMAA79, s. 50[1][b]). Similarly, Crown land may be designated a controlled site (PMR86, s. 1[7]). However, any operations to be carried out on Crown land also requires the specific consent of the Crown (AMAA79, s. 50[3–4]).

Curtilage is a term from English land law relating to the extent of that land. Features forming part of the land within the curtilage of a property may be taken into account for the purposes of the listing of a building (PLBC90, s. 1[3][b]). Objects and structures which have been part of the land within the curtilage of the property since 1 July 1948 will form part of a listed building (PLBC90, s. 1[5][b]). Easements relate to rights attaching to a property such as access, light and so on. The Secretary of State has the right to acquire easements over land adjoining monuments which are in state ownership or guardianship (AMAA79, s. 16). Such easements may be granted by the limited owners of such land (AMAA79, s. 18[2]).

CONSEQUENCES OF CATEGORIZATION

Allocation to institutions

State authorities
The Crown is the highest authority in the British constitution. While Parliament is always supreme, this is a Parliament comprising Lords, Commons and the Crown in the person of the monarch. Accordingly, all state organs and offices are subsidiary to the Crown. It is the Crown which holds the right to the title of Treasure Trove items. These are items only of gold or silver (Overton82), never of antiquities of other metals (Overton80). The Crown also holds the right to acquire the

rights to wrecks through purchase by the Board of Trade out of the proceeds of salvage monies (MS94, s. 528). The Board of Trade also holds the power to control imports and exports (IECP39, s. 1). The Treasury must give its consent to the purchase by the Board of Trade of wrecks on behalf of the Crown (MS94, s. 528). Officers of the Valuation Office of the Inland Revenue Department of the Treasury are authorized to enter land for the purposes of survey and valuation in connection with the proposed acquisition of any land (AMAA79, s. 43[2]).

For historical reasons and the purposes of constitutional nicety, there is deemed to be only one Secretary of State, although the functions of that office – comprising not only functions *sensu strictu* but also powers and duties (AMAA79, s. 61[1]) – are now shared by a number of individuals. The majority of responsibilities for the archaeological heritage and historic environment are currently held by the National Heritage Secretary, although many also devolve on to the Environment Secretary and some on to the President of the Board of Trade and the Transport Secretary. The Secretary of State together with the Chancellor of the Duchy of Lancaster (who may be the same individual) are the responsible Ministers for the National Heritage Memorial Fund (NHMF) and are empowered to pay state funds in to that body (NH80, s. 2[1]). Their consent is required to allow the NHMF to retain any property on which work has been funded by the NHMF (NH80, s. 4[3]) and gifts made to the NHMF (NH80, s. 5[3]).

The duties of the Secretary of State (that is, those functions that must be performed) comprise those that relate to scheduled and guardianship monuments, and to listed buildings. The first comprise the preparation of the schedule of monuments of national importance (AMAA79, s. 1) and to publish the schedule when first compiled (AMAA79, s. 1[7]), the requirement to inform owners of monuments affected by any change in the schedule (AMAA79, s. 1[6]), to superintend work on scheduled monuments when thought advisable (AMAA79, s. 25[2]) and to compensate developers for their financial losses in respect of grants of scheduled monument consent (AMAA79, s. 7–9). Duties in respect of guardianship monuments comprise the requirement to maintain them (AMAA79, s. 13[1]) and to allow public access (AMAA79, s. 19[1]). Duties in respect of listed buildings comprise the preparation of the list (PLBC90, s. 1), and to take into account various additional factors when doing so (PLBC90, s. 1[2–3]). There is a duty to consult certain statutorily authorized bodies before finally approving the list (PLBC90, s. 1[4]) or prior to making a restricted area order (PW73, s. 1[4]). In addition, local authorities must be notified of the appointment of any investigating authority for an AAI within their area (AMAA79, s. 34[3]).

The many and wide non-mandatory powers of the Secretary of State relate to duties in relation to monuments, buildings, locations and movable objects. These include the power to exclude and add monuments to the schedule (AMAA79, s. 1[5]), to publish amendments to the schedule which only then become evidence of a monument's inclusion (AMAA79, s. 1[7–8]), to grant written consent to works to be carried out on a specific scheduled monument (AMAA79, s. 2[3]) or a class of scheduled monuments (AMAA79, s. 3), to modify or revoke any such consent (AMAA79, s. 4[3]), to conduct urgent work on a scheduled monument for its preservation (AMAA79, s. 5), and to authorize entry on to land where a scheduled monument is situated (AMAA79, s. 6). The Secretary of State has the power to acquire an ancient monument compulsorily (AMAA79, s. 10), by agreement with the owner (AMAA79, s. 11[1]) or by gift (AMAA79, s. 11[3]) and to accept guardianship of an ancient monument (AMAA79, s. 12[1]). Powers in relation to an ancient monument extend to any land adjoining that monument (AMAA79, s. 15), to requisition information concerning the ownership of land (AMAA79, s. 57) and to the power to acquire easements (AMAA79, s. 16). The Secretary of State has a general power to control and manage guardianship monuments (AMAA79, s. 13[2]) and to enter into agreements with the owners of monuments – a necessary corollary of the power to accept monuments into guardianship, although this is also a power more generally applicable (AMAA79, s. 17[1] and s. 17[4]). The general powers to control and manage guardianship monuments (AMAA79, s. 13[2]) extend to powers to control public access thereto (AMAA79, s. 19[2]), to make provision or provide facilities for public access (AMAA79, s. 20), and to oversee local authority regulations concerning restrictions on public access (AMAA79, s. 19[8]). Once under control, the ownership or guardianship of a monument may be transferred to or from a local authority (AMAA79, s. 21[1]) subject to the consent of the owner of a guardianship monument (AMAA79, s. 21[2]). In addition to all these, the Secretary of State may give advice on matters relating to ancient monuments (AMAA79, s. 25[1]), charge for such advice (AMAA79, s. 25[3]) and superintend works on ancient monuments (AMAA79, s. 25[2]). The general power to dispose of land is also granted (AMAA79, s. 30[1]) although in the case of land including a monument, this must be done only on certain terms (AMAA79, s. 30[3]).

A building preservation notice issued by a local authority can be overturned by the Secretary of State (PLBC90, s. 3[2–6]) or the Secretary of State may issue a certificate stating that a building will not be listed (PLBC90, s. 6). The Secretary of State may make grants to the Redundant Churches Fund (RC69, s. 1) and may be authorized by the court to take a place of public religious worship as a gift or otherwise than for full consideration (RC69, s. 4).

The Secretary of State has the power to designate AAIs (AMAA79, s. 33[1]), vessels for protection (PMR86, s. 1[2][a]), controlled sites (PMR86, s. 1[2][b]), restricted areas (PW73, s. 1[1]) and prohibited areas (PW73, s. 2[1]); and to substitute a later date than 1914 (but no earlier one) for the protection of vessels and aircraft lost while on military service (PMR86, s. 1[8]). Consequent powers include those of revoking or varying orders designating AAIs, but only so long as the AAI is reduced in size (requiring a new contiguous AAI to be created to increase the area so covered) (AMAA79, s. 33[4]) and to appoint (AMAA79, s. 34[1]) or cancel the appointment of an investigating authority for an AAI (AMAA79, s. 34[2]), to limit its powers (AMAA79, s. 38[8]), including those of entry (AMAA79, s. 39[3]), or – where none has been appointed – to act in that capacity (AMAA79, s. 34[4]). The Secretary of State may receive operations notices where the developer of an AAI is the local authority (AMAA79, s. 35[5]) and issue regulations on the action to be taken on the receipt of an operations notice (AMAA79, s. 36[6]), including the power to authorize entry to property which is the site of operations within an AAI (AMAA79, s. 40). The Secretary of State may also simply direct that limitations on the operations to be carried out within an AAI shall not apply (AMAA79, s. 37[2–4]). Licences for acts in restricted areas may be granted (PW73, s. 1[3]); similarly, licences for work to be carried out in a protected place or a controlled site (PMR86, s. 4[1]) and such grants may be made the subject of payment (PMR86, s. 5[3]). Authority may be given to a person to search and seize property in relation to offences committed in a protected place or controlled site (PMR86, s. 6[8]).

The Secretary of State may give written consent to the use of a metal detector on a protected place (AMAA79, s. 42[1]), may authorize persons to survey and value land for the purpose of acquisition (AMAA79, s. 43[2]), and authorize those persons to search and bore over the objections of any statutory undertakers holding that land (AMAA79, s. 44[9]). In terms of archaeological investigations, relevant powers are to finance them (AMAA79, s. 45[1]) and publish them (AMAA79, s. 45[3]). The Secretary of State may make grants to the Architectural Heritage Fund (AMAA79, s. 49) and may also receive grants and loans for the acquisition or taking into guardianship of monuments (NH80, s. 3[6]).

'Negative' powers of the Secretary of State consist of the lack of power to include dwellings in the schedule of monuments of national importance (AMAA79, s. 1[4]) and not to hold any object of archaeological or historic interest without the consent of the owner

(AMAA79, s. 54[2]). Actions of the Secretary of State in relation to the designation of an AAI or the grant of scheduled monument consent are subject to judicial review (AMAA79, s. 55), but not those relating to guardianship monuments or regulations concerning operations within an AAI.

Quasi-state institutions
Certain functions exercisable by the Secretary of State for the Environment (one specific 'member' of the unitary Secretary of State) in respect of ancient monuments and historic buildings situated in England have been delegated to the Historic Buildings and Monuments Commission for England (HBMCE) (NH83, s. 34), a body to be at least partly funded from the Treasury by the Secretary of State (NH83, s. 38). The functions of the HBMCE include powers and duties (AMAA79, s. 61[1]) but not those 'of making regulations or other instruments of a legislative character' (NH83, s. 34[4][a]) or those relating to royal palaces (NH83, s. 34[4][b]). Accordingly, the HBMCE has no powers in relation to scheduling or designation orders of any kind, from which it follows that monuments falling within the wider definition of 'ancient monument' (NH83, s. 33[8] and 34[3]) but outside the definition of 'monument' (AMAA79, s. 61[7–10]) are not eligible for scheduling: this exclusion covers flint scatters, refuse spread over fields, relict landscapes and so on. The three duties of the HBMCE are limited to England and are 'to secure the preservation of ancient monuments [in the broader sense] and historic buildings' (NH83, s. 33[1][a]), 'to promote the preservation and enhancement of . . . conservation areas' (NH83, s. 33[1][b]) and 'to promote the public's enjoyment of, and advance their knowledge of, ancient monuments and historic buildings . . . and their preservation' (NH83, s. 33[1][c]). These duties are subsidiary to a narrower range of functions (NH83, s. 33[1]). These functions – to which must be added those delegated by the Secretary of State for the Environment – cover the provision of educational facilities and services, the giving of advice and the funding of research in relation to ancient monuments, historic buildings and conservation areas (NH83, s. 33[2][a–c]), the maintenance of records in relation to ancient monuments and historic buildings (NH83, s. 33[2][d]) but not conservation areas, and the giving of guidance to local planning authorities in relation to the listing of buildings (PLBC90, s. 1[1]). For the purpose of exercising these functions, the HBMCE is granted certain powers, including those to make contracts, to acquire and dispose of property in the form of both land for offices and other property, to do other things that are deemed necessary or expedient by the HBMCE (NH83, s. 33[5]), to charge for their services (NH83, s. 33[6]), with the consent of the Secretary of State

to borrow money (NH83, s. 33[7]), to form companies (NH83, s. 35), to authorize persons to enter land in order to inspect it (NH83, s. 36), and may be empowered by the Secretary of State to take responsibility for monuments only partly situated in England (NH83, s. 37).

The Royal Commission on Historical Monuments for England (RCHME) was established in 1908 to record the historic monuments and buildings of England. Accordingly, the RCHME may authorize persons to enter the site of any operations in an AAI for the purpose of recording matters of archaeological or historical interest (AMAA79, s. 40[b])'.

The National Heritage Memorial Fund (NHMF) has been established in succession to the National Land Fund as a 'memorial to those who have died for the United Kingdom' (NH80, s. 1[1]) and is administered by and vested in its Trustees (NH80, s. 1[2]) who owe a mandatory duty to prepare and lay accounts yearly before the Ministers responsible for the Fund, who in turn must lay them before Parliament (NH80, s. 7). The purpose of the Fund is to make grants and loans to eligible institutions for the purposes of the acquisition, maintenance or preservation of land, buildings, structures, objects, and collections of importance to the national heritage (NH80, s. 3[1–2]) and having regard to their public access and display (NH80, s. 3[3]), but not in respect of former places of public religious worship (RC69, s. 6). In this respect, the Trustees may impose conditions on such grants or loans (NH80, s. 3[4]), use the monies of the Fund to acquire, maintain or preserve any property themselves (NH80, s. 4[1]) and accept gifts to the Fund but may retain such property only so long as the Ministers responsible for overseeing the Fund may allow (NH80, s. 4[3]), or invest unused funds with the consent of the Treasury (NH80, s. 6). The institutions eligible for grants or loans from the Fund are museums, art galleries or libraries holding collections of objects (NH80, s. 3[6][a]), bodies preserving public amenities (NH80, s. 3[6][b]), nature conservation bodies (NH80, s. 3[6][c]) and the Secretary of State in respect of guardianship monuments or the acquisition of historic buildings or ancient monuments (NH80, s. 3[6][d]).

The Coroner has jurisdiction concerning Treasure Trove inquests and has a duty to enquire into any treasure found in his district and who may be the Finders of that treasure (CA88, s. 30). The Coroner's jury has to decide as a question of fact if the items in question contain a substantial amount of gold or silver (Overton82).

Like the Secretary of State, local authorities – that is, county or district councils (AMAA79, s. 61[1]) – have duties and powers in respect of the historic environment. While the scheduling of monuments is exclusively the province of the national authority, local authorities have the power to acquire ancient monuments (in the narrower sense of a particular type of monument [AMAA79, s. 61(12)]) by agreement (AMAA79, s. 11[2]) and by way of gift (AMAA79, s. 11[3]), and also the power to accept such ancient monuments into guardianship (AMAA79, s. 12[2]). The power to list buildings is also reserved to the national authority, but is carried out 'with a view to the guidance' of local authorities in respect to their 'functions . . . in relation to buildings of special architectural or historic interest' (PLBC90, s. 1[1]). Accordingly, local authorities owe a duty to such buildings within their jurisdiction and listing by the Secretary of State marks such buildings as the object of that duty. Other explicit duties (that is, mandatory acts) follow either from discretionary powers or that wider duty. The power to accept monuments into guardianship creates a duty to maintain any such guardianship monument (AMAA79, s. 13[1]) and the acquisition or acceptance of guardianship over an ancient monument carries with it the right of public access (AMAA79, s. 19[1]). The power to dispose of land comprising an ancient monument which has been acquired or taken into guardianship carries the duty to consult with the Secretary of State prior to disposal (AMAA79, s. 30[1]) and only to do so on such terms as will in their opinion ensure the preservation of the monument (AMAA79, s. 30[3–4]). The listing of a building by the Secretary of State requires the relevant local authority to notify this fact to the owners of the building (PLBC90, s. 2[3][b]).

Local authorities have the power to control and manage ancient monuments in their guardianship (AMAA79, s. 13[2]), to enter into guardianship agreements (AMAA79, s. 17[2]), and to regulate public access to monuments in their care or ownership (AMAA79, s. 19[2]) subject to confirmation by the Secretary of State (AMAA79, s. 19[8]). They may acquire or take into guardianship land adjoining such monuments (AMAA79, s. 15) together with easements over such land (AMAA79, s. 16), and accordingly have powers to requisition information concerning the ownership of land (AMAA79, s. 57). They may provide facilities for public access (AMAA79, s. 20), and contribute towards the cost of preservation, maintenance or management of any ancient monument (in the narrower sense) in their area (AMAA79, s. 24[4]). A local authority may designate an AAI (AMAA79, s. 33[2]), subject to judicial review (AMAA79, s. 55), and accordingly is empowered to receive an operations notice (AMAA79, s. 35[5]) unless the local authority is itself the developer, in which case the notice must be delivered to the Secretary of State (AMAA79, s. 35[5][c]), and to institute proceedings for operations within an AAI for non-service of an appropriate operations notice (AMAA79, s. 35[10]). They have the power to finance (AMAA79, s. 45[2]) and publish the results of

(AMAA79, s. 45[3]) archaeological investigations, but may not un-
reasonably hold objects of archaeological or historic interest without the
owner's consent (AMAA79, s. 54[2]). Any local authority other than a
county council may serve a building preservation notice (thus providing
a temporary listing) (PLBC90, s. 3[1]) but this may be overturned by the
Secretary of State (PLBC90, s. 3[6]). Certain local authorities possess
powers of compulsory purchase (AMAA79, s. 39[5]) which entitle them
to serve an operations notice in respect of proposed works in an AAI
(AMAA79, s. 39[1]), although not without the consent of the Crown in
the case of Crown land (AMAA79, s. 50[3]), and to authorize entry on
to land proposed to be acquired for the purpose of valuation (AMAA79,
s. 43[2]).

Any person the Secretary of State considers competent to carry out
archaeological investigations may be appointed by the Secretary of State
as an investigating authority in relation to an AAI (AMAA79, s. 34[1]).
The Secretary of State may also cancel any such appointment
(AMAA79, s. 34[2]), and if no such appointment is made, the Secretary
of State is the relevant authority (AMAA79, s. 34[4] and 41[2]). While
local authorities must be informed of any such appointment or
cancellation (AMAA79, s. 34[3]), they do not have a similar power.
Investigating authorities may delegate their powers in writing to another
(AMAA79, s. 34[5]). The investigating authority may authorize works
within an AAI (AMAA79, s. 37[1]), and where operations within an
AAI are due to commence after clearance of the site, the developer must
inform the investigating authority of the end of clearance operations
(AMAA79, s. 35[7]). The investigating authority has an absolute power
to enter the site of any operations within an AAI for the purposes of
inspection (AMAA79, s. 38[1][a] and 39[1]), observation (AMAA79, s.
38[1][b]) and to exercise its right to excavate (AMAA79, s. 38[6]). In
order to exercise its right to excavate the site of any operations within
an AAI (AMAA79, s. 38[2]), the investigating authority must serve
notice of its intention on the developer (AMAA79, s. 38[3][a]), on the
local authority and on the Secretary of State (AMAA79, s. 38[3][b]) no
later than four weeks after the date of service of the operations notice by
the developer (AMAA79, s. 38[3]). After a further six weeks (earlier if
agreed between the investigating authority and the developer
[AMAA79, s. 38(4)(c)] or clearance operations are being carried out in
advance of works [AMAA79, s. 38(5)]), the investigating authority has
four months and two weeks to excavate the site (AMAA79, s. 38[4]). All
an investigating authority's powers of entry and excavation are
ultimately subject to control by the Secretary of State (AMAA79, s.
38[8] and 39[3]).

The Church of England – to which all ecclesiastical property belongs

(AMAA79, s. 51[5]) – is represented by its various arms. The Church Commissioners are the body on which any notice concerning ecclesiastical property must be served (AMAA79, s. 51[1]), are generally to be treated as the holders of such land in fee simple (AMAA79, s. 51[2]), and are both the recipients of compensation (AMAA79, s. 51[3]) and the payers of compensation (AMAA79, s. 51[4]) where relevant. The Diocesan Synod has responsibility for schemes for the inspection of churches in its area (ICM55, s. 1[1]). Where such inspections do not take place at least every five years, the parochial church council is required to take this on (ICM55, s. 2[1]), and where no such council exists, the churchwardens shall act in its stead (ICM55, s. 4). The advisory committee for the care of churches in a diocese (ICM55, s. 6) must approve the appointment of the architect obliged to report on the condition of churches once in every five years (ICM55, s.1[2][c]). The architect so appointed must report to the archdeacon and the parochial church council (ICM55, s. 1[2][d]). Where others fail to act in relation to the inspection of churches, the archdeacon is empowered to act in their stead (ICM55, s. 2).

Statutory undertakers are persons authorized by statute law to provide means of transport or power or water supply (AMAA79, s. 61[2][a]), certain named bodies carrying out such functions (AMAA79, s. 61[2][b]) and others to be included by the Secretary of State (AMAA79, s. 61[2][c]). They are qualified to issue an operations notice for work within an AAI (AMAA79, s. 36[2]) and, if it will interfere with their operations, are authorized to object to any searching or boring of a site by officers of the Inland Revenue Valuation Office (AMAA79, s. 44[9][b]).

Interpretation powers of institutions

The opinion of the Secretary of State determines the national importance of monuments (AMAA79, s. 1[3]), the public interest of an ancient monument (AMAA79, s. 61[12]) and the historical, archaeological or artistic importance of a wreck (PW73, s. 1[1]). Together with that of the HBMCE the opinion of the Secretary of State determines the special architectural or historic interest of buildings (PLBC90, s. 1[1]), and the opinion of the HBMCE alone may judge the historic, architectural, traditional, artistic, or archaeological interest of ancient monuments and the historic or architectural interest of buildings (NH83, s. 33[8]). The opinion of a local authority may decide the architectural or historic interest of a building subject to the overriding opinion of the Secretary of State (PLBC90, s. 3[2]), and the opinion of the Trustees of the NHMF decides the outstanding scenic, historic, aesthetic, architectural or scientific interest of items that may be the subject of grants or loans

(NH80, s. 3[1]) and the importance of such items to the national heritage (NH80, s. 3[2]).

Independent bodies and persons
The Redundant Churches Fund (RC69, s. 1) and the Architectural Heritage Fund (AMAA79, s. 49[1–2]) are both eligible for grants from the Secretary of State. Persons or bodies thereof who have special knowledge of or interest in buildings of architectural or historic interest must be consulted by the Secretary of State before approving any listed buildings (PLBC90, s. 1[4]).

A developer is 'any person carrying out or proposing to carry out any operations' (AMAA79, s. 35[3] and 41[1][a]). It is the duty of the developer to serve an operations notice in respect of works to be carried out within an AAI (AMAA79, s. 35[5]) and to notify the investigating authority of the end of clearance operations (AMAA79, s. 35[7]). If some other person – such as the owner of the land (AMAA79, s. 36[1]) – serves the operations notice, then the developer must be authorized to carry out the works referred to in the accompanying certificate (AMAA79, s. 36[3][c]).

Owners and occupiers of property share a number of legislative provisions in common. They must be informed of the entry of a monument on to the schedule (AMAA79, s. 1[6]), of a building on to the list (PLBC90, s. 2[3][b]), of any class order of scheduled monument consent affecting them (AMAA79, s. 3[4]), of any works to preserve a monument (AMAA79, s. 5[1]) and must give consent to the erection of markers (AMAA79, s. 6[5]). They may require evidence of a person's authority to enter their property (AMAA79, s. 44[3]) but may be required by the Secretary of State or the local authority to give proof of their interest in any land (AMAA79, s. 57[1]). The owner of an object must give consent to its custody where this is 'unreasonable' (AMAA79, s. 54[2]) and must consent to any transfer of a guardianship monument between the Secretary of State and a local authority or vice versa (AMAA79, s. 21[2]). The grant of a licence to conduct prohibited works on a controlled site or a vessel given protection does not affect ownership rights (AMAA79, s. 4[6]). An owner, however, cannot grant the guardianship of a monument without the occupier also being party to the guardianship deed (AMAA79, s. 12[4]), and where there is no occupier must be informed of any restrictions on permission to conduct unauthorized works in an AAI (AMAA79, s. 37[4]). An occupier alone has the power to enter into agreement with the Secretary of State or a local authority in relation to an ancient monument (AMAA79, s. 17[1–2]) and need be the only person to be notified of restrictions on permission to carry out unauthorized works in an AAI (AMAA79, s.

37[4]). The occupier's consent is required for entry to any land except for the purposes of valuation (AMAA79, s. 44[1]). Persons with interests in property include those who are owners and occupiers (AMAA79, s. 12[3] and 61[3]) but not exclusively. Any such person is qualified to receive compensation concerning a scheduled monument (AMAA79, s. 7[1] and 9[1]), may appoint the Secretary of State (AMAA79, s. 12[1]) or a local authority (AMAA79, s. 12[2]) the guardian of an ancient monument together with any adjoining land (AMAA79, s. 15), and may terminate such guardianship unless bound by the guardianship deed (AMAA79, s. 14[1]). Any person with an interest in land may issue the certificate to accompany an operations notice (AMAA79, s. 36[1]). A limited owner of property – that is, a body corporate, a life tenant, or a trustee (AMAA79, s. 18[3–4]) – may enter into a guardianship deed (AMAA79, s. 18[1]), may grant easements or rights over land (AMAA79, s. 18[2][a]) or enter into an agreement for the management of an ancient monument (AMAA79, s. 18[2][b]).

Physical consequences
General prohibitions may be the subject of an agreement concerning the management of an ancient monument (AMAA79, s. 17[4][e]), while specific prohibitions include excavating, salvage or diving on a controlled site or protected place (PMR86, s. 2[3]), the export of scheduled goods (EGCO87, s. 2) and bans placed by the Board of Trade on the importation or exportation of certain goods (IECP39, s. 1).

Physical changes wrought by institutions
An archaeological investigation 'of any land, objects or other material' consists of 'obtaining and recording information . . . discovering and revealing and . . . recovering and removing any objects or other material of archaeological or historical interest situated in, on or under the land; and examining, testing, treating, recording and preserving any such objects or material' (AMAA79, s. 61[4]). It specifically includes the right to excavate (AMAA79, s. 26[2]), to remove samples for testing (AMAA79, s. 44[5]) and accordingly to take into custody objects of archaeological and historical interest (AMAA79, s. 54[1]). The focus on the specific recovery of objects may be seen as a limiting factor so far as archaeology is concerned, but there is no reason why the references to 'other material' cannot be taken to include other sources of archaeological data, such as ecofacts and other contextual information. The Secretary of State has the power to make such investigations a condition of scheduled monument consent (AMAA79, s. 2[5]), and may authorize such an investigation into any ancient monument (in the narrower sense). Those deemed competent to carry out such

investigations may be appointed investigating authorities for AAIs (AMAA79, s. 34[1]). Both the Secretary of State and local authorities may finance such investigations (AMAA79, s. 45[1–2]) and publish their results (AMAA79, s. 45[3]).

Inspections, observation and archaeological examinations are to be differentiated from investigations. An inspection includes recording of matters of archaeological or historical interest and to determine whether excavation is desirable (AMAA79, s. 38[1][a]) as well as the observation of operations within an AAI (AMAA79, s. 38[1][b]). Such inspections may be carried out by investigating authorities upon notification that a (local) authority with powers of compulsory purchase intends to carry out operations on a site (AMAA79, s. 39[1]) and by any person authorized by the Secretary of State or the RCHME on a site covered by an operations notice (AMAA79, s. 40[a–b]). The Secretary of State may authorize inspections of scheduled monuments (AMAA79, s. 6) and of any ancient monument (in the narrower sense) (AMAA79, s. 26[1]), for which purpose it includes excavation for the purpose of archaeo-logical investigation (AMAA79, s. 26[2]), so long as consent to do so on the land has been obtained (AMAA79, s. 26[3]). Schemes for the inspection of churches at least once every five years must be put into effect (ICM55, s. 1). Investigating authorities have the power to carry out observations on operations by developers within AAIs (AMAA79, s. 38[1]) and by local authorities with the power of compulsory purchase on sites subject to such purchase (AMAA79, s. 39[1]). Such observations include the power to take into custody objects of archaeological and historical interest (AMAA79, s. 54[1]). An archaeological examination includes 'any examination or inspection of land . . . for the purpose of obtaining and recording any information of archaeological or historical interest' (AMAA79, s. 61[5]), together with the right to remove samples (AMAA79, s., 44[5]) and to take into custody objects (AMAA79, s. 54[1]). They may be made the subject of a condition of the grant of scheduled monument consent (AMAA79, s. 2[5]) or carried out by local authorities or the Secretary of State on guardianship monuments (AMAA79, s. 13[4][a–b]).

Only objects of archaeological or historical interest may be taken into custody (AMAA79, s. 54[1]) so long as there is no unreasonable reten-tion without the consent of the owner (AMAA79, s. 54[2]) but this statutory right is overborne by the rules of Treasure Trove (AMAA79, s. 54[3]). Samples 'of any description' may be removed both in the process of archaeological investigation and examination (AMAA79, s. 44[5]). An excavation can be a monument (AMAA79, s. 61[7][a]) and includes the right to take objects into temporary custody (AMAA79, s. 54[1]), but otherwise remains undefined. It may be ordered as a condition of the grant of scheduled monument consent (AMAA79, s. 2[5]), and both the Secretary of State and local authorities have the right to carry them out on guardianship monuments (AMAA79, s. 13[4][b]). The Secretary of State has power to authorize excavations of ancient monuments (in the narrower sense) (AMAA79, s. 26[1]) subject to consent (AMAA79, s. 26[3]), and investigating authorities have power to carry them out within set time limits on sites within AAIs where an operations notice has been served (AMAA79, s. 38[2–6]). Excavations are prohibited on controlled sites, if conducted to find an aircraft or vessel lost on military service, or to interfere with or enter such an aircraft or vessel (PMR86, s. 2[3]).

The law grants a power of entry for various purposes to a number of authorities, all such powers including the right to take objects into temporary custody (AMAA79, s. 54[1]) and to take such assistance or equipment as may be reasonably required (AMAA79, s. 44[4]). The Secretary of State may authorize such power for the purposes of conducting urgent works on (AMAA79, s. 5) or inspection of the condition of (AMAA79, s. 6) a scheduled monument, the inspection of an ancient monument (in the narrower sense) (AMAA79, s. 26[1]), for observation of operations in an AAI (AMAA79, s. 40), or for the valuation of land (AMAA79, s. 43[2]). A local authority has such power in relation to a guardianship monument (AMAA79, s. 13[5]). An investigating authority has such power for the purposes of inspection or observation of operations within an AAI (AMAA79, s. 38[1]) and excavation within the time limits provided (AMAA79, s. 38[6]) but may only be exercised within one month of notification in the case of works conducted by authorities with powers of compulsory purchase (AMAA79, s. 39[2]) and within any limits placed upon such powers by the Secretary of State (AMAA79, s. 39[3]). The RCHME may authorize a power of entry for the purpose of inspecting any buildings or structures on the site of operations within an AAI (AMAA79, s. 40[b]) and the Valuation Office of the Inland Revenue may exercise such a power for the purpose of the valuation of land (AMAA79, s. 43) without the consent of the owner (AMAA79, s. 44[1]). Limitations on such powers include the need to obtain specific authority to enter Crown land (AMAA79, s. 50[2]), there is no power to enter a dwelling without the consent of the owner except for the purpose of valuation by the Valuation Office of the Inland Revenue (AMAA79, s. 44[1]) and without service of the appropriate notice – fourteen days in the case of works (AMAA79, s. 43[2][a], otherwise twenty-four hours (AMAA79, s. 43[2][b]) except in the case of urgent work on a scheduled monument where the notice period is seven days (AMAA79, s. 43[2] and 5[1]). Occupiers can legitimately require evidence of authority to enter

(AMAA79, s. 44[3]), and may make reasonable requirements to prevent interference with works on the site (AMAA79, s. 44[6]), but such requirements must not frustrate the purpose of the entry (AMAA79, s. 44[7]). Obstruction of persons with a power of entry is an offence (AMAA79, s. 44[8]), but compensation may be claimed in respect of any damage caused in pursuance of the exercise of such power (AMAA79, s. 46). Valuation includes the power of survey (AMAA79, s. 43[1]), which itself includes a power both to search and to bore for the purpose of establishing the nature of the subsoil or for minerals (AMAA79, s. 43[3]), although proper notice of any such intentions must be served (AMAA79, s. 44[9][a]) and they may be prevented by statutory undertakers (AMAA79, s. 44[9][b]). The officers of the Customs and Excise have a power of search for prohibited goods (ECGO87, s. 7[1]), as do persons authorized by the Secretary of State for the purposes of determining the commission of an offence in relation to a controlled site or the site of a vessel or aircraft lost on military service (PMR86, s. 6[1]). Persons so authorized by the Secretary of State (PMR86, s. 6[8]) have a power of boarding vessels to determine if an offence in relation to a controlled site or the site of a vessel or aircraft lost while on military service has been committed (PMR86, s. 6[1]), although permission to board must first be obtained and may only be requested if there are reasonable grounds to believe that an offence has been or was to be committed (PMR86, s. 6[2]). A power of boarding includes a power to seize objects (PMR86, s. 6[3]), and to use reasonable force (PMR86, s. 6[4]).

The purpose of designating a restricted area is the protection of a historic wreck (PW73, s. 1[2][b]) from unauthorized interference (PW73, s. 1[1][b]) until that protection is no longer required (PW73, s. 3[2][a]), and both the protection it provides and the need for the preservation of the aircraft or vessel it contains determine the size of a controlled site (PMR86, s. 1[5]). Preservation is the purpose of the compulsory acquisition of an ancient monument (AMAA79, s. 10) and adjoining land (AMAA79, s. 15), of the carrying out of urgent works on scheduled monuments by the Secretary of State (AMAA79, s. 5), of the erection of markers concerning scheduled monuments (AMAA79, s. 6[5]), of the removal of a guardianship monument (AMAA79, s. 13[4][c]), and is a duty of the HBMCE in relation to ancient monuments (in the wider sense) (NH83, s. 33[1][a]) and conservation areas (NH83, s. 33[1][b]). It may be made provision for in an agreement to manage an ancient monument (AMAA79, s. 17[4][a]), may be the purpose of a grant from the NHMF (NH80, s. 3[1] and 4[1]) and the desirability of preserving an object or feature external to a building may be taken into account for the purpose of listing (PLBC90, s. 1[3][b]).

The needs of preservation must be taken into account before terminating the guardianship of an ancient monument (AMAA79, s. 14[3]) or the disposal of land (AMAA79, s. 30[3]) unless this is no longer deemed practicable (AMAA79, s. 30[4]). The HBMCE is charged with the duty of promoting the public's knowledge of the preservation of ancient monuments and historic buildings (NH83, s. 33[1][c]), and grants from the NHMF are made to institutions which preserve features 'for the public benefit' (NH80, s. 3[6][a]) or public amenities (NH80, s. 3[6][b]). Ancient monuments are not only subject to preservation but also to maintenance, which is non-exclusively defined as including 'fencing, repairing, and covering in and . . . protecting . . . from decay or injury' (AMAA79, s. 13[7] and 32[1]). It is a duty of both the Secretary of State and local authorities to maintain guardianship monuments (AMAA79, s. 13[1]), it is the purpose of acquiring land adjoining guardianship monuments or those acquired (AMAA79, s. 15[1][a]), and may be provided for in any agreement concerning an ancient monument (AMAA79, s. 17[4][a]). The Secretary of State (AMAA79, s. 24[2]) and local authorities (AMAA79, s. 24[4]) may contribute towards the cost of maintaining ancient monuments (AMAA79, s. 24), the funds of any charity may be applied for the preservation of any building or objects (RC69, s. 5[1]) or parts of a building (RC69, s. 5[2]) formerly used for public religious worship acquired by the Secretary of State (RC69, s. 5), the NHMF may provide grants for the purposes of the preservation of buildings or objects (NH80, s. 3[1]) and make such preservation a condition of any such grant (NH80, s. 3[4][a][ii]) and the Trustees of the NHMF may use the funds of the Fund for that purpose (NH80, s. 4[1]). Similarly, the safe keeping of an object may be made the condition of an NHMF grant (NH80, s. 3[4][a][ii]).

The provision of objects for places of public religious worship out of charitable funds is allowed (NH80, s. 5[1–2]), and the provision of educational facilities for ancient monuments, historic buildings and conservation areas is one of the functions of the HBMCE (NH83, s. 33[2][a]). The public use of land can be a criterion for the receipt of a loan or grant from the NHMF (NH80, s. 3[6]).

Physical changes wrought by others
Causing damage is an offence in relation to scheduled monuments (AMAA79, s. 2[2]), protected monuments (AMAA79, s. 28[1]), protected places and controlled sites (PMR86, s. 2[2]), and in a restricted area (PW73, s. 1[3]), especially by the deposit of materials on to a wreck (PW73, s. 1[3][c]). Due diligence to avoid damage to a scheduled monument is a defence against prosecution (AMAA79, s. 2[2]), and compensation is payable for damage to property in the exercise of

powers of entry (AMAA79, s. 46). Demolition constitutes work in relation to a listed building (PLBC90, s. 7) and part of clearance in relation to buildings in an AAI (AMAA79, s. 41[1][d]). It is an offence against a scheduled monument (AMAA79, s. 2[2]) and if unauthorized against a listed building (PLBC90, s. 7), although this restriction does not apply in the case of a redundant building (RC69, s. 2). The threat of demolition of a non-listed building may give rise to the service of a building preservation notice (PLBC90, s. 3[1]) or, if applied for, a certificate of non-listing (PLBC90, s. 6[1][a]). The destruction of a scheduled monument (AMAA79, s. 2[2]) or a protected monument (AMAA79, s. 28[1]) is an offence, as is the obliteration of a wreck in a restricted area (PW73, s. 1[3][c]). Tipping is defined as 'tipping soil or spoil or depositing building or other materials or matter (including waste materials or refuse) on any land' (AMAA79, s. 61[1]) and constitutes operations within an AAI (AMAA79, s. 35[2]). It is an offence against a scheduled monument (AMAA79, s. 2[2]) and includes depositing, which is an offence if it obliterates a wreck in a restricted area (PW73, s. 1[3][c]) or obstructs access to it (PW73, s. 1[3][c]). Obstruction of a person with a power of entry is an offence (AMAA79, s. 44[8]), as is that of a person authorized by licence in a restricted area (PW73, s. 1[6]). Flooding – that is 'covering land with water or any other liquid or partially liquid substance' (such as mud) (AMAA79, s. 61[1]) – constitutes operations in an AAI (AMAA79, s. 35[2]) and is an offence against a scheduled monument (AMAA79, s. 2[2]).

The clearance of a site covers the demolition and removal of buildings and other materials to clear the surface but not the levelling of the surface or the removal of materials from below the surface (AMAA79, s. 41[1][d]). Details of any such clearance must be given by a developer conducting operations within an AAI (AMAA79, s. 35[4][a]), and the investigating authority must be notified of their completion (AMAA79, s. 35[7]) or the effect will be as if no operations notice has been served (AMAA79, s. 35[8]). The date of completion of such clearance is the earliest date on which the investigating authority may excavate (AMAA79, s. 38[5]). Clearance operations are operations relating to site clearance (AMAA79, s. 41[1][e]) and operations are those that disturb the ground (AMAA79, s. 35[2][a]), or involve flooding (AMAA79, s. 35[2][b]) or tipping (AMAA79, s. 35[2][c]), and require specific authority on Crown land unless the Crown is the developer (AMAA79, s. 54[1]). Carrying out operations in an AAI within six months of serving an operations notice, or without serving one at all, is an offence (AMAA79, s. 35[1]). Persons with a power of entry to undertake operations on an ancient monument also have the power to take into temporary custody objects (AMAA79, s. 54[1]). To disturb the ground is to conduct operations (AMAA79, s. 35[2]), although to have taken all reasonable precautions to avoid doing so is an effective defence (AMAA79, s. 37[5]). Exempt operations (AMAA79, s. 39[1]) are those consented to by an investigating authority for an AAI (AMAA79, s. 37[1]) and those classed as such by the Secretary of State (AMAA79, s. 37[2]). In addition, where all reasonable precautions were taken to avoid disturbing the ground (AMAA79, s. 37[5]), where the developer had no reason to know the operations were conducted in an AAI (AMAA79, s. 37[6][a]) or where such operations were urgently necessary for reasons of safety and written notification was given as soon as practicable (AMAA79, s. 37[6][b]), the ban on operations in AAIs does not apply.

Works include any operations including those of flooding, tipping, agriculture and forestry (AMAA79, s. 61[1]) together with searching and boring (AMAA79, s. 44[9][a]), alteration or extension (PLBC90, s. 8[1]) or demolition (PLBC90, s. 8[2]). They are an offence in relation to scheduled monuments (AMAA79, s. 2[2]) unless they are authorized and all conditions complied with (AMAA79, s. 2[3]) or are urgently necessary (AMAA79, s. 2[9]), and they may be the subject of an agreement concerning an ancient monument (AMAA79, s. 17[4][b]). The Secretary of State may conduct urgent works for the preservation of a scheduled monument (AMAA79, s. 5), may authorize the inspection of any works undertaken on a scheduled monument (AMAA79, s. 6), must superintend works on any ancient monument if thought advisable (AMAA79, s. 25[2]) and may do so on any ancient monument if so invited (AMAA79, s. 25[2]). Conditions may be placed by owners or occupiers upon works by state agencies to avoid interference (AMAA79, s. 44[6]) but they may never frustrate the purpose of such works (AMAA79, s. 44[7]), and legally conducted works may always be carried out in a controlled site or on a crashed, sunk or stranded military aircraft or vessel (PMR86, s. 2[8]). Compensation may be payable by the Secretary of State in the case of refusal to allow permission for works on a scheduled monument (AMAA79, s. 7). Excepted works are works for which scheduled monument consent has been granted (AMAA79, s. 28[2]) and are therefore not prohibited. It is specifically the execution of works on a listed building which is the offence (PLBC90, s. 7 and 8).

The alteration of a listed building constitutes unauthorized work unless consent has been given (PLBC90, s. 7), and both that and the alteration of a scheduled monument (AMAA79, s. 2[2]) are offences, although not in the case of a redundant building (RC69, s. 2). Plans to alter a non-listed building may give rise to a preservation notice (PLBC90, s. 3[1]) or a certificate of non-listing from the Secretary of State (PLBC90, s. 6[1]). Similarly, the extension of a listed building constitutes unauthorized work − unless consent has been given − which is an offence (PLBC90, s. 7), although not in the case of a redundant building (RC69, s. 2). Plans to extend a non-listed building may give rise to a certificate of non-listing from the Secretary of State (PLBC90, s. 6[1]). It is an offence to make any addition to a scheduled monument (AMAA79, s. 2[2][b]). In cases where urgent preservation is required, a building preservation notice may be affixed to an object on the building (PLBC90, s. 4[1]). The deliberate inclusion of a quantity of gold or silver is not in itself sufficient to render an item Treasure Trove (Overton82).

The purpose of designating a restricted area is to prevent unauthorized interference with a wreck of historical, archaeological or artistic importance (PW73, s. 1[1][b]), and similarly the designation of a prohibited area that of a dangerous wreck (PW73, s. 2[1]). Such interference is comprised of tampering with, damaging or removing any part of the wreck or object in it (PW73, s. 1[3][a]), carrying out diving or salvage operations or using equipment for that purpose (PW73, s. 1[3][b]), or depositing anything on the wreck (PW73, s. 1[3][c]). Tampering with an aircraft or vessel is an offence in a controlled site (PMR86, s. 2[1][a] and 2[2]), a protected place (PMR86, s. 2[1][b] and 2[2]) and in a restricted area (PW73, s. 1[3][a]). The repair of a scheduled monument is an offence unless authorized (AMAA79, s. 2[2][b]), but that of the object of an NHMF loan or grant may be a condition for the release of those funds (NH80, s. 3[4][a][ii]), and where a place of public religious worship is taken by the Secretary of State, charitable funds for its repair or any part of it (but not that of objects) may continue to be applied for that purpose (RC69, s. 5[1] and 5[2]).

The unearthing of remains is an offence in a protected place and a controlled site (PMR86, s. 2[2]). The removal of a scheduled monument is an offence unless authorized (AMAA79, s. 2[2]), as is the removal of objects found by metal detector in a protected place (AMAA79, s. 42[2]), remains from a protected place or controlled site (PMR86, s. 2[2]) or from within a restricted area (PW73, s. 1[3][a]). Buildings may be removed as part of clearance operations (AMAA79, s. 41[1][d]), the Secretary of State or a local authority may remove a guardianship monument for the purposes of preservation (AMAA79, s. 13[4][c]), the Secretary of State may contribute towards the cost of such removal (AMAA79, s. 24[2]), and samples taken during an investigation or examination may be removed (AMAA79, s. 44[5]). Salvage services are those which are provided and which incur salvage monies (MS94, s. 510[2]). Salvage operations are generally prohibited in a restricted area (PW73, s. 1[3][b]) but competence in the field of historic wrecks is of relevance for the grant of a licence for that purpose (PW73, s. 1[5][a][i]). Salvage operations for the purpose of investigating or recording the remains in a controlled site are prohibited (PMR86, s. 2[3][a]), as are those involving tampering with, damaging, moving, removing or unearthing the remains of or entering into the vessel in a protected place (PMR86, s. 2[3][b] referring to 2[2]).

Moving the remains in a controlled site or protected place is an offence (PMR86, s. 2[2]). Exportation includes 'in relation to a ship or aircraft the taking . . . out of the United Kingdom of the ship or aircraft notwithstanding that [it] is conveying goods or passengers, and whether or not it is moving under its own power' (EGCO87, s. 1[2]) and the exportation of goods is subject to regulation or prohibition by the Board of Trade (IECP39, s. 1). The delivery of goods subject to such regulation to someone other than is specified by the regulation constitutes the offence of the conveyance of prohibited goods (IECP39, s. 3[2]).

It is an offence to enter a hatch or opening in an aircraft or vessel which crashed while on military service (PMR86, s. 2[2][b]) or is in a prohibited area (PW73, s. 2[3]). Diving is prohibited on a controlled site for the purposes of investigation or recording (PMR86, s. 2[3]), in a protected place if it involves entry on or physical changes to the remains located there (PMR86, s. 2[3][b]), and in a restricted area if for the purpose of exploring the wreck or removing objects from it (PW73, s. 1[3][b]). It is an offence to use a metal detector – a 'device designed or adapted for detecting or locating any metal or mineral in the ground' (AMAA79, s. 42[2]) – on a protected place (AMAA79, s. 42[1]).

Public access is a right to monuments owned and in the guardianship of the Secretary of State and local authorities (AMAA79, s. 19[1]) except where there is danger to the monument or the public (AMAA79, s. 19[6] and 19[2]) or is excluded by the guardianship deed (AMAA79, s. 19[9]), may be the subject of an agreement concerning the management of an ancient monument (AMAA79, s. 17[4][c]), may be provided for in a scheme for the Secretary of State to acquire a place of public religious worship (RC69, s. 4[2]), may be taken into account for the purposes of an NHMF grant or loan (NH80, s. 3[3]) or be a condition of such grant or loan (NH80, s. 3[4][a][i]), and may be the purpose of the acquisition of land adjoining a monument subject to control by the Secretary of State or a local authority (AMAA79, s. 15[1][b]). The Secretary of State and local authorities have the power to make provision and provide facilities for public access to monuments (AMAA79, s. 20) and may charge entry fees (AMAA79, s. 19[5]). The public display of a building or object may be taken into account for an NHMF grant or loan (NH80, s. 3[3]) or be a condition for any such grant or loan (NH80, s. 3[4][a][i]).

Moral consequences

Moral changes wrought by institutions alone
A scheme of control of the import and export of goods consists in their regulation by the Board of Trade (IECP39, s. 2). Restricting the use to which an ancient monument can be put may form part of an agreement for its management (AMAA79, s. 14[4][d]). The Secretary of State may superintend works on any ancient monument if requested (AMAA79, s. 25[2]), and if thought desirable, must do so on a scheduled monument (AMAA79, s. 2[2]).

The Secretary of State may acquire compulsorily (AMAA79, s. 10), by agreement (AMAA79, s. 11[1]) or by gift (AMAA79, s. 11[3]) an ancient monument, or by agreement or gift a building of outstanding historic interest together with contiguous land (HBAM53, s. 5[1]), and a local authority may acquire such monuments by agreement (AMAA79, s. 11[2]) or by gift (AMAA79, s. 11[3]), together with adjoining land (AMAA79, s. 15), although any acquisition of Crown land requires specific authority (AMAA79, s. 50[2]), and ancient monuments so acquired may be transferred into and out of local authority and Secretary of State control (AMAA79, s. 21). The Secretary of State may also acquire places of public religious worship under the authority of the court (RC69, s. 4–5), and the NHMF may make grants for the purpose of the acquisition of items (NH80, s. 3[1]) and may acquire them in its own right (NH80, s. 4[1]). A limited owner may enter into an agreement with a local authority or the Secretary of State in respect of the acquisition of rights over land (AMAA79, s. 18[2]), and officers of the Inland Revenue Valuation Office have a right of entry on to land subject to acquisition by the Secretary of State for the purpose of valuation (AMAA79, s. 43[1]). The Secretary of State may accept as a gift an ancient monument (AMAA79, s. 11[3]), land adjoining it (AMAA79, s. 15), and buildings no longer required as places of public religious worship (RC69, s. 4[1]). Local authorities may take as gifts ancient monuments (AMAA79, s. 11[3]) and adjoining land (AMAA79, s. 15), and the Trustees of the NHMF may accept a gift – including devises (NH80, s. 5[4]) – of money or property so long as it is unconditional (NH80, s. 5[1–2]) but they may not retain property other than money except as the Ministers allow (NH80, s. 5[3]). The Board of Trade may purchase for the Crown wrecks out of the proceeds of salvage (MS94, s. 528).

A site in the ownership of a local authority or the Secretary of State is a protected place (AMAA79, s. 42[2]), and such ownership is created by any of compulsory purchase, agreement, gift or transfer between the Secretary of State and local authority or vice versa or between local authorities (AMAA79, s. 32[3] referring to s. 10, 11 and 21), although no rights of ownership can be exercised in respect of a guardianship monument without the consent of all those affected by the guardianship deed (AMAA79, s. 21[2]). There is a right of public access to all such monuments (AMAA79, s. 19[1]), and they may be transferred between the Secretary of State and local authorities, or vice versa or between local authorities (AMAA79, s. 21[1]). The NHMF has no power of ownership of any property acquired by purchase or gift except as allowed by the responsible Ministers (NH80, s. 4[3] and 5[3]).

Agreements may relate to the acquisition of an ancient monument (AMAA79, s. 11[1–2]) and adjoining land (AMAA79, s. 15), the maintenance, carrying out of works on, public access to, restrictions on use of, prohibitions concerning, or making payments in relation to an ancient monument or adjoining land (AMAA79, s. 17[4][a–f]), the renunciation of guardianship of an ancient monument (AMAA79, s. 14[1]) although a local authority requires the consent of the Secretary of State (AMAA79, s. 14[2]) and arrangements must be made for the future preservation of the monument (AMAA79, s. 14[3]), or for the acquisition by the Secretary of State of former places of public religious worship (RC69, s. 4–5) so long as they are held in trust for charity (RC69, s. 4[1]). A guardianship deed (AMAA79, s. 12[6]), including one made by a limited owner (AMAA79, s. 18), may appoint the Secretary of State or a local authority guardian of an ancient monument (AMAA79, s. 12[1–2]) or land in its vicinity (AMAA79, s. 15) including the seabed (AMAA79, s. 53[3]), placing them under a duty to maintain it (AMAA79, s. 13[1]) as a protected place (AMAA79, s. 42[2]) and, subject to the safety of the public and the monument (AMAA79, s. 19[2]), to allow public access (AMAA79, s. 19[1]) unless excluded by the deed (AMAA79, s. 19[9]), granting them full control and management of the monument (AMAA79, s. 13[2]) with the power to do all things necessary with respect to it (AMAA79, s. 13[3]) including examination (AMAA79, s. 13[4][a]), opening or excavation (AMAA79, 13[4][b]), removal for the purpose of preservation (AMAA79, s. 13[4][c]), entry (AMAA79, s. 13[5]), transfer with the owners' consent (AMAA79, s. 21[2]) to or from a local authority or the Secretary of State (AMAA79, s. 21[1]), or renunciation with the owners' agreement (AMAA79, s. 14). A scheme may be for the inspection of churches (ICM55, s. 1[1]) which comes into effect from the date of signature of the Chair of the Diocesan Synod (ICM55, s. 1[4]), must provide for a fund to pay for such inspection (ICM55, s. 1[2][a–b]), the appointment of an architect (ICM55, s. 1[2][c]) and for the distribution of the inspection report to the archdeacon and the parochial church council (ICM55, s. 1[2][d]), or a scheme of control by the Board of Trade of the import and export of goods (IECP39, s. 2), or for the acquisition by the Secretary of State of places of public religious worship no longer in use which are held in trust by charities but not churches (RC69, s. 4[1]) which may provide for the building's restoration as a place of public religious worship (RC69, s. 4[3]) and includes rights of way (RC69, s. 4[2]). The disposal of land is a power of the Secretary of State and local authorities (AMAA79, s. 30) subject to the need to preserve any ancient monument on the land (AMAA79, s. 30[3–4]) and in the case of local authorities to the consent of the Secretary of State (AMAA79, s. 30[2]), and the disposal of property may be a condition of a grant or loan from the NHMF (NH80, s. 3[4][a][iii]).

Those to be consulted in relation to the listing of buildings include those persons or bodies with special knowledge or interest in buildings of architectural or historical interest (PLBC90, s. 1[4]). Information, instruction and educational services relating to ancient monuments, historic buildings and conservation areas must be provided to the public by the HBMCE (NH83, s. 33[2][a]), and inquiries into treasure and its finders is the jurisdiction of the Coroner (CA88, s. 30). While the purpose of listing is to provide guidance to local planning authorities (PLBC90, s. 1[1]), advice may be given or provided at a cost (AMAA79, s. 25[3]) by the Secretary of State in relation to the treatment of an ancient monument (AMAA79, s. 25[1]) or to any person concerning ancient monuments, historic buildings or conservation areas by the HBMCE (NH83, s. 33[2][b]). The power to survey land – which includes to search and bore to ascertain the nature of the subsoil or the presence of minerals (AMAA79, s. 43[3]) – is given to those authorized by the Secretary of State or officers of the Inland Revenue Valuation Office (AMAA79, s. 43[2]) for the valuation of land to be acquired (AMAA79, s. 43[1]). Reports of the inspection of churches are to be sent to relevant archdeacons and parochial church councils (ICM55, s. 1[2]), while records may be made and kept by the HBMCE concerning ancient monuments and historic buildings (NH83, s. 33[2][d]), and the recording of matters of archaeological and historical interest is the purpose of the inspection of land believed to contain an ancient monument (AMAA79, s. 26[1]), a site in an AAI in respect of which an operations notice has been served (AMAA79, s. 38[1] and 40), and land in an AAI due for compulsory purchase (AMAA79, s. 39[1]). The list of buildings of special architectural or historical importance must be published to local authorities, the HBMCE and may be to the public (PLBC90, s. 2), and local authorities and the Secretary of State may publish the results of archaeological investigations (AMAA79, s. 45[3]).

The schedule of monuments compiled by the Secretary of State in a form thought fit (AMAA79, s. 1[1]) and published from time to time

(AMAA79, s. 1[7]), published amendments to which shall constitute evidence (AMAA79, s. 1[8]), must include all monuments included in previous schedules (AMAA79, s. 1[2][a–b]) and may include any others which appear to the Secretary of State to be of national importance (AMAA79, s. 1[3]), including those on Crown lands (AMAA79, s. 50[1][a]) and on the seabed (AMAA79, s. 53[1]) where they are to be described as lying off the coast (AMAA79, s. 53[2]), but in no case dwellings (AMAA79, s. 1[4]). A designation order may relate to an AAI (AMAA79, s. 33[3] and 61[1]) made by the Secretary of State which may be revoked or reduced in size but not increased (AMAA79, s. 33[4]), or to a vessel lost while on military service or a controlled site which is made by statutory instrument (PMR86, s. 1[2]). A building preservation notice served on owners by the local planning authority (PLBC90, s. 3), while in force, requires the building to be treated as if listed (PLBC90, s. 3[5]), in urgent cases may be affixed to an object on the building (PLBC90, s. 4[1]) but may be revoked by the Secretary of State by listing the building or by notification that such listing will not take place (PLBC90, s. 3[4]).

The purpose of scheduled monument consent from the Secretary of State as written authority to conduct specific works on a specific scheduled monument (AMAA79, s. 2[3] and 3[5]) constitutes such work as excepted works (AMAA79, s. 28[2]), is to ensure the benefit of the monument and all interested persons (AMAA79, Sch. 1, para. 1[2]), expires after five years if no work is undertaken (AMAA79, s. 4[1]) unless it is for a fixed term (AMAA79, s. 4[2]), may be modified or revoked by the Secretary of State (AMAA79, s. 4[3–4]), and is not to be confused with any term of any agreement for the management of an ancient monument (AMAA79, s. 17[8]). A class order of consent for works of a particular kind on a particular kind of scheduled monument may be made by the Secretary of State (AMAA79, s. 3), but such orders are not to be taken as scheduled monument consent (AMAA79, s. 3[5]). Current such consents cover agricultural, horticultural or forestry works, mining by the National Coal Board, repair and maintenance work on canals by the British Waterways Board, the repair of machinery, work essential for health or safety, and works by the HBMCE (AMCCO81 and AMCCO84). Planning permission is required for the alteration, extension or demolition of a listed building (PLBC90, s. 6[1][a]) and may result in the issue of a certificate of non-listing (PLBC90, s. 6[1]). A certificate from a person with an interest in the site or power to acquire it compulsorily (AMAA79, s. 36[1]) or a statutory undertaker (AMAA79, s. 36[2]), signed by the issuer and confirming their interest in the site and specifically authorizing the developer to carry out operations within an AAI (AMAA79, s. 36[3]), must accompany the operations notice (AMAA79, s. 35[4][b]), and to make any knowingly false or misleading statement in the certificate is an offence (AMAA79, s. 36[4]). A licence issued by the Secretary of State is required for any person in a restricted area to tamper with, damage or remove any part of any wrecked vessel, to dive or conduct salvage operations, or to deposit anything (PW73, s. 1[3]), and such licences may only be granted to those who appear to be competent to conduct salvage operations in respect of historic wrecks (PW73, s. 1[5][a][i]) or have some other legitimate reason to do so (PW73, s. 1[5][a][ii]) and may be conditional or varied or revoked on one week's notice (PW73, s. 1[5][b]). The grant of a licence is a defence in respect of offences in relation to the remains of aircraft and vessels lost while on military service, controlled sites and protected places (PMR86, s. 2[4]), and such licences may be granted by the Secretary of State (PMR86, s. 4[1]) to particular persons or a class of persons or in an order designating a controlled site (PMR86, s. 4[2]), may be conditional (PMR86, s. 4[3]), shall continue in force until the earlier of revocation or expiry (PMR86, s. 4[4]), must be published to the licensee and to others affected by it (PMR86, s. 4[5]), but does not affect any rights of ownership (PMR86, s. 4[6]). Export licences are required for the export of scheduled goods or their passage as ships' stores (EGCO87, s. 4[a]). Conditions may be imposed on any grant or loan by the Trustees of the NHMF, especially in relation to public access, maintenance, disposal and repayment (NH80, s. 3[4]), and attached to any scheduled monument consent (AMAA79, s. 2[4]), any class order (AMAA79, s. 3), consent to use a metal detector on a protected place (AMAA79, s. 42[4]), and on licences to conduct works on aircraft and vessels lost while on military service, protected places and controlled sites (PMR86, s. 4[2]), in which case failure to comply is an offence (AMAA79, s. 2[3 and 6] and 42[5]).

The service of a notice to excavate on the developer and local authority – or the Church Commissioners in the case of ecclesiastical property (AMAA79, s. 51[1]) – no later than four weeks after service of an operations notice (AMAA79, s. 38[3]) authorizes an investigating authority to excavate on the site of works in an AAI (AMAA79, s. 38[2]). An operations notice (AMAA79, s. 35[3] and 41[1]) must be in the prescribed form (AMAA79, s. 35[4][c]), specify the operations, the site, the dates, and timings to which it relates (AMAA79, s. 35[4][a]), accompany the certificate authorizing the developer to proceed (AMAA79, s. 35[4][b] and 36) and a certificate of authority if the works are on Crown land (AMAA79, s. 50[3]), be served by the developer on the local authority or the Secretary of State if the local authority is the developer (AMAA79, s. 35[5]), but is invalidated if the completion of clearance operations is not notified to the investigating authority

(AMAA79, s. 35[8]) or if operations are conducted during the period allowed for excavation by the investigating authority (AMAA79, s. 38[7]).

The Secretary of State may make financial contributions towards the acquisition (AMAA79, s. 24[1]), removal for preservation (AMAA79, s. 24[2]) or the provision by a local authority of facilities for the public (AMAA79, s. 24[3]) in respect of any ancient monument except a dwelling house (AMAA79, s. 24[5]), towards the cost of archaeological investigations (AMAA79, s. 45[1]) and the publication of those undertaken at public expense (AMAA79, s. 45[3]), and may make grants to the Architectural Heritage Fund (AMAA79, s. 49) and the Redundant Churches Fund so long as the latter do not exceed £200,000 (RC69, s. 1[1–2]). Local authorities may contribute towards the cost of preservation, maintenance and management of ancient monuments (AMAA79, s. 24[4]) and archaeological investigations (AMAA79, s. 45[2]) and their publication (AMAA79, s. 45[3]), the HBMCE may finance research into ancient monuments, historic buildings and conservation areas (AMAA79, s. 33[2][c]), and the Treasury may levy charges in respect of any scheme of control over the import or export of goods (IECP39, s. 2). Schemes for the inspection of churches must provide for their financing (ICM55, s. 1[2]), and the assets of trusts for places of religious worship acquired by the Secretary of State must be applied to the repair of the building or the maintenance of objects located inside (RC69, s. 5[1]) or the repair of parts of the building (RC69, s. 5[2]), but their acquisition may not be financed out of the National Land Fund (now the NHMF) (RC69, s. 6). The Secretary of State and local authorities may accept voluntary contributions towards any costs in relation to ancient monuments (AMAA79, s. 31). The NHMF may make grants for the acquisition, maintenance and preservation of buildings, land or objects (NH80, s. 3[1]) but these may only be made in respect of any property which is of importance to the National Heritage (NH80, s. 3[2]) and after having regard to public access and display (NH80, s. 3[3]), may be made with conditions (NH80, s. 3[4]), to a Trust established to receive the money (NH80, s. 3[5]) or to certain specified types of body (NH80, s. 3[6]) which may be neither non-UK bodies nor profit-making (NH80, s. 3[7]). The HBMCE may make grants for the upkeep of historic buildings (HBAM53, s. 3A) and the Secretary of State to the Redundant Churches Fund so long as these do not exceed £200,000 (RC69, s. 1[1–2]). The NHMF may make loans for the acquisition, maintenance and preservation of buildings, land or objects (NH80, s. 3[1]) but these may only be made in respect of any property which is of importance to the National Heritage (NH80, s. 3[2]) and after having regard to public access and display (NH80, s.

3[3]), may be made with conditions (NH80, s. 3[4]), to a Trust established to receive the money (NH80, s. 3[5]) or to certain specified types of body (NH80, s. 3[6]) which may be neither non-UK bodies nor profit-making (NH80, s. 3[7]), and the HBMCE may make loans for the upkeep of historic buildings (HBAM53, s. 3A). The conditions attached to an NHMF grant or loan may include that of repayment (NH80, s. 3[4][b]) and while the Trustees have powers of investment of funds, these are limited and must be exercised with the consent of the Treasury (NH80, s. 6).

Salvage is defined as the expenses incurred in providing salvage services, and accordingly is the amount paid to the salvagors of wrecks (MS94, s. 510[2]), and it is out of the proceeds of the sale of wrecks that the Board of Trade may purchase wrecks for the Crown (MS94, s. 528). The power to enter land for the purpose of its valuation (AMAA79, s. 43[1]) is granted to officers of the Inland Revenue Valuation Office and those authorized by the Secretary of State or a local authority planning to acquire the land (AMAA79, s. 43[2]). Payments may be the subject of an agreement relating to the management of an ancient monument (AMAA79, s. 17[4][f]), may be charged by the Secretary of State for the grant of a licence to conduct operations at the site of a vessel lost while on military service, a protected place or a controlled site (PMR86, s. 5[3]), may be made by the responsible Ministers into the NHMF (NH80, s. 2[1]) and represent all amounts received by the Trustees of the NHMF (NH80, s. 2[2]). Compensation is payable in respect of a refusal of scheduled monument consent, a grant of consent with conditions attached (AMAA79, s. 7), or for its revocation (AMAA79, s. 9), may be recovered where consent is granted (AMAA79, s. 8), must be claimed as prescribed (AMAA79, s. 47[1]), is payable in respect of loss or damage as a result of the depreciation of the value of land (AMAA79, s. 27[2]) which requires a power of entry for its assessment (AMAA79, s. 43[1]) and where damage to land or chattels takes place in the course of valuation is further payable (AMAA79, s. 46[1]), is payable to the Church Commissioners in respect of ecclesiastical property (AMAA79, s. 51[3–4]), and to the Secretary of State or a local authority where damage is caused to a guardianship monument (AMAA79, s. 29). Penalties for offences consist exclusively of fines for damage to a scheduled monument (AMAA79, s. 2[10]), ignoring regulations regarding public access (AMAA79, s. 19[7]), non-service of an operations notice (AMAA79, s. 35[9]) or making a false statement therein (AMAA79, s. 36[4]), for unauthorized use of a metal detector in a protected place (AMAA79, s. 42[1]) and removal of objects so found (AMAA79, s. 42[3]), or for failure to comply with the conditions of any consent to use a metal detector at a protected place (AMAA79, s. 42[5]), for obstruction of a person with a power of entry (AMAA79, s. 44[8]), for failure to disclose information concerning the ownership of land (AMAA79, s. 57[2]) or a mis-statement (AMAA79, s. 57[3]), for offences in protected places or controlled sites (PMR86, s. 2[7]) or for making false statements in relation to such offences (PMR86, s. 5[2]), for the import or export of prohibited goods (IECP39, s. 3[1]), for trading with the enemy (IECP39, s. 7[2]), for providing false information in an application for an export licence (EGCO87, s. 6), for not allowing a search by the Customs and Excise (EGCO87, s. 7[3]) and making a false declaration to them (EGCO87, s. 7[3]), and for offences in relation to restricted areas and prohibited areas (PW73, s. 3[4]).

Moral changes wrought by institutions and others
Any proposed development requires planning permission and where it involves the alteration, extension or demolition of a building this may give rise to a certificate of non-listing (PLBC90, s. 6[1]). Any treasure – such as gold or silver coins in an urn (Overton80, p. 875E) – that is found is the subject of a Coroner's inquiry (CA88, s. 30), and if in a rural location will be classed as having been hidden (Overton80, p. 875F). Any building in danger of demolition or alteration that would affect any special historical or architectural interest it may have may be subject to a building preservation notice (PLBC90, s. 3[1]), while a wreck may present a danger to life or property (PW73, s. 2[1]) and if no longer a danger may have any prohibited area order revoked (PW73, s. 3[2]).

To issue false statements, information or documents is an offence in respect of an application for a licence to conduct works in a controlled site or protected place (PMR86, s. 5[1]). Those with a special interest in buildings of historical or architectural interest are to be consulted before listing (PLBC90, s. 1[4]) and the list itself is subject to public inspection (PLBC90, s. 2[4]).

The insurance (NH80, s. 3[4][a][ii]) or lending (NH80, s. 3[4][a][iii]) of items may be a condition of an NHMF loan or grant, while bequests are included as gifts to the NHMF (NH80, s. 5[4]). The forfeit of goods may be the penalty for the carriage of prohibited goods (IECP39, s. 3[1]) or of goods falsely declared to be for a particular destination (IECP39, s. 7[1]).

Defences against conviction which require to be proved consist of taking due diligence to avoid damage to an ancient monument (AMAA79, s. 2[7]), having no knowledge or reason to know of the presence of an ancient monument (AMAA79, s. 2[8]), the conducting of urgent necessary works on an ancient monument (AMAA79, s. 2[9]), having no knowledge of nor intention nor being reckless as to destroy or damage a protected monument (AMAA79, s. 28[1]), conducting excepted works (AMAA79, s. 28[2]) having the consent of the investigating authority (AMAA79, s. 37[1]) or of the Secretary of State (AMAA79, s. 37[2]) for works in an AAI, taking all precautions to avoid disturbing the ground in an AAI (AMAA79, s. 37[5]), not knowing nor having reason to believe land was in an AAI or urgent necessity (AMAA79, s. 37[6]) (and therefore not both at one time), not using a metal detector on a protected site to find archaeological objects (AMAA79, s. 42[6]), taking reasonable precautions to ensure that the site of metal detector use was not a protected site (AMAA79, s. 42[7]), obtaining a licence for works on a controlled site or protected place (PMR86, s. 2[4]) or honestly believing the site not to be a protected place (PMR86, s. 2[5]) or conducting works for reason of safety, health or to avoid damage (PMR86, s. 2[6]), and for dealing with an emergency (PW73, s. 3[3][a]), meeting the conditions of another Act of Parliament (PW73, s. 3[3][b]) or for reasons of necessity brought about by weather or navigational hazards (PW73, s. 3[3][c]) in a restricted area.

Appendix 3
Ascribed values

TYPES OF VALUE

Amenity and use values

Treasure Trove is the ultimate valuation of a movable object, determines its future fate as a 'treasure' for display in a museum and overrides the power of any authority to take objects into custody (AMAA79, s. 54[3]). It is the product of the Coroner's inquiry (CA88, s. 30), and extends only to items of gold or silver rather than antiquities in general, does not consist of rigid rules to define the presence of precious metal (Overton80), but items must be 'substantially' of silver or gold (Overton82). Monuments appearing to the Secretary of State to be of national importance are those that may be included in the schedule (AMAA79, s. 1[3]), and importance to the national heritage is the ultimate criterion for the award of a grant from the NHMF (NH80, s. 3[2]). These terms remain undefined except to the extent that the NHMF replaced the National Land Fund as a memorial to those who died for the United Kingdom (NH80, s. 1[1]).

A vessel which is of public interest may be treated as a monument (AMAA79, s. 61[8]), while a monument is held to be of public interest because of its historic, architectural, traditional, artistic or archaeological interest (AMAA79, s. 61[12]) and a collection or group of objects of public benefit by virtue of its historic, artistic or scientific interest (NH80, s. 3[6][a]), thus defining these terms by reference to other value ascriptions. Amenities are to be 'enjoyed' by the public (NH80, s. 3[6][b]) and thus qualify for loans and grants from the NHMF (NH80, s. 3[6]), and promotion of public knowledge and the public enjoyment of ancient monuments and historic buildings is one of the duties of the HBMCE (NH83, s. 33[1][c]).

The scenic interest of land may qualify for a grant or loan from the NHMF (NH80, s. 3[1][a]). It is the duty of the HBMCE to promote the appearance of conservation areas (NH83, s. 33[1][b]) together with their character (NH83, s. 33[1][b]), and it is the character of listed buildings as of special architectural or historic interest that constitutes their importance (PLBC90, s. 3[1] and 7).

Scientific values

Land, buildings or structures of aesthetic interest may be the subject of grants or loans from the NHMF (NH80, s. 3[1][a]) together with objects of artistic interest (NH80, s. 3[1][b]), which is also a criterion for classifying a monument, site or feature as an ancient monument (AMAA79, s. 61[12][b] and NH83, s. 33[8]). Artistic importance is the criterion for protecting a wreck or its contents (PW73, s. 1[1][b]) and selecting salvagors on the basis of their competence to deal with such material (PW73, s. 1[5][a][b]). The architectural interest of a monument may allow it to be classified as ancient (AMAA79, s. 61[12][b] and NH83, s. 33[8]) or that of land, buildings or structures to be the subject of a grant or loan from the NHMF (NH80, s. 3[1][a]), while buildings of such special interest shall be listed (PLBC90, s. 1[1]), and this requires taking into account the contribution of the exterior of the building to a group of buildings of which it is part (PLBC90, s. 1[3][a]), features external to the building which may be of such interest in their own right (PLBC90, s. 1[3][b]), and the contribution such interest makes to the character of the building (PLBC90, s. 3[1][b]).

The archaeological interest of a monument, site or feature is a criterion for classifying it as ancient (AMAA79, s. 61[12][b] and NH83, s. 33[8]), and matters of such interest are the purpose of archaeological inspections (AMAA79, s. 26[1], 38, 39, and 40), while the removal of objects of such interest from a protected place by the use of a metal detector is an offence (AMAA79, s. 42). Wrecks or their contents of such importance may be subject to protection (PW73, s. 1[1][b]) and potential salvagors must be competent to deal with such material (PW73, s. 1[5][a][i]). Matters of historical interest are to be recorded during inspections (AMAA79, s. 26[1], 38, 39 and 40), it is an offence to remove objects of historical interest from protected sites while using a metal detector (AMAA79, s. 42), and such importance of a wreck or its contents may make it eligible for protection (PW73, s. 1[1][b]) while its salvagors must be competent to deal with such material (PW73, s. 1[5][a][ii]). The historic interest of a monument or other site or feature is a criterion for classifying it as ancient (AMAA79, s. 61[12][b] and NH83, s. 33[8]), for the making of a grant or loan by the NHMF in respect of land, structures, buildings or objects (NH80, s. 3[1]) and for listing buildings (PLBC90, s. 1[1]) after taking into account the contribution of its exterior to such interest of the group of buildings to which it belongs (PLBC90, s. 1[3][a]), any features external to the building (PLBC90, s. 1[3][b]) and its character as a building of such interest (PLBC90, s. 3[1]). The traditional interest of a monument may make it eligible for classification as ancient (AMAA79, s. 61[12][b] and NH83, s. 33[8]).

The scientific interest of land and objects may make them eligible to be the subject of a grant or loan from the NHMF (NH80, s. 3[1][a–b]) while bodies engaged in nature conservation are eligible recipients of such loans or grants (NH80, s. 3[6][c]).

None of these value terms is given a strict definition.

LEVELS OF VALUE

To appear to the Secretary of State to be of national importance is the criterion for inclusion on the schedule of monuments (AMAA79, s. 1[3]) while importance to the national heritage is the ultimate criterion for a grant or loan from the NHMF (NH80, s. 3[2]). Wrecks of vessels or objects contained in them which are of archaeological, artistic or historical importance are subject to protection, while interest in land or land–based buildings, features, matters or objects may be aesthetic (NH80, s. 3[1]), artistic (AMAA79, s. 61[12] and NH80, s. 3[1]), archaeological (AMAA79, s. 26[1], 38, 39, 40, 42 and 61[12]), architectural (AMAA79, s. 61[12]; NH80, s. 3[1]; PLBC90, s. 1[1], 1[3], 1[4], 3[1] and 7), historic (AMAA79, s. 61[12]; NH80, s. 3[1]; NH83, s. 33 and PLBC90, s. 1[1], 1[3], 1[4], 3[1] and 7), historical (AMAA79, s. 26[1], 38, 39, 40 and 42), scenic (NH80, s. 3[1]), scientific (NH80, s. 3[1]), traditional (AMAA79, s. 61[12] and NH83, s. 33[8]) and ultimately public – a term which is defined in terms of the other interests listed here (AMAA79, s. 61[8] and 61[12]).

The qualification outstanding may be applied to scenic, historic, aesthetic, architectural, scientific and artistic interest in order for such items to qualify for NHMF funding (NH80, s. 3[1]) and the qualification special to historic buildings, their exteriors and attachments to qualify them for listing (PLBC90, s. 1). Accordingly, outstanding or special interest ranks equally with national importance and in the case of wrecks importance generally, while a type of interest alone and unqualified does not.

The value of a building's exterior may contribute to that of the group of buildings of which it is a part (PLBC90, s. 1[3][a]), and a substantial amount of gold or silver content is required for judgement of an object as Treasure Trove (Overton82). Unauthorized works that would affect the character of a building as of special architectural or historic interest are an offence (PLBC90, s. 7), while the enhancement of conservation areas is one of the duties of the HBMCE (NH83, s. 33[1][b]) and the restoration of former places of religious worship allowed for (RC69, s. 4[3]). Such treatments thus allow for the movement of specific items up and down value scales, although none of these terms is given a precise operational definition.

COMPONENT VALUES
Components of the archaeological heritage which may be granted
national status comprise land, buildings, structures, objects, collections
and groups of objects (NH80, s. 3[1]), works, caves, excavations,
vehicles, vessels, aircraft and machinery (AMAA79, s. 61[7]). Those that
may be considered treasure comprise coins and other objects
substantially of gold or silver (Overton80 and Overton82).

Those that may be archaeological comprise vessels (AMAA79, s. 61[7]
and PW73, s. 1[1][b]), matters which are the subject of inspections
(AMAA79, s. 26[1], 38, 39 and 40), objects (AMAA79, s. 42 and PW73,
s. 1[1][b]), buildings, structures, works, caves, excavations, vehicles,
aircraft, machinery, land (AMAA79, s. 61[7]), sites, gardens and areas
(NH83, s. 33[8]). Those that may be historic are vessels (AMAA79, s.
61[7]), caves, excavations, vehicles, machinery (AMAA79, s. 61[7]), land,
structures, works (AMAA79, s. 61[7], NH83, s. 33[8] and NH80, s.
3[1]), buildings (AMAA79, s. 61[7]), PLBC90, s. 1[1] and NH80, s.
3[1]), the exterior of a building (PLBC90, s. 1[3][a]), features external to
buildings (PLBC90, s. 1[3][b]), sites, gardens and areas (NH83, s. 33[8]).
Those that may be historical comprise vessels (PW73, s. 1[1][b]), matters
which are the subject of inspections (AMAA79, s. 26[1], 38, 39 and 40)
and objects (AMAA79, s. 42 and PW73, s. 1[1][b]). Those that may be
traditional comprise buildings, caves, excavations, vehicles, vessels, aircraft, machinery, land (AMAA79, s. 61[7]), structures, works (AMAA79,
s. 61[7] and NH83, s. 33[8]), sites, gardens and areas (NH83, s. 33[8]).

Those that may be architectural comprise caves, excavations, vehicles,
vessels, aircraft, machinery (AMAA79, s. 61[7]), land (AMAA79, s. 61[7]
and NH80, s. 3), structures, works (AMAA79, s. 61[7] and NH83, s.
33[8]), buildings (PLBC90, s. 1[1] and NH83, s. 33[8]), the exterior of a
building (PLBC90, s. 1[3][a]), features external to a building (PLBC90, s.
1[3][b]), sites, gardens and areas (NH83, s. 33[8]). Those that may be
artistic comprise vessels (AMAA79, s. 61[7] and PW73, s. 1[1][b]),
buildings, caves, excavations, vehicles, aircraft, machinery, land
(AMAA79, s. 61[7]), objects (NH80, s. 3[1] and PW73, s. 1[1][b]),
collections or groups of objects (NH80, s. 3[1]), structures, works
(AMAA79, s. 61[7] and NH83, s. 33[8]), sites, gardens and areas (NH83,
s. 33[8]). Those that may be aesthetic or scenic comprise land, buildings
and structures (NH80, s. 3[1]).

Those that may be scientific comprise land, buildings, structures,
objects and collections or groups of objects (NH80, s. 3[1]) and those
that may be of public interest comprise vessels (AMAA79, s. 61[8]),
buildings, structures, works, caves, excavations, vehicles, vessels, aircraft,
machinery and land (AMAA79, s. 61[7]).

References

Adams, W. Y. and Adams, E. W. 1991. *Archaeological Typology and Practical Reality: A Dialectical Approach to Artifact Classification*. Cambridge: Cambridge University Press.

Adovaiso, J. M. and Carlisle, R. C. 1988. Some thoughts on cultural resource management archaeology in the United States. *Antiquity* 62, 72–87.

Alexander, J. 1989. A suggested training scheme for archaeological resource managers in tropical countries. In Cleere, H. F. (ed.) *Archaeological Heritage Management in the Modern World*. One World Archaeology 9. London: Unwin Hyman, 280–4.

All England Law Reports. London: Butterworth.

All England Law Reports. Annual Review 1990. 1991. London: Butterworth.

Amigoni, D. 1991. Life histories and the cultural politics of historical knowing: the Dictionary of National Biography and the late nineteenth-century political field. In Dex, S. (ed.) *Life and Work History Analyses: Qualitative and Quantitative Developments*. Sociological Review Monograph 37. London: Routledge.

Andah, B. W. (ed.) 1990. Cultural resource management: an African dimension. Forum on Cultural Resource Management at the Conference in Honour of Prof. Thurstan Shaw. *West African Journal of Archaeology* 20.

Appadurai, A. 1986a. Introduction: commodities and the politics of value. In Appadurai, A. (ed.) *The Social Life of Things: Commodities in Social Perspective*. Cambridge: Cambridge University Press, 3–63.

Appadurai, A. (ed.) 1986b. *The Social Life of Things: Commodities in Social Perspective*. Cambridge: Cambridge University Press.

The Archaeological Journal. London: The Royal Archaeological Institute.

Ashley-Smith, J. n.d. The ethics of conservation. *The Conservator* 1, 1–5.

Ashworth, J. G. and Tunbridge, J. E. 1990. *The Tourist-Historic City*. London: Belhaven.

Atiyah, P. S. 1983. *Law and Modern Society*. London: Opus.

Aubert, V. 1969. Law as a way of resolving conflicts: the case of a small industrialised society. In Nader, L. (ed.) *Law in Culture and Society*. Chicago: Aldine.

Barrett, J. 1987. Fields of discourse: reconstituting a social archaeology. *Critique of Anthropology* 7(3), 5–16.

Barton, R. 1990. An influential set of chaps: the X-Club and Royal Society politics 1864–85. *British Journal of the History of Science* 23, 53–81.

Bastick, T. 1982. *Intuition: How We Think and Act*. Chichester: John Wiley and Sons.

Batisse, M. 1980. A new partnership in the making. *Unesco Courier*, August 1980, 5.

Benn, S. I. and Gaus, G. F. 1983a. The liberal conception of the public and the private.

In Benn, S. I. and Gaus, G. F. (eds) *Public and Private in Social Life*. London: Croom Helm, 31–65.

Benn, S. I. and Gaus, G. F. 1983b. The public and the private: concepts and action. In Benn, S. I. and Gaus, G. F. (eds) *Public and Private in Social Life*. London: Croom Helm, 3–27.

Benn, S. I. and Gaus, G. F. (eds) 1983c. *Public and Private in Social Life*. London: Croom Helm.

Berger, P. L. (with Berger, B. and Kellner, H.) 1973. *The Homeless Mind: Modernisation and Consciousness*. Harmondsworth: Penguin.

Bernstein, B. 1971, 1972, 1973. *Class, Codes and Behaviour: I, II and III*. London: RKP.

Biddle, M. 1989. The Rose reviewed: a comedy (?) of errors. *Antiquity* 63, 753–60.

Binford, L. R. 1962. Archaeology as anthropology. *American Antiquity* 28, 217–25.

Binford, L. R. 1983. *Working at Archaeology*. Studies in Archaeology. San Diego: Academic Press.

Binford, L. R. 1989. *Debating Archaeology*. Studies in Archaeology. San Diego: Academic Press.

Binney, M. and Burman, P. 1977. *Chapels and Churches: Who Cares? An Independent Report*. London: British Tourist Authority.

Boulting, N. 1976. The law's delays: conservationist legislation in the British Isles. In Fawcett, J. (ed.) *The Future of the Past: Attitudes to Conservation 1174–1974*. London: Thames and Hudson, 9–33.

Bourdieu, P. 1977. *Outline of a Theory of Practice*. Trans. R. Nice. Cambridge: Cambridge University Press.

Bourdieu, P. 1984. *Distinction: A Social Critique of the Judgment of Taste*. Trans. R. Nice. London: RKP.

Boyce, D. G. 1986. The marginal British: the Irish. In Colls, R. and Dodd, P. (eds) *Englishness: Politics and Culture 1880–1920*. London: Croom Helm, 230–53.

Bradley, R. 1983. Archaeology, evolution and the public good: the intellectual development of General Pitt-Rivers. *The Archaeological Journal* 140, 1–9.

British Archaeological News. London: Council for British Archaeology.

Brown, A. E. (ed.) 1991. *Garden Archaeology*. CBA Research Report 78. London: Council for British Archaeology.

Brown, G. M. 1990. Valuation of genetic resources. In Orians, G. H., Brown, G. M., Kunin, W. E. and Swierzbinski, J. E. (eds) *The Preservation and Valuation of Genetic Resources*. Seattle and London: University of Washington Press, 203–45.

Buck, L. and Dodd, P. 1991. *Relative Values, or, What's Art Worth?* London: BBC Books.

Burnham, B. 1974. *The Protection of Cultural Property: Handbook of National Legislations*. Paris: International Council of Museums (ICOM).

Byrne, D. 1991. Western hegemony in archaeological heritage management. *History and Anthropology* 5, 269–76.

Cannadine, D. 1983. The context, performance and meaning of ritual: the British monarchy and the 'invention of tradition'. In Hobsbawm, E. and Ranger, T. (eds) *The Invention of Tradition*. Cambridge: Cambridge University Press, 101–64.

Carman, J. 1990a. Commodities, rubbish and treasure: valuing archaeological objects. *Archaeological Review from Cambridge* 9.2, 195–207.

Carman, J. 1990b. A role for the Chartered Secretary in archaeology. *Administrator: The Journal of the Institute of Chartered Secretaries and Administrators*, January 1990, 16–17.

Carman, J. 1991. Beating the bounds: archaeological heritage management as archaeology, archaeology as social science. *Archaeological Review from Cambridge* 10.2, 175–84.

Carman, J. 1992. Review of I. Bapty and T. Yates (eds) *Archaeology After Structuralism: Poststructuralism and the Practice of Archaeology* and F. Baker and J. Thomas (eds) *Writing the Past in the Present*. *Archaeological Review from Cambridge* 11.2, 411–16.

Carman, J. 1993. The P is silent – as in archaeology. *Archaeological Review from Cambridge* 12.1, 39–53.

Carman, J. in press. Wanted: archaeologists not bureaucrats. In Cleere, H. F. and Fowler, P. J. (eds) *Training Heritage Managers*. The Heritage: Care, Preservation, Management. London: Routledge.

Chapman, W. 1989. The organisational context in the history of archaeology: Pitt-Rivers and other British archaeologists in the 1860s. *The Antiquaries Journal* 69.1, 23–42.

Chippindale, C. 1983a. The making of the first Ancient Monuments Act, 1882, and its administration under General Pitt-Rivers. *Journal of the British Archaeological Association* 136, 1–55.

Chippindale, C. 1983b. Stonehenge, General Pitt-Rivers and the first Ancient Monuments Act. *Archaeological Review from Cambridge* 2.1, 59–65.

Chippindale, C. 1989. Editorial. *Antiquity* 63, 411–13.

Chippindale, C. and Gibbins, D. 1990. Heritage at sea: proposals for the better protection of British archaeological sites underwater. *Antiquity* 64, 390–400.

Clark, A. 1990. *Seeing Beneath the Soil: Prospecting Methods in Archaeology*. London: Batsford.

Clarke, D. L. 1978. *Analytical Archaeology*. 2nd edition revised by Bob Chapman. London: Methuen.

Cleere, H. F. (ed.) 1984a. *Approaches to the Archaeological Heritage*. New Directions in Archaeology. Cambridge: Cambridge University Press.

Cleere, H. F. 1984b. Great Britain. In Cleere, H. F. (ed.) *Approaches to the Archaeological Heritage*. New Directions in Archaeology. Cambridge: Cambridge University Press, 54–62.

Cleere, H. F. 1984c. World cultural resource management: problems and perspectives. In Cleere, H. F. (ed.) *Approaches to the Archaeological Heritage*. New Directions in Archaeology. Cambridge: Cambridge University Press, 125–31.

Cleere, H. F. (ed.) 1989a. *Archaeological Heritage Management in the Modern World*. One World Archaeology 9. London: Unwin Hyman.

Cleere, H. F. 1989b. Introduction: the rationale of archaeological heritage management. In Cleere, H. F. (ed.) *Archaeological Heritage Management in the Modern World*. One World Archaeology 9. London: Unwin Hyman, 1–19.

Clifford, J. 1988. *The Predicament of Culture: Twentieth Century Ethnography, Literature and Art*. Cambridge, MA: Harvard University Press.

Collis, R. 1986. Englishness and the political culture. In Colls, R. and Dodd, P. (eds) *Englishness: Politics and Culture 1880–1920*. London: Croom Helm, 29–61.

Colls, R. and Dodd, P. (eds) 1986. *Englishness: Politics and Culture 1880–1920*. London: Croom Helm.

Cooper, M. 1992. Theory and archaeological management. Paper given at the Annual Conference of the Theoretical Archaeology Group, Leicester, December.

Cooper, M., Firth, A., Carman, J. and Wheatley, D. (eds) 1995. *Managing Archaeology*. London: Routledge.

Countryside Commission. 1989. *A People's Charter: Forty Years of the National Parks and Access to the Countryside Act 1949*. J. Blunden and N. Curry (eds). London: HMSO.

Cox, M., Straker, V. and Taylor, D. (eds) 1995. *Wetland Archaeology and Nature Conservation*. London: HMSO.

Cracknell, S. and Corbishley, M. (eds) 1986. *Presenting Archaeology to Young People*. CBA Research Report 64. London: Council for British Archaeology.

Creamer, H. 1990. Aboriginal perceptions of the past: the implications for cultural resource management in Australia. In Gathercole, P. and Lowenthal, D. (eds) *The Politics of the Past*. One World Archaeology 12. London: Unwin Hyman, 130–40.

Cross, Sir R. 1987. *Statutory Interpretation*. By John Ball and Sir George Engle. London: Butterworth.

Cunningham, R. D. 1979. Why and how to improve archaeology's business work. *American Antiquity* 44, 572–4.

Czaplicki, J. S. 1989. A contractor's perspective of two approaches to cultural resource management. In Cleere, H. F. (ed.) *Archaeological Heritage Management in the Modern World*. One World Archaeology 9. London: Unwin Hyman, 236–55.

Daniel, G. A. 1978. *150 Years of Archaeology*. London: Duckworth.

Daniel, G. and Renfrew, C. 1988. *The Idea of Prehistory*. Edinburgh: Edinburgh University Press.

Darvill, T. 1987. *Ancient Monuments in the Countryside: An Archaeological Management Review*. English Heritage Archaeological Report No. 5. London: English Heritage.

Darvill, T. 1995. Preparing archaeologists for management. In Cooper, M. A., Firth, A., Carman, J. and Wheatley, D. (eds) *Managing Archaeology*. London: Routledge.

Darvill, T. C., Parker-Pearson, M., Smith, R. W. and Thomas, R. M. 1978. *New Approaches to Our Past: An Archaeological Forum*. Southampton: Southampton University Archaeological Society.

Darvill, T., Saunders, A. and Startin, B. 1987. A question of national importance: approaches to the evaluation of ancient monuments for the Monuments Protection Programme in England. *Antiquity* 61, 393–408.

Darvill, T., Gerrard, C. and Startin, B. 1993. Identifying and protecting historic landscapes. *Antiquity* 67, 563–74.

Davis, H. A. 1989a. Is an archaeological site important to science or to the public, and is there a difference? In Uzzell, D. L. (ed.) *Heritage Interpretation: Volume 1: The Natural and Built Environment*. London: Belhaven Press, 96–9.

Davis, H. A. 1989b. Learning by doing: this is no way to treat archaeological resources. In Cleere, H. F. (ed.) *Archaeological Heritage Management in the Modern World*. One World Archaeology 9. London: Unwin Hyman, 275–9.

Davis, J. B. 1856. On some of the bearings of ethnology upon archaeological science.

Paper presented to the Section of Antiquities of the Archaeological Institute, Edinburgh, July. *The Archaeological Journal* 13, 315–27.

Deane, P. 1978. *The Evolution of Economic Ideas.* Modern Cambridge Economics. Cambridge: Cambridge University Press.

Department of the Environment. 1990. *Archaeology and Planning: Planning Policy Guidance Note no. 16* (PPG16). London: Department of the Environment, November.

Department of Trade and Industry/Reviewing Committee on the Export of Art. 1985. *Notice to Exporters: Export of Antiques, Collector's Items (Including Works of Art, Archaeological Material, Documents and Photographs).* London: HMSO.

Dictionary of National Biography from the earliest time to 1900. Sir L. Stephen and Sir S. Lee (eds). London: Oxford University Press.

Dixon, K. A. 1977. Applications of archaeological resources: broadening the basis of significance. In Schiffer, M. B. and Gumerman, G. J. (eds) *Conservation Archaeology: A Guide for Cultural Resource Management Studies.* New York: Academic Press, 277–92.

Douglas, M. (ed.) 1982. *Essays in the Sociology of Perception.* London: RKP.

Douglas, M. and Isherwood, B. 1979. *The World of Goods: Towards an Anthropology of Consumption.* Harmondsworth: Allen Lane.

Dunnell, R. C. 1984. The ethics of archaeological significance decisions. In Green, E. L. (ed.) *Ethics and Values in Archaeology.* New York: Free Press, 62–74.

Dunnell, R. C. and Dancey, W. S. 1983. The siteless survey: a regional scale data collection strategy. In Schiffer, M. B. (ed.) *Advances in Archaeological Method and Theory* 6. San Diego: Academic Press, 267–87.

Edelman, M. 1967. *The Symbolic Uses of Politics.* Urbana: University of Illinois Press.

Edelman, M. 1971. *Politics as Symbolic Action: Mass Arousal and Quiescence.* Institute for Research on Poverty Monograph Series. Chicago: Markham.

Edgeworth, M. 1990. Analogy as practical reason: the perception of objects in excavation practice. *Archaeological Review from Cambridge* 9.2, 243–51.

Embree, L. 1990. The structure of American theoretical archaeology: a preliminary report. In Pinsky, V. and Wylie, A. (eds) *Critical Traditions in Contemporary Archaeology.* New Directions in Archaeology. Cambridge: Cambridge University Press, 28–37.

English Heritage. 1991a. *Exploring Our Past: Strategies for the Archaeology of England.* London: English Heritage.

English Heritage. 1991b. *The Management of Archaeological Projects.* London: English Heritage.

Erickson, F. 1976. Gatekeeping encounters: a social selection process. In Sanday, P. R. (ed.) *Anthropology and the Public Interest.* New York: Academic Press, 111–45.

Erickson, F. and Schulte, J. 1982. *The Counsellor as Gatekeeper: Social Interaction Interviews.* Language, thought and culture: advances in the study of cognition. New York: Academic Press.

Erskine May. 1989. *Erskine May's Treatise on The Law, Privileges, Proceedings and Usage of Parliament.* 21st edition. Boulter, C. J. (ed.). London: Butterworth.

Fawcett, J. (ed.) 1976. *The Future of the Past: Attitudes to Conservation 1174–1974.* London: Thames and Hudson.

Foley, R. 1981. *Off-site Archaeology and Human Adaptation in Eastern Africa.* BAR

International Series 97. Cambridge Monographs in African Archaeology 3. Oxford: BAR.

Foley, R. 1987. *Another Unique Species: Patterns in Human Evolutionary Ecology.* Harlow: Longman.

Foucault, M. 1970. *The Order of Things: An Archaeology of the Human Sciences.* French edition 1966 entitled *Les Mots et les Choses.* London: Tavistock.

Foucault, M. 1973. *The Birth of the Clinic: An Archaeology of Medical Perception.* French edition 1963 entitled *Naissance de la Clinique.* Trans. A. M. Sheridan. London: Tavistock.

Foucault, M. 1977. *Discipline and Punish: The Birth of the Prison.* French edition 1975 entitled *Surveiller et punir: naissance de la prison.* Trans. A. Sheridan. London: Allen Lane.

Fowler, D. D. 1982. Cultural resources management. In Schiffer, M. B. (ed.) *Advances in Archaeological Method and Theory* 5. San Diego: Academic Press, 1–50.

Fowler, D. D. 1984. Ethics in contract archaeology. In Green, E. L. (ed.) *Ethics and Values in Archaeology.* New York: Free Press, 108–16.

Fowler, D. D. 1986. Conserving American archaeological resources. In Meltzer, D. J., Fowler, D. D. and Sabloff, J. A. (eds) *American Archaeology Past and Future: A Celebration of the Society for American Archaeology 1935–1985.* Washington: Smithsonian Institution Press, 135–62.

Fowler, D. D. 1987. Uses of the past: archaeology in the service of the State. *American Antiquity* 52.2, 229–48.

Fowler, P. J. 1992. *The Past in Contemporary Society: Then, Now.* The Heritage: Care, Preservation, Management. London: Routledge.

Franks, A. W. 1852. The collection of British antiquities in the British Museum. *The Archaeological Journal* 9, 7–15.

Franks, A. W. 1853. On the additions to the collection of national antiquities in the British Museum. *The Archaeological Journal* 10, 1–13.

Franks, A. W. 1854. The additions to the collections of national antiquities in the British Museum. *The Archaeological Journal* 11, 23–32.

Gale, A. 1990. The marine SMR. *Antiquity* 64, 400–2.

Gandara, M. 1990. La arqueología social latinoamericana en el contexto de la teoría arqueológica actual. Paper given to the Second World Archaeological Congress, Barquisimeto, Venezuela, September.

Gaze, J. 1988. *Figures in a Landscape: A History of the National Trust.* London: Barrie & Jenkins/National Trust.

Gero, J. 1990. Gender division of labour in the construction of archaeological knowledge in the United States. Paper given to the Second World Archaeological Congress, Barquisimeto, Venezuela, September.

Gero, J. 1991. Railroading epistemology: paleoindians and women. Paper given at the Interpretive Archaeologies Conference, Cambridge, England, September.

Giddens, A. 1984. *The Constitution of Society: Outline of the Theory of Structuration.* Cambridge: Polity Press.

Giddens, A. 1987. *Social Theory and Modern Sociology.* Cambridge: Polity Press.

Goffman, E. 1961. *Encounters: Two Studies in the Sociology of Interaction.* London: Allen Lane.

Goffman, E. 1969. *The Presentation of Self in Everyday Life*. London: Allen Lane.

Goldstein, J. H. 1990. The prospects for using market incentives for conservation of biological diversity. In Orians, G. H., Brown, G. M., Kunin, W. E. and Swierzbinski, J. E. (eds) *The Preservation and Valuation of Genetic Resources*. Seattle and London: University of Washington Press, 246–81.

Grady, M. A. 1977. Significance evaluation and the Orme Reservoir project. In Schiffer, M. B. and Gumerman, G. J. (eds) *Conservation Archaeology: A Guide for Cultural Resource Management Studies*. New York: Academic Press, 259–68.

Green, E. L. (ed.) 1984. *Ethics and Values in Archaeology*. New York: Free Press.

Greenfeld, L. 1989. *Different Worlds: A Sociological Study of Taste, Choice and Success in Art*. Cambridge: Cambridge University Press.

Greenfield, J. 1989. *The Return of Cultural Treasures*. Cambridge: Cambridge University Press.

Greeves, T. 1989. Archaeology and the Green movement: a case for perestroika. *Antiquity* 63, 659–65.

Greffe, X. 1990. *La valeur économique du patrimoine: la demande et l'offre de monuments*. Paris: Anthropo-Economica.

Gurr, A. 1994. Static scenes at the Globe and the Rose Elizabethan theatres. *Antiquity* 68, 146–7.

Halsbury's Statutes. 1989 reissue. *Halsbury's Statutes of England and Wales*. London: Butterworth.

Hammond, G. N. 1982. Treasure Trove: ancient law to preserve archaeological relics. *Antiquity* 56, 58–60.

Hansard (JHC). Journals of the House of Commons. Printed by the authority of the House of Commons. London: H. Hansard and Sons.

Hansard (JHL). Journals of the House of Lords. Printed by the authority of the House of Lords. London: H. Hansard and Sons.

Harrison, B. and Mockett, H. 1990. Women in the factory: the state and factory legislation in nineteenth century Britain. In Jamieson, L. and Carr, H. (eds) *State, Private Life and Political Change*. London: Macmillan, 137–62.

Haskell, F. 1980. *Rediscoveries in Art: Some Aspects of Taste, Fashion and Collecting in England and France*. The Wrightman Lectures 1973. Oxford: Phaidon.

Hickman, P. P. 1977. Problems of significance: two case studies of historical sites. In Schiffer, M. B. and Gumerman, G. J. (eds) *Conservation Archaeology: A Guide for Cultural Resource Management Studies*. New York: Academic Press, 269–76.

Hill, Sir G. 1936. *Treasure Trove in Law and Practice from the Earliest Time to the Present Day*. Oxford: Clarendon.

Hobsbawm, E. 1990. *Nations and Nationalism Since 1780: Programme, Myth, Reality*. Cambridge: Cambridge University Press.

Hobsbawm, E. and Ranger, T. (eds) 1983. *The Invention of Tradition*. Cambridge: Cambridge University Press.

Hodder, I. 1982. *Symbols in Action: Ethnoarchaeological Studies of Material Culture*. New Studies in Archaeology. Cambridge: Cambridge University Press.

Hodder, I. 1986. *Reading the Past: Current Approaches to Interpretation in Archaeology*. Cambridge: Cambridge University Press.

Hodder, I. (ed.) 1987. *Archaeology as Long-Term History*. New Directions in Archaeology. Cambridge: Cambridge University Press.

Hodder, I. (ed.) 1991. *Archaeological Theory in Europe: The Last Three Decades*. London: Routledge.

Hooper-Greenhill, E. 1992. *Museums and the Shaping of Knowledge*. London: Routledge.

Hudson, K. 1987. *Museums of Influence*. Cambridge: Cambridge University Press.

Hughes, M. and Rowley, L. (eds) 1986. *The Management and Preservation of Field Monuments*. Oxford: Oxford University Department of External Studies.

Hutton, B. 1986. *Recording Standing Buildings*. Sheffield: Department of Archaeology and Prehistory/RESCUE: The Trust for British Archaeology.

ICOMOS. 1990. *Guide to Recording Historic Buildings*. London: Butterworth.

IFA (Institute of Field Archaeologists). n.d. *By-laws of the Institute of Field Archaeologists: Code of Conduct*. Birmingham: IFA.

IFA (Institute of Field Archaeologists) and English Heritage. 1993. Project Management in Archaeology. Two-day course held at Bournemouth University, February.

Kennet, W. 1972. *Preservation*. London: Temple Smith.

Kent, S. 1990. Activity areas and architecture: an interdisciplinary view of the relationship between use of space and domestic built environment. In Kent, S. (ed.) *Domestic Architecture and the Use of Space: An Interdisciplinary Cross-cultural Study*. New Directions in Archaeology. Cambridge: Cambridge University Press, 1–8.

King, T. F., Hickman, P. P., and Berg, G. 1977. *Anthropology in Historic Conservation: Caring for Culture's Clutter*. Studies in Archaeology. New York: Academic Press.

Knudson, R. 1986. Contemporary cultural resource management. In Meltzer, D. J., Fowler, D. D., and Sabloff, J. A. (eds) *American Archaeology Past and Future: A Celebration of the Society for American Archaeology 1935–1985*. Washington: Smithsonian Institution Press, 135–62.

Kopytoff, I. 1986. The cultural biography of things: commoditisation as a process. In Appadurai, A. (ed.) *The Social Life of Things: Commodities in Social Perspective*. Cambridge: Cambridge University Press, 64–91.

Kristiansen, K. 1989. Perspectives on the archaeological heritage: history and future. In Cleere, H. F. (ed.) *Archaeological Heritage Management in the Modern World*. One World Archaeology 9. London: Unwin Hyman, 23–9.

Kroll, E. M. and Price, T. D. 1991. Introduction. In Kroll, E. M. and Price, T. D. (eds) *The Interpretation of Archaeological Spatial Patterning*. New York: Plenum Press, 1–3.

Kropotkin, P. 1972. *Mutual Aid: A Factor of Evolution*. New York: New York University Press.

Kuper, A. and Kuper, J. (eds) 1985. *The Social Science Encyclopedia*. London: RKP.

Lamberg-Karlovsky, C. C. (ed.) 1989. *Archaeological Thought in America*. Cambridge: Cambridge University Press.

Last, J. 1991. Walking/digging/building: an archaeology of modern art. *Archaeological Review from Cambridge* 10.2, 185–201.

Layton, R. (ed.) 1989a. *Conflict in the Archaeology of Living Traditions*. One World Archaeology 8. London: Unwin Hyman.

Layton, R. (ed.) 1989b. *Who Needs the Past? Indigenous Values and Archaeology*. One World Archaeology 5. London: Unwin Hyman.

Leone, M. and Potter, P. B. 1992. Legitimation and the classification of archaeological sites. *American Antiquity* 57, 137–45.

Levine, P. 1986. *The Amateur and the Professional: Antiquarians, Historians and Archaeologists in Victorian England 1838–1886.* Cambridge: Cambridge University Press.

Lipe, W. D. 1974. A conservation model for American archaeology. *The Kiva* 39, 213–43.

Lipe, W. D. 1977. A conservation ethic for American archaeology. In Schiffer, M. B. and Gumerman, G. J. (eds) *Conservation Archaeology: A Handbook for Cultural Resource Management Studies.* Studies in Archaeology. New York: Academic Press, 19–42.

Lipe, W. D. 1984. Value and meaning in cultural resources. In Cleere, H. F. (ed.) *Approaches to the Archaeological Heritage.* New Directions in Archaeology. Cambridge: Cambridge University Press, 1–10.

Lowenthal, D. 1985. *The Past Is a Foreign Country.* Cambridge: Cambridge University Press.

Lubbock, Sir J. 1894. *The Use of Life.* London: Macmillan.

Lubbock, Sir J. 1900. *Prehistoric Times: As Illustrated by Ancient Remains and the Manners and Customs of Modern Savages.* 6th edition (revised). Oxford: Williams and Norgate.

Lubbock, Sir. J. et al. 1887. *Mr. Gladstone and the Nationalities of the United Kingdom: A Series of Letters to the "Times"* . . . *with Rejoinders.* . . . London: Bernard Quantick.

Luce, R. D. and Raiffa, H. 1957. *Games and Decisions: Introduction and Critical Survey.* New York: John Wiley and Sons.

McGimsey, C. R. 1972. *Public Archaeology.* New York: Seminar Books.

McGimsey, C. R. 1984. The value of archaeology. In Green, E. L. (ed.) *Ethics and Values in Archaeology.* New York: Free Press, 171–4.

McGimsey, C. R. and Davis, H. A. (eds) 1977. *The Management of Archaeological Resources: The Airlie House Report.* Washington: Society for American Archaeology.

Malaro, M. C. 1985. *A Legal Primer on Managing Museum Collections.* Washington: Smithsonian Institution Press.

Mallet, Sir B. 1934. Political and economic. In Grant Duff, U. (Mrs A.) (ed.) *The Life-Work of Lord Avebury.* London: Watts and Co., 35–66.

MARS News Release. 1994. *MARS: A National Census of Archaeological Sites.* Bournemouth: Monuments at Risk Survey News Release, July.

Marsden, B. M. 1984. *Pioneers of Prehistory: Leaders and Landmarks in English Archaeology (1500–1900).* Ormskirk: G. W. and A. Hesketh.

Marsden, P. 1972. Archaeology at sea. *Antiquity* 46, 198–202.

Merriman, N. 1991. *Beyond the Glass Case: The Past, The 'Heritage' and the Public in Britain.* Leicester Museum Studies. Leicester: Leicester University Press.

Messenger, P. M. 1989. *The Ethics of Collecting Cultural Property.* Albuquerque: University of New Mexico Press.

Mills, N. T. W. n.d. *Information Management, Cultural (Especially Archaeological) Resources and the Tourist and Leisure Services Industries.* CRUS Working Paper 4. Sheffield: CRUS.

Moore, S. F. 1978. *Law As Process: An Anthropological Approach.* London: RKP.

Moore, V. 1990. *A Practical Approach to Planning Law.* 2nd edition. London: Blackstone Press.

Morris, W. 1892. *News from Nowhere, or, An Epoch of Rest, Being Some Chapters from a Utopian Romance*. 3rd edition. London: Reeves and Turner.

Muckelroy, K. 1978. *Maritime Archaeology*. New Studies in Archaeology. Cambridge: Cambridge University Press.

Murray, T. 1990. The history, philosophy and sociology of archaeology: the case of the Ancient Monuments Protection Act (1882). In Pinsky, V. and Wylie, A. (eds) *Critical Traditions in Contemporary Archaeology*. New Directions in Archaeology. Cambridge: Cambridge University Press, 55–67.

Nader, L. (ed.) 1969. *Law in Culture and Society*. Chicago: Aldine.

National Rivers Authority (NRA) 1991. *The Water Environment, Our Cultural Heritage*. Proceedings of a Conference held at the National Exhibition Centre, Birmingham, June. Solihull: NRA.

National Trust for Historic Preservation. 1980. *Preservation: Towards an Ethic in the 1980s*. Washington: Preservation Press.

Newan, K. S. 1983. *Law and Economic Organisation: A Comparative Study of Preindustrial Societies*. Cambridge: Cambridge University Press.

Newcombe, R. M. 1979. *Planning the Past: Historical Landscape Resources and Recreation*. Studies in Historical Geography. London: William Dawson.

Newton, C. 1851. On the study of archaeology. Paper read at the Oxford Discourse of The Archaeological Institute, 18 June 1850. *The Archaeological Journal* 8, 1–26.

O'Keefe, P. J. and Prott, L. V. 1984. *Law and the Cultural Heritage: Volume 1: Discovery and Excavation*. Abingdon: Professional Books.

Ordeshook, P. C. 1986. *Game Theory and Political Theory: An Introduction*. Cambridge: Cambridge University Press.

Orrell, J. and Gurr, A. 1989. What The Rose can tell us. *Antiquity* 63, 421–9.

Oxford English Dictionary. 1971. Oxford: Oxford University Press.

Palmer, N. E. 1981. Treasure Trove and the protection of antiquities. *Modern Law Review* 44, 178–87.

Palmer, N. E. 1989. Museums and cultural property. In Vergo, P. (ed.) *The New Museology*. London: Reaktion Books, 172–204.

Palmer, N. E. 1991. The law of cultural property and international cultural relations. *World Archaeological Bulletin* 5, 33–41.

Parnell, A. C. 1987. *Building Legislation and Historic Buildings*. London: Architectural Press.

Patrik, L. E. 1985. Is there an archaeological record? In Schiffer, M. B. (ed.) *Advances in Archaeological Method and Theory* 8. New York: Academic Press, 27–62.

Perkin, H. 1989. *The Rise of Professional Society: England Since 1880*. London: Routledge.

Piggott, S. 1989. *Ancient Britons and the Antiquarian Imagination: Ideas from the Renaissance to the Regency*. London: Thames and Hudson.

Price, H. M. III 1990. *Disputing the Dead: US Law on Aboriginal Remains and Grave Goods*. London: University of Missouri Press.

Price, N. P. S. 1984. Conservation on excavations and the 1956 Unesco recommendation. In Price, N. P. S. (ed.) *Conservation on Archaeological Excavations with Particular Reference to the Mediterranean Area*. Rome: ICCROM, 145–52.

Priddy, D. 1991. The protection of historic gardens. In Brown, A. E. (ed.) *Garden*

Archaeology. CBA Research Report 78. London: Council for British Archaeology, 190–1.

Purdue, M., Young, E. and Rowan-Robinson, J. 1989. *Planning Law and Procedure*. London: Butterworth.

Raab, L. M. 1984. Towards an understanding of the ethics and values of research design in archaeology. In Green, E. L. (ed.) *Ethics and Values in Archaeology*. New York: Free Press, 75–88.

Rahtz, P. 1976. *Rescue Archaeology*. Harmondsworth: Penguin.

Rahtz, P. 1991. *Invitation to Archaeology*. 2nd edition. Oxford: Blackwell.

Rathje, W. L. 1981. A manifesto for modern material culture studies. In Gould, R. A. and Schiffer, M. B. (eds) *Modern Material Culture: The Archaeology of Us*. Studies in Archaeology. New York: Academic Press, 51–6.

Renfrew, C. and Bahn, P. 1991. *Archaeology: Theories, Methods and Practice*. London: Thames and Hudson.

Renfrew, J. (ed.) 1991. *New Light on Early Farming: Recent Developments in Palaeoethnobotany*. Edinburgh: Edinburgh University Press.

Rigaud, J.-P. and Simek, J. F. 1991. Interpreting spatial patterns at the Grotte XV: a multiple method approach. In Kroll, E. M. and Price, T. D. (eds) *The Interpretation of Archaeological Spatial Patterning*. New York: Plenum Press, 199–220.

Roberts, S. 1979. *Order and Dispute: An Introduction to Legal Anthropology*. Harmondsworth: Penguin.

Robinson, J. and Eatwell, J. 1973. *An Introduction to Modern Economics*. Revised edition. London: McGraw-Hill.

Rodwell, W. (with Rodwell, K.) 1977. *Historic Churches: A Wasting Asset*. CBA Research Report 19. London: Council for British Archaeology.

Rodwell, W. 1981. *The Archaeology of the English Church*. London: Batsford.

Rowley, R. T. and Breakell, M. (eds) 1977. *Planning and the Historic Environment* (2 volumes). Oxford: Department of Extra-Mural Studies.

Sanday, P. R. (ed.) 1976. *Anthropology and the Public Interest*. New York: Academic Press.

Saunders, A. D. 1983. A century of ancient monuments legislation 1882–1982. *The Antiquaries Journal* 63, 11–29.

Schaafsma, C. F. 1989. Significant until proven otherwise: problems versus representative samples. In Cleere, H. F. (ed.) *Archaeological Heritage Management in the Modern World*. One World Archaeology 9. London: Unwin Hyman, 38–51.

Schiffer, M. B. 1972. Archaeological context and systemic context. *American Antiquity* 37, 156–65.

Schiffer, M. B. 1987. *Formation Processes of the Archaeological Record*. Albuquerque: University of New Mexico Press.

Schiffer, M. B. and Gumerman, G. J. (eds) 1977. *Conservation Archaeology: A Handbook for Cultural Resource Management Studies*. Studies in Archaeology. New York: Academic Books.

Schiffer, M. B. and House, J. H. 1977. An approach to assessing significance. In Schiffer, M. B. and Gumerman, G. J. (eds) *Conservation Archaeology: A Handbook for Cultural Resource Management Studies*. Studies in Archaeology. New York: Academic Books, 249–58.

Schlanger, N. and Sinclair, A. 1990. Introduction: technology in the humanities. *Archaeological Review from Cambridge* 9.1, 3–4.

Schwarz, M. and Thompson, M. 1990. *Divided We Stand: Redefining Politics, Technology and Social Choice*. Hemel Hempstead: Harvester Wheatsheaf.

Scollar, I., Tabbagh, A., Hesse, A. and Herzog, I. 1990. *Archaeological Prospecting and Remote Sensing*. Topics in Remote Sensing. Cambridge: Cambridge University Press.

Scovill, D. H., Gordon, G. J. and Anderson, K. 1977. Guidelines for the preparation of statements of environmental impact on archaeological resources. In Schiffer, M. B. and Gumerman, G. J. (eds) *Conservation Archaeology: A Handbook for Cultural Resource Management Studies*. Studies in Archaeology. New York: Academic Books, 43–62.

Shanks, M. 1992. *Experiencing the Past: On the Character of Archaeology*. London: Routledge.

Shanks, M. and Tilley, C. 1987a. *Reconstructing Archaeology: Theory and Practice*. New Studies in Archaeology. Cambridge: Cambridge University Press.

Shanks, M. and Tilley, C. 1987b. *Social Theory and Archaeology*. Cambridge: Polity Press.

Shannon, R. 1976. *The Crisis of Imperialism 1865–1915*. The Paladin History of England. St Albans: Paladin.

Sills, D. L. 1968. *International Encyclopaedia of the Social Sciences*. New York: Macmillan.

Silverman, S. and Parezo, N. J. (eds) 1992. *Preserving the Anthropological Record*. New York: Wenner-Gren Foundation for Anthropological Work.

Smith, C. W. 1989. *Auctions: The Social Construction of Value*. Hemel Hempstead: Harvester Wheatsheaf.

Smith, L. 1993. Heritage management as postprocessual archaeology? Paper given as a Graduate Seminar, Department of Archaeology, University of Cambridge, May.

Smith, L. in press. Significance concepts in Australian management archaeology. In Clark, A. and Smith, L. (eds) *Issues in Management Archaeology*. St Lucia: Tempus Publications, University of Queensland.

Snyder, F. G. 1989. Thinking about 'Interests': legislative process in the European community. In Starr, J. and Collier, J. F. (eds) *History and Power in the Study of Law*. New Directions in Legal Anthropology. London: Cornell University Press, 168–98.

Somerset County and District Councils. 1989. *Protecting the Historic and Architectural Heritage of Somerset*. Written by R. Lillford and R. Croft. Taunton: County and District Councils of Somerset.

Sparrow, C. 1982. Treasure Trove: a lawyer's view. *Antiquity* 56, 199–201.

Startin, B. 1992. The monuments protection programme: archaeological records. In National Museum of Denmark *Sites and Monuments: National Archaeological Records*. Copenhagen: National Museum of Denmark, 201–6.

Startin, B. 1993. Assessment of field remains. In Hunter, J. and Ralston, I. (eds) *Archaeological Resource Management in the UK: An Introduction*. Stroud: Allan Sutton/ IFA, 184–96.

Startin, B. 1995. The monuments protection programme: protecting what, how, and for whom? In Cooper, M. A., Firth, A., Carman, J. and Wheatley, D. (eds) *Managing Archaeology*. London: Routledge.

Stead, I. M. 1991. The Snettisham treasure: excavations in 1990. *Antiquity* 65, 447–65.

Stocking, G. W. Jnr. 1987. *Victorian Anthropology*. New York: Free Press.

Suddards, R. W. 1988. *Listed Buildings: The Law and Practice of Historic Buildings, Ancient Monuments and Conservation Areas.* London: Sweet and Maxwell.

Tainter, J. A. and Lucas, J. G. 1983. Epistemology of the significance concept. *American Antiquity* 48, 707–19.

Tatton-Brown, T. 1991. Building the tower and spire of Salisbury Cathedral. *Antiquity* 65, 74–96.

Thapar, B. K. 1984. India. In Cleere, H. F. (ed.) *Approaches to the Archaeological Heritage.* New Directions in Archaeology. Cambridge: Cambridge University Press, 63–72.

Thompson, M. 1979. *Rubbish Theory: The Creation and Destruction of Value.* Oxford: Clarendon.

Thompson, M. 1982. A three-dimensional model. In Douglas, M. (ed.) *Essays in the Sociology of Perception.* London: RKP, 31–63.

Thompson, M. 1990. The management of hazardous wastes and the hazards of wasteful management. In Bradby, H. (ed.) *Dirty Words: Writings on the History and Culture of Pollution.* London: Earthscan Publications, 115–38.

Thompson, M., Ellis, R. and Wildavsky, A. 1990. *Cultural Theory.* Boulder, CO: Westview Press.

Tite, M. S. 1972. *Methods of Physical Examination in Archaeology.* London: Seminar Press.

Torres de Arauz, R. 1987. Legal foundations: the government's role and responsibilities. In Wilson, R. L. and Loyola, G. (eds) *Rescue Archaeology: Papers from the First New World Conference on Rescue Archaeology.* Washington: Preservation Press, 59–66.

Trigger, B. 1989. *A History of Archaeological Thought.* Cambridge: Cambridge University Press.

US Department of the Interior. 1989–90. *Federal Historic Preservation Laws.* Compiled by S. K. Blumenthal, National Park Service, Cultural Resources Programs. Washington: US Department of the Interior.

Uzzell, D. L. (ed.) 1989. *Heritage Interpretation: Volume 1: The Natural and Built Environment.* London: Belhaven Press.

Wainwright, G. J. 1989. Saving the Rose. *Antiquity* 63, 430–5.

Walsh, K. 1992. *The Representation of the Past: Museums and Heritage in the Post-modern World.* The Heritage: Care, Preservation, Management. London: Routledge.

Weber, M. 1968. *Economy and Society: Volume 1.* New York: Bedminster Press.

Weekly Law Reports. London: The Incorporated Council of Law Reporters for England and Wales.

Wester, K. W. 1990. The current state of cultural resource management in the United States. In Andah, B. W. (ed.) Cultural resource management: an African dimension. Forum on Cultural Resource Management at the Conference in Honour of Prof. Thurstan Shaw. *West African Journal of Archaeology* 20, 80–8.

Wildesen, L. E. 1980. Cultural resource management: a personal view. *Practising Anthropology* 2.2.10, 22–3.

Williams, S. A. 1978. *The International and National Protection of Movable Cultural Property: A Comparative Study.* New York: Oceana Publications.

Wilson, R. L. (ed.) 1987. *Rescue Archaeology: Proceedings of the Second New World Conference on Rescue Archaeology.* Dallas, TX: Southern Methodist University Press.

Wilson, R. L. and Loyola, G. (eds) 1982. *Rescue Archaeology: Papers from the First New World Conference on Rescue Archaeology.* Washington: Preservation Press.

Woodcock, G. 1975. *Anarchism: A History of Libertarian Ideas and Movements.* Harmondsworth: Pelican.

Wright, P. 1985. *On Living in an Old Country: The National Past in Contemporary Britain.* London: Verso.

Yeo, S. 1986. Socialism, the State and some oppositional Englishmen. In Colls, R. and Dodd, P. (eds) *Englishness: Politics and Culture 1880–1920.* London: Croom Helm, 308–69.

Young, L. 1994. Significance, connoisseurship and facilitation: new techniques for assessing museum acquisitions. *Museum Management and Curatorship* 13, 191–9.

Ziedler, J. A. 1982. Pot-hunting and vandalism: an Ecuadorian example. In Wilson, R. L. and Loyola, G. (eds) *Rescue Archaeology: Papers from the First New World Conference on Rescue Archaeology.* Washington: Preservation Press, 49–58.

Index